ELECTIONEERI

ELECTIONEERING

A Comparative Study
of Continuity and Change

edited by
DAVID BUTLER
and
AUSTIN RANNEY

CLARENDON PRESS · OXFORD
1992

Oxford University Press, Walton Street, Oxford OX2 6DP
Oxford New York Toronto
Delhi Bombay Calcutta Madras Karachi
Petaling Jaya Singapore Hong Kong Tokyo
Nairobi Dar es Salaam Cape Town
Melbourne Auckland
and associated companies in
Berlin Ibadan

Oxford is a trade mark of Oxford University Press

Published in the United States
by Oxford University Press, New York

British Library Cataloguing in Publication Data
Data available

Library of Congress Cataloging in Publication Data
Data available
ISBN 0–19–827375–4

Typeset by Cambridge Composing (UK) Ltd
Printed and bound in
Great Britain by Biddles Ltd,
Guildford & King's Lynn

Acknowledgements

Many academic colleagues have contributed to the chapters in this book, and we and our fellow authors wish to thank them. We have in particular to acknowledge the assistance of Barbara Glass in Berkeley and Audrey Skeats in Oxford.

David Butler
Nuffield College
Oxford

Austin Ranney
Institute of Governmental Studies
University of California, Berkeley

1 September 1991

Contents

Notes on Contributors

ALAN ANGELL, University Lecturer in Latin American Politics and Fellow of St Antony's College, Oxford.

LARRY M. BARTELS, Professor of Politics, Princeton.

DAVID BUTLER, Fellow of Nuffield College, Oxford.

JEAN and MONICA CHARLOT, Professors of Politics, University of Paris.

GERALD L. CURTIS, Professor of Political Science, Columbia University, New York.

PETER ESAIASSON, Lecturer in Political Science, University of Gothenburg.

JODY FOSTER, University of California, Berkeley.

STEPHEN GUNDLE, Fellow of University College, Oxford.

COLIN A. HUGHES, Professor of Political Science, University of Queensland.

MAX KAASE, Professor of Political Science, University of Mannheim.

DENNIS KAVANAGH, Professor of Politics, Nottingham University.

MARIA D'ALVA KINZO, Professor of Political Science, São Paulo University, Brazil.

JAMES MANOR, Professorial Fellow, Institute of Development Studies, University of Sussex.

CHRISTOPHER MUSTE, University of California, Berkeley.

AUSTIN RANNEY, Emeritus Professor of Political Science, University of California, Berkeley.

DIEGO URBANEJA, Editor of *El Diario*, Caracas; formerly Professor of Political Science, Central University of Venezuela.

1

Introduction

DAVID BUTLER and AUSTIN RANNEY

Elections can produce high drama or infinite tedium, but they are the key institutions of representative democracy. Elections, when they are open and competitive, allow voters to decide which persons or parties shall control their government. For all but a handful of citizens, voting in national elections is the most important form of political participation; for most it is the only form. Consequently, the recent holding of free elections in formerly authoritarian nations, such as Argentina, Chile, Czechoslovakia, Poland, Spain, and the Soviet Union, provided the clearest evidence of their movement towards democracy.

However, the free and secret casting of ballots, and their honest counting, are only part of what makes elections democratic. Equally important are the preceding campaigns mounted by parties and candidates to maximize their votes. For citizens' votes to register meaningful decisions they should have real alternatives to choose between and they should be able to learn what policies the contestants are likely to pursue if successful; in an ideal world they should also have sufficient information about the character and background of the contenders to assess how honestly and effectively they will perform in office.

The making of voting choices is not, of course, confined to the formal period of campaigning. Some people are set in one party loyalty for a lifetime by their family and their social background. Those who do change party loyalties are swayed as much by events over the years as by the epiphenomena of campaigns; information about elected persons and their challengers is presented continuously between elections in the daily coverage of public affairs by the news media. But research shows that almost everywhere most citizens' interest in politics is considerably increased during election campaigns, and it is then that they learn much of what they know about candidates and issues.

The information generated in campaigns comes from two sources: the electioneering activities of parties and candidates, and the coverage of those activities by the news media (although the latter can sometimes be regarded as part of the former). This book attempts to describe and explain the significant changes in election-eering in major democratic countries over the last half-century. 'Electioneering' includes all the activities directed at voters by all the contestants. Obviously, electioneering is not confined to elec-tion campaigns; it goes on all the time and can involve pursuing local office or fighting a referendum. But in this book our main focus is on campaigns for election at the national level and on activities pursued during the final period of formal campaigning.

Three kinds of people are involved in elections: the contestants, the media, and the voters. Each has a different stake in the situation; each takes a different approach.

For most contestants, leaders, candidates, party officials, and volunteer workers, the main purpose is to win elections. Their advertisements, parades, and meetings, their press conferences and television presentations are all intended to attract the greatest possible number of voters to turn out on election day. In most countries there are, of course, some contestants who know that they have no chance but who nevertheless electioneer. This book necessarily focuses on those parties and candidates who campaign on the premiss that they will achieve reasonable success. Success is usually judged by winning or losing, but sometimes what matters is to have put on 'a good campaign'—either one that is praised by journalists, academics, and other campaigners for its intrinsic quality or one that produces a vote which, win or lose, is higher than expected.

The news media have other goals. Their main purpose is to provide the best possible coverage by publishing or broadcasting accurate, interesting, and illuminating descriptions of the campaign activities and of their likely impact on the outcome. Some media in some countries are corrupt and partisan. But for most of those who control the media, success tends to be measured by the number of readers and viewers who are attracted, and to a smaller degree, by the critical assessments of their coverage.

The third group, ordinary citizens, if they follow an election at all, are concerned to acquire information about the contest that may be useful for making voting decisions or interesting for its own sake (elections, one must acknowledge, are for many people a spectator sport as much as a way of choosing a government). They measure success in electioneering by the extent to which it proves non-boring, non-offensive, and informative.

This book is a comparative study. We have asked experts on ten major countries or regions to describe how electioneering has changed over the last couple of generations. Although we suggested some common questions, we made no attempt to impose a common form on their treatment.

Ten years ago we collaborated on a book, *Democracy at the Polls*, in which we commissioned synoptic chapters, each of which gave a world-wide view of a particular aspect of electioneering—such as party finance, candidate selection, press and broadcasting.[1] It seemed a valuable exercise, but we were aware of the difficulty of isolating any one aspect of a country's electioneering from its total political culture. We traced elements of similarity and difference within different democracies but we could hardly offer a balanced picture of what was happening within any one country.

Ten years later, a different approach seemed appropriate. We wanted to look at national experiences in more depth, at how particular electioneering devices fit within a particular political tradition and set of institutions.

But we also wanted to look at electioneering over the last forty years, to see how the innovations in technique and style which we personally had observed becoming part of the electoral scene had been absorbed in different settings. The changes have been far-reaching, but they have come in different ways and at different speeds in different countries.

Our appendix presents in schematic form for each of the countries covered in the book a number of facts relevant to electioneering. Also, each chapter has a brief bibliography. However, there is no bibliography for our introduction and conclusion because there are virtually no books that deal comparatively with questions about electioneering. There are a number of useful comparative studies of political parties, electoral systems, party finance, and polling.[2] Electioneering has so far largely escaped this approach, and we hope that this book will help to fill the gap.

In this chapter and in our conclusion, we offer some general comparative observations. We do believe that seeing how another country behaves can throw a flood of light on how one's own country manages its affairs. But we must be totally receptive to diversity and not assume the existence of some latent universal model.

A particular difficulty in the comparative study of politics lies in the presidential–parliamentary divide, the fundamental contrast between America and the rest of the world. We are, all of us, more ethnocentric than we realize. Few Americans appreciate how unique is their system, with its separated powers, its primaries, its loose-linked federal party structure. Few Europeans, accustomed to the conventions of parliamentary democracy and strong party discipline, understand the gulf between their political institutions and those of the United States.

In eleven chapters we could not cover all the major democracies of the world. We apologize to Canadians and to Spaniards, to the people of the Low Countries and the Caribbean, to the Irish, the Greeks, and the Israelis for not discussing their variants of election-eering. This book deals with most of the major democracies of the world, but it still represents a collection of case-studies rather than a comprehensive report. And each case-study is a highly personal analysis of a particular society.

This book is about continuity and about change. Each of its chapters stress how strong national traditions can be; each points to ways in which the conduct of elections has been transformed between 1950 and 1990. In most countries the formal framework of law under which elections are conducted has changed little. It is the practices of politicians and the media, exploiting technical innovations and marketing approaches, that have altered the appearance of elections.

At the centre electioneering has become much more sophisti-cated. The old pros of fifty years ago have been replaced by a large army of specialized advisers from the media as well as from polling and from advertising. The academic and journalistic worlds have produced a new breed of campaign analysts and critics. Elections, once oddly amateur and instinctive, have become increasingly technical and self-conscious operations.

But even in this new world some electioneering fundamentals remain. The basic targets are unchanged:

(1) Uncommitted voters (who are there to be won).
(2) Hostile voters (who must be converted).
(3) Loyal voters (whose loyalty must be reinforced).
(4) All potential supporters (who must be activated to go to the polls).

However, the assumptions that most observers and practitioners made about elections forty years ago are under increasing challenge. Consider the traditional assumptions:

1. Elections were conducted by partisan politicians within a party framework. Strategy was determined mainly by party leaders and candidates. Electioneering tactics were executed mainly by party activists.

2. In parliamentary democracies, campaigns were essentially party-centred, seeking to maximize support for the party and its candidates as a package rather than for particular candidates. Although party leaders might receive special attention, the main emphasis was on electing a party to rule rather than on electing individuals to seats in parliament. In the United States, by contrast, the separate election of executives and of legislators and the low discipline and decentralization of the parties placed a higher emphasis on individual candidates. Yet even in the United States most campaigns focused more on support for a party's whole ticket than on plugging individual candidatures.

3. The main source of information about how voters were reacting and what they would do on election day was the 'feel' that local leaders and editors could claim on the basis of long experience in the community.

4. Most voters were committed to a particular party. Campaigners were often restrained from trying to persuade them to switch since that might only stir them to go out to record their customary partisanship.

5. Electioneering normally consisted of:

   (*a*) Circulating written documents—party manifestos, candidate biographies, position papers, and fly-sheets.
   (*b*) Door-to-door canvassing by party volunteers, intended mainly to identify potential voters so that they could be reminded to vote on election day; secondary goals included soliciting contributions from the faithful, persuading 'leaners' to cross over and 'waverers' to hold firm.

(c) Holding public meetings, at which party candidates and leaders spoke, and organizing rallies and parades at which partisans could demonstrate their enthusiasm for their side, creating the impression that the party's 'bandwagon' was rolling to victory. The party faithful also showed their colours in window stickers and campaign buttons to show the flag and accelerate the bandwagon.

(d) Using billboards, posters, and newspaper advertisements to reinforce the party appeal.

(e) Door-knocking on election day to get known supporters to the polling booth.

6. Parties often provided poll-watchers to observe the casting and counting of votes to prevent election stealing.

7. The candidates and party leaders based their campaign strategy and tactics upon certain widely held views about what determined the voters' preferences and motivated them to get to the polls:

(a) 'Attack, don't defend.' Because people tend to have a low opinion of politicians, they are more likely to believe bad things about the opposition than good things about their own side. Hence the 'anti' vote is easier to attract than the 'pro' vote. Rubbishing opponents is more effective than selling one's own side. Fear is easier to excite than affection.

(b) 'Most people vote their pocket books.' They use their votes not to testify to their commitment to socialism or capitalism or any other abstraction but to defend and improve their personal economic well-being. If things are going well for them, they vote to keep the status quo. If things are going badly, they vote to expel those who are mismanaging the economy and replace them with others 'who can't do worse and might do better'.

(c) 'Play the sectarian card.' Voters with strong ethnic or religious affiliations can be stirred to support those whom they feel will give their groups respect or material help and to oppose those who are painted as hostile or disrespectful to their group. Parties, whenever the system allows, should therefore seek 'balanced tickets' to show they are not excluding any significant ethnic or religious groupings.

(d) 'Get the bandwagon rolling.' It helps to convince voters that your side is going to win. Voters like to be on the victorious side.

(e) 'Pile up endorsements.' Most voters know little about the candidates and issues. They depend upon the advice of trusted newspapers or known public figures to help them separate the good from the bad. It is desirable to get candidates and issues supported by as much of the media and as diverse a body of ethnic and other group leaders as possible.

(f) 'Stir them up.' Many voters are uninterested in politics. If left alone they may not bother to vote. They must be persuaded that the outcome of the election will have important consequences for them and that a particular vote will bring good things, or prevent bad things.

(g) 'Personal contact wins votes.' People are more likely to vote for people they know. Candidates appearing on the doorstep or seen at meetings show that they care enough about the voters to make the effort; they help voters to accept them as human beings rather than remote names or faces on posters.

(h) 'Run scared.' Voters are mysterious and changeable. Therefore, no matter how far candidates or parties feel they are ahead, they should always fight hard to the end. Whether or not the opposition is mounting a big campaign, letting up is always dangerous.

Much of this folk-wisdom (familiar at least to those active in American and British campaigns in 1950) would still be accepted today. We shall see in the chapters that follow how opinion polls and academic research have confirmed some of these beliefs and shown that others were untrue or unimportant. We shall also see how politicians have been educated by the new insights which social psychology and market research have offered. We shall see how new methods of communications and changing social conditions have transformed the receptiveness of the electorate to older types of campaign stimuli.

Commentators in many countries encapsulate these changes in a complaint against 'the Americanization of politics'. Certainly most of the important technological developments in electioneering have their origin in the United States:

(1) Opinion polls, public and private;
(2) Telephone canvassing;
(3) Computers;
(4) Direct mail;
(5) Fax machines;
(6) Campaign consultants;
(7) Market research;
(8) Television saturation.

In all these fields, the United States has been a pioneer. In almost all of them, other democracies have followed ten or twenty years later. 'Sound-bite', 'photo-opportunity', and 'news management', are all phrases of American origin that are today heard in every election strategy conference in Western Europe.

At a less material level, the decline of canvassing and of attendance at political meetings seems to have occurred first in the United States. The dwindling influence of party leaders in the design and direction of electioneering and their replacement by professional consultants from advertising agencies has certainly been more evident in America than anywhere else. The transformation of election finance in terms of the amount spent, of the legal restrictions, and of the possibility of public subsidy has taken different forms in every country, but the American example looms large in most debates on the subject.

This book explores the extent of this 'Americanization' and its limits. In preparing it, we have come to feel that the variations in the ways in which the new techniques have interacted with different political cultures is as interesting as the changes themselves.

The chapters that follow have no standard pattern. In Chapters 2–11 the authors describe different countries and have different styles of approach. Yet they all address a common set of questions: how were election campaigns conducted forty years ago? How are they conducted today? How has the institutional framework changed? How and when have the new techniques of electioneering been absorbed? What difference, if any, do they make? Each chapter provides an up-to-date account of how electioneering practices and impact have changed in a country or a region since 1945. But in Chapter 12, Larry M. Bartels notes the widespread labelling of changes in electioneering in other democracies as their 'Americanization', and forcefully challenges the conventional belief that in the United States electioneering has changed in function as well as in form and that electioneering plays a major role in determining election outcomes.

Because the new techniques were largely developed first in America, we begin with an account of the situation in the United States and follow with Latin America, the area most strongly influenced in institutions and techniques by the American example. We then turn to the Westminster model and to its adaptations in Australasia and India before turning to the countries of continental Europe. Our country descriptions end with Japan, in many ways the most exceptional of our examples. Two analytical chapters provide the conclusion: Larry Bartels's argument that electioneering matters less than many suppose and our own more general assessment of the diversities and similarities revealed in these pages.

Notes

1. David Butler, Howard R. Penniman, and Austin Ranney (eds.), *Democracy at the Polls: A Comparative Study of Competitive National Elections* (Washington, DC: American Enterprise Institute for Public Policy Research, 1981).
2. For example, on political parties: L. Epstein, *Political Parties in Western Democracies* (New York: Praeger, 1967); G. Sartori, *Parties and Party Systems* (Cambridge: Cambridge University Press, 1976); M. Duverger, *Political Parties: Their Organization and Activity in the Modern State*, trans. B. and R. North (London: Methuen, 1954); and R. Michels, *Political Parties: A Sociological Study of the Oligarchical Tendencies of Modern Democracy*, trans. E. Eden (New York: Hearst's 1915). On elections: V. Bogdanor and D. Butler, *Democracy and Elections* (Cambridge: Cambridge University Press, 1983); E. Lakeman, *How Democracies Vote*, 4th edn. (London: Faber, 1984); and Butler, Penniman, and Ranney, *Democracy at the Polls*. D. Nohlen, *Elections and Election Systems* (Bonn: Friedrich Ebert Stiftung, 1984); D. Rae, *The Political Consequences of Electoral Laws* (New Haven, Conn.: Yale University Press, 1971); S. Rokkan, *Citizens, Elections, Parties* (Oslo: Universitetsforlaget, 1970); and R. Taagepera and M. Shugart, *Seats and Votes* (New Haven, Conn.: Yale University Press, 1989). For political finance: A. Heidenheimer

(ed.), *Comparative Political Finance* (Lexington, Mass: D. C. Heath, 1971); and H. Alexander (ed.), *Comparative Political Finance in the 1980s* (Cambridge: Cambridge University Press, 1989). On polls: R. Worcester, *Public Opinion Polling: An International Review* (New York: St Martin's Press, 1982).

2

The United States

JODY FOSTER and CHRISTOPHER MUSTE

Introduction

Campaigning and electioneering in the United States have undergone tremendous change since 1945. The changes have been driven by a host of factors, including declining party identification and participation in the electorate, the growing impact of the media and other communication technologies, the greater involvement of independent, professional consultants and technical experts in the management of campaigns, changes in the laws regarding elections and campaign finance, the extended duration of campaigns, and the increased resources available to incumbent candidates.

These developments have generated considerable controversy among political analysts over their sources, significance, and implications. However, nearly all analysts agree that the net result has been the creation of a campaign process that is far more candidate-centred than before. In recent decades, candidates have been campaigning less as representatives of party organizations and more as individuals offering their personal political expertise to voters.

This chapter outlines the changes which have produced this new style of American electioneering and analyses some of the implications for the functioning of the electoral process and the political system. Before turning to the analysis of modern American campaigns, however, it may be helpful to review briefly some basic aspects of the political environment which distinctively shape elections in the United States.

The authors would like to acknowledge Bruce Cain and Austin Ranney for their helpful advice and assistance. We would also like to thank Marcia K. Meyers for insightful criticism and support.

First, it should be kept in mind that the electoral task in the United States is more demanding than in m st other modern democracies. The sheer number of elected positions is huge. A government which is based on separation of executive, legislative, and judicial powers and a separate constituency for each branch requires a lot of elections to keep the system operating. At the federal level the electorate must choose a President every four years and members of the two houses of Congress every two years: thus, in November of even-numbered years all 435 seats of the House of Representatives (apportioned among the states according to population) and one-third of the 100 seats in the Senate (two from each state) are scheduled for elections. At the local level, voters must choose state governors, two houses of state legislators (usually), and many country, city, judicial, and municipal officers. Moreover, while most US elections (except some at the city and county level) are based on single-member districts and plurality voting, each type of election has its own distinct constituency and electoral calendar, which do not necessarily coincide with those of other offices.

The voter's task is made more arduous by the commitment to popular participation institutionalized in the American electoral system. For many elected offices the voters are asked not only to choose the winner in the general election, but also first to select the party nominees in primary elections. In addition, many states hold votes not just on candidates but on issues as well, in the form of initiatives, referendums, and recalls.

Hence, American voters typically face several elections during a year and frequently must mark a 'long ballot'. For example, California voters were faced with fifty-seven decisions on the November 1988 ballot alone. The number and complexity of elections in the USA may partially account for the contradiction between the American ideal of popular participation and the reality that voter turn-out is relatively low compared to other democracies.[1]

Moreover, the Democrats and the Republicans, the political parties responsible for organizing these numerous elections and helping voters to determine and express their preferences in voting, are widely perceived as weak and declining intermediaries in the process.[2] The two major parties in the USA are quite different from those in most other Western democracies. For a variety of reasons, including the historical antipathy towards 'factions' and the federal structure of the government which allows fifty diverse states to regulate the political parties, US parties have developed as decentralized, quasi-public institutions with a less programmatic basis and fewer formal membership processes than the parties of other countries.[3]

Moreover, although the USA is called a two-party system because there are only two major organized parties, the reality is more complicated. Until fairly recently, parties at the national level existed primarily in the form of 'presidential' parties organized every four years to elect a President and write a national platform, while state and local organizations constituted the real organizational base of the parties.[4] The nature and ideology of the two parties varies widely from state to state, however. Any given state might be dominated by only one party, or might have a party which carries the Democratic party label but promotes policy positions closer to those of the national Republican party. This aspect of the American political system is caricatured when political scientists say that the USA in fact has a 100-party system.

Although the state and local organizations are losing influence to candidates' own organizations and to other kinds of political intermediaries, it should be kept in mind that, for the most part, the federal campaigns described in this chapter are still waged in state-level battles. Even the one office based on a nation-wide constituency, the presidency, is conducted state by state. Since the electoral college apportions votes on a state-by state, 'winner take all' basis, candidates must pursue a states-based strategy aimed at winning a majority of state electoral votes regardless of the national popular vote. Thus, candidates pay more attention to large and marginal states, which provide the highest return in electoral votes.[5]

This should not be taken to mean, however, that what is true of campaigns for federal office is necesarily true of campaigns for state offices. The specific campaigning strategies described in this chapter have been distinctively shaped by the nature of federal elections, which typically involve larger and less homogeneous districts, much larger amounts of money and incumbent resources, and a greater degree of 'professionalism' than do elections for state office. These scale differences necessarily alter the specific strategies likely to be pursued in campaigns. However, the general trend of candidate-centred campaigning appears to be emerging in campaigns for state offices as well, albeit in a muted form.[6]

This chapter analyses the trend toward candidate-centred campaigning in the United States. After a general discussion, two subsequent sections look specifically at how this trend is expressed in presidential elections and congressional elections. More space is devoted to the analysis of presidential campaign strategies because of the dominating nature of this campaign in the American electoral landscape.

Candidate-centred Campaigning

The sea-change in electioneering which has occurred over the last forty years can be highlighted by contrasting the 1948 and 1952 presidential campaigns. The political historian Robert Dinkin uses these elections to mark the divide between what he calls the 'merchandised style' of campaigning which dominated the first half of the twentieth century and the 'mass media age' style which has dominated since.[7]

In 1948 Harry Truman achieved one of the greatest upsets in the history of presidential campaigns by effectively marshalling the electioneering tools available to him at that time: whistle-stop speeches, radio advertising, and grass-roots organizations. Truman undertook an extensive and exhausting tour of the country by special train, stopping in hundreds of towns to make speeches criticizing the 'do-nothing' Republicans; he based his campaign message on reminding farmers, labourers, and consumers of their gains under the New Deal; and he convinced party regulars and union officials to put their organizations to work getting out the Democratic vote.

In 1952, the campaign environment facing Dwight Eisenhower and Richard Nixon was basically the same, with the exception that television had arrived on the scene. But a few significant differences from the 1948 election subtly prefigured the forthcoming electioneering changes. While Truman had years of previous political experience and service in party organizations, Eisenhower had never been in politics before. While Truman promoted the policies of his party, Eisenhower appealed to voters on the basis of his celebrity status as a World War II military hero. And, finally, while

Eisenhower campaigned basically as Truman had, travelling the country by train (in fact, his was the last presidential campaign which did so), when the campaign was rocked by embarrassing financial revelations about Nixon, the negative public reaction was overcome by Nixon's nationally televised speech naming his dog Checkers as the only campaign gift he had accepted.

Thus, when we think of 1948 we recall Truman's whistle-stop tour and the speeches about the New Deal, but when we think of 1952, we picture Nixon on a television screen giving the Checkers speech. These contrasting images suggest the important changes which transformed electioneering in the ensuing forty years. That is, candidates secured nomination and campaigned on the basis of their personal records and organizations rather than on the basis of partisan appeals to the electorate; and second, campaign strategies and success were increasingly driven by the television media. Clearly, these two developments are connected, but the causal directions go both ways. Moreover, the developments have been influenced by changes in other components of the campaign environment.

Several factors are usually cited for the increasing independence of candidates from party organizations. One of the most important has been the slowly expanding use of primaries over the last half-century to determine party nominees for elections at all levels. Primaries enable candidates to pursue and secure nomination without relying on party support. Candidate independence has also been encouraged by the decreasing partisanship of the electorate, which has resulted in increased split-ticket voting and voting based on personal rather than partisan records.[8]

At the same time, several developments increased the effectiveness of candidates' private campaign organizations. Advances in computer and communication technologies provided many new tools for independent campaigning. Polling previously had been used primarily by news organizations to predict winners. By the late 1960s and 1970s, however, the costs of polls declined somewhat and the capacity to identify weaknesses and strengths in support increased. As a result, polling became integrated into the development of campaign strategy.

Computer-generated mailings made direct communication with voters effective for the first time, both for selling the candidates and their issues and for raising money. Appeals using direct mail and other 'narrowcasting' media allow candidates to reach a small, carefully targeted segment of the public. The messages are crafted to appeal to the interests of the targeted group, often in emotional language. While such messages might elicit a negative reaction from the general public or be viewed as catering to special interests, they can increase contributions, solidify electoral support, and win new voters and activists to the campaign.

Finally, air transportation has vastly expanded the possible locations a candidate or a candidate's family representatives can visit during the campaign. By the 1960s, presidential candidates travelled primarily in planes which were equipped to satisfy the needs of the accompanying press entourage. Squeezing many campaign stops into a candidate's day requires a great deal of precise planning if the candidate is to come across well to the present audience, and more importantly to any media audience. Candidates are thus advised to stump loudly and carry a large staff. Thus, campaigns rely upon a large staff, expert in doing the necessary advance work to ensure that not only does the candidate's appearance go well but that necessary media accommodations are made.

The factor most significant in encouraging all these campaigning trends is television. Indeed, the effect of the mass media on elections in the United States has come under increasing scrutiny in the past few years largely because of the increase in the number of functions the media perform in campaigns, and the perception that many features of the American electoral landscape have developed in response to media activities.

The term 'mass media' encompasses news provided by commercial and non-commercial organizations, and advertising purchased by candidates and parties. The primary function of the media in election campaigns is communication between the campaigns and the public. The decline of political parties as organizations effective at mobilizing large numbers of campaign workers and voters, and the rise of candidate-centred campaigns have both resulted from and contributed to a greater reliance on mass media to reach potential voters.

Campaigns have two avenues of access to the media. One is through the paid medium of advertising, in which campaigns may purchase television and radio time, and newspaper and magazine space to disseminate their message to the public. The other route is via the free coverage of the campaigns provided by the electronic and print news organizations. The type of access that a campaign seeks most will depend on the office being sought, the nature of the political jurisdiction, and the resources of the campaign.

Television exposure is now the main medium for presidential campaigns. In state-wide senate and gubernatorial races, heavy use of television is now commonplace, and has driven campaign costs in some cases up to tens of millions of dollars. Many candidates for the US House of Representatives find the costs of television campaigning are prohibitive in large urban areas, where House districts are typically only a fraction of the whole area and purchasing air time is extremely expensive.[9]

However, many House candidates feel they have to pay the price, as do many candidates for local office, and will often devote considerable time and money to getting their message across on television.[10] The most obvious consequence of greater reliance on television is the need for large amounts of money to buy air time, to produce the commercials, and to develop the strategy and campaign themes expressed by the commercials. The importance of media costs is shown by studies which report that about half of spending in most campaigns for national office goes for advertising and production costs.[11]

Using paid advertisements is not the only way for a campaign to reach the public, or even the best. It is an article of faith among campaign consultants that 'free' advertising—the appearance of the candidate in news stories—has more impact on the public than campaign commercials. This is primarily due to the greater credibility enjoyed by reporters presenting a story than by an obviously biased political advertisement.[12] Some candidates, frequently challengers who possess little money, place a great deal of emphasis on stimulating reportage of their campaigns. They often hire consultants to get their message on newscasts and in newspapers. This has some costs but not nearly so much as would be required by the production of commercials and the purchase of air time and print space.

The attempts by the campaigners to control the information flowing to the media can be effective in discouraging journalists from exploring issues which the campaigners want raised. Campaigners try to make the press travelling with them physically comfortable, throw parties for them, and develop personal friendships. This makes strategic sense, since journalists may be less likely to seek out or report damaging material about people they consider their friends. Cultivating friendships also increases the sting when the campaigners criticize the media for not being hard enough on their opponents or being too critical of their own candidate, since the criticism can take on a personal aspect in addition to the professional one. Campaigns also feed material to journalists on a schedule which makes it easy for them to meet their deadlines.[13] The strategy of helping the news media is becoming a matter of course in campaigns and is continued by candidates if they are elected to office.

Managing campaigns today is a matter of responding to these new circumstances. Substantial efforts are made to build up campaign organizations that are capable of raising large sums of money, ensuring that the news-gathering media present their candidates in the best possible light, and producing paid advertisements which mesh with the messages presented to the news organizations. The increasing technical sophistication required to utilize such tools effectively has led to less reliance on party regulars to perform campaign tasks. At great cost, candidates turn to professional campaign managers, strategists, fund-raisers, pollsters, and political advertising experts to help them run successful campaigns.[14]

The costs of utilizing these technological advances in campaigning have had important consequences for the electoral system. The cost of campaigns at every level of government increased dramatically from 1964 to 1984: the total spent by all candidates for all offices in the USA rose from $200 million to $1,800 million, a factor of nine.[15] As costs began rising, candidates initially responded by pursuing a wide variety of independent fund-raising strategies based on direct mail, telephone soliciting, fundraising dinners and telethons. Public concern about the vastly increased scale of political fund-raising and the tendency for a lot of money to be collected from a few wealthy 'fat cat' donors led to the enactment of campaign-finance reforms in the early 1970s intended to encourage more dispersed fund-raising.

The reforms did achieve this goal, but also had two other effects. First, they increased the ability of both presidential and congressional candidates to amass financial support independently of party organizations, thus contributing to the candidate-centred trend in electioneering. They also dramatically increased the fund-raising advantages of incumbent congressional candidates over challengers, since incumbents enjoy far greater communication access to voters and can offer potentially greater rewards to donors. The tendency of incumbents to secure re-election increased dramatically over this period, and is generally characterized both as a result of the trends causing increased partisan independence of candidates and as a contributing factor in their continuing development. The growing incumbency advantage has also raised concerns about how the new campaigning strategies affect the responsiveness of the political system.[16]

Such concerns have been fanned by perceptions that trends in the electorate have also encouraged the independence of candidates from party organizations as well as the electoral security of incumbents. Levels of voter turnout and partisan identification in the electorate have been declining since the early 1960s. The exact parameters and causes of these declines are debated. However, increased social and geographic mobility have clearly served to undercut traditional partisan connections.[17]

A shrinking electorate which relies less on party as a voting cue is likely to be more responsive to targeted appeals based on the personal characteristics and records of candidates. Moreover, research also indicates that most of the public has little political information and makes political decisions more on the basis of group affiliations than from informed deliberation, a characteristic which also encourages susceptibility to well-targeted appeals.[18]

These characteristics of the electorate—low turnout, weak party identification, and low levels of political cognition—have all influenced the strategies adopted in political campaigns. The effect of variations in turnout on political campaigning is particularly significant. Candidates need to win votes, not approval from those who will not vote. Research has shown that those who vote tend to have a different demographic profile from the general public: they are better off, better educated, and older.[19]

The representatively skewed electorate has an effect on political campaigns. Campaign strategies and messages are increasingly geared towards those who do vote, in part because campaign technologies have become sophisticated enough to permit greater targeting. The increase in 'narrowcasting' as a marketing technique has encouraged this targeting, as smaller and more homogeneous demographic and attitudinal groups can be reached with the campaign messages. Better techniques of direct mail solicitation have improved the focus and efficiency of appeals for votes, contributions, and even registration assistance and absentee voting. These avenues of communication enable the campaign to tailor the message to fit more closely the attitudes of the target group, and remove this part of the campaign from the public to a more private sphere. For example, a campaign might send a piece of fund-raising mail to members of an issue-interest group such as an environmental or religious organization, playing to that special audience and making claims that might alienate other voters in the general public who will never see the mailing.

Both targeted messages and the ones directed at the general public have often been criticized for appealing to the lowest common denominator in the electorate. Most recently, political commentators have expressed concern over the increased reliance on 'negative' campaigning based on undermining support for the opponent rather than promoting one's own candidate. Those who run such campaigns are quick to respond that negative messages have the greatest impact on the electorate. They argue that since the ultimate goal of any campaign is to win, any strategy that seems to work will and should be used; if negative campaigning is to stop, then the electorate must stop responding more readily to negative than to positive messages.

However, the public response to negative advertisement need not involve any change in vote choice to have an important effect on the election result. For example, the heavy use of negative advertisements by a Republican gubernatorial candidate in a heavily Democratic county in the 1974 Ohio elections resulted in a decline in turnout of 19 per cent over the previous election, more than enough to account for the Republican's slim margin of victory.[20]

Thus, electorate and media behaviour interact with one another, but the causal connections between the two are not clear and simple. For example, since the introduction of television to campaigning in the 1950s, presidential campaigns have increasingly communicated with voters via television, particularly in light of the declining significance of party cues. Likewise, television has become the news source most relied upon by the public.[21] But an important consequence of this increasing reliance on television may be a less informed voting public. A number of studies have pointed out the more limited substantive content of television compared to newspapers.[22] In addition, people who get their news primarily from television have been shown to have less comprehension of news stories than those who rely on print media.[23]

In sum, the rise of the candidate-centred campaign is reflected in changes in the electorate as well. The public increasingly focuses on candidate qualities such as issue positions, character, experience, and appearance, relies less on party affiliation and other cues in making vote choice, has a limited interest in gathering and digesting political information, is declining in voting turnout, and displays differential participation rates among major groups in society.

Whether the main causal direction runs from campaign to voter, or vice versa, or relates to the decline of other cue-providing political institutions, the fact is that all three have been involved in the development of a new kind of electioneering. The characteristics of the electorate and campaign incentive structure interact to produce increasingly expensive candidate-centred campaigns which devote less attention to issues and encourage weaker party affiliation among voters.

Presidential Elections

Many of the elements of the candidate-centred campaign are more visible in presidential elections than those for other offices. The presidency, as the most powerful office in the USA, is the focus of attention of the political parties, the national press, and those who believe the system needs reform. For this reason, innovations in campaigning and campaign technology, in press coverage, and in reform efforts usually occur first in presidential campaigns.

The rapid escalation in costs of presidential campaigns has been outlined above. Reactions to these increasing costs, and to the means by which funds have been raised, have prompted attempts to regulate the raising and spending of money in campaigns. In 1974, partly in response to the money-laundering scandals associated with Watergate, Congress amended the 1971 Federal Election Campaign Act, in order to achieve a comprehensive reform of the financing system for both presidential and congressional elections.

The amended FECA provided for federal public funding of presidential elections.

The presidential funding system is divided into two stages: during the nomination process, matching funds are provided to candidates who satisfy certain eligibility requirements; following the national conventions, the federal government provides an equal amount of money to each of the major-party candidates to conduct the general election campaign. Federal law prohibits the national party committees and candidates which accept these funds from spending any additional funds on the campaign.[24]

Candidates in the primary elections qualify for the matching funds by raising (in 1988, for example) $5,000 in small donations of $250 or less from each of twenty states during the primaries. To receive the money, the candidate must accept general spending limits (approximately $28 million during the pre-nomination campaign in 1988) as well as spending limits in certain states. This system gives an advantage to candidates who already have established a wide base of support prior to the primaries, whether that support was achieved through prior national exposure or through extensive personal campaigning and organizing in a number of states. The candidate's ability to continue raising funds during the course of the primary campaign is dependent on success in the primaries. Some candidates who have built successful fund-raising organizations have seen their sources of private donations dry up following one or two poor showings in the early primaries.[25]

The primary campaign component of the federal funding rules has come under criticism. The need to raise money in small donations in many states has extended the campaign season earlier and earlier before the first primary contests, as candidates campaign for funds. The need for money also diverts the attention of candidates from focusing on issues to fund-raising, as they seek to keep pace with the rules governing eligibility for matching funds. Although some critics have focused on the role of PACs (political action committees) as contributors, there is less criticism today about the role of 'big money' in the primary system: since small contributions are favoured, a greater number of people are giving than prior to the reforms.[26] The system also makes it possible for less well-known candidates who can marshal some public support to attempt a campaign; this has helped to increase the number of candidates in the race for the nomination, and hence the choices confronting the voter.

After the nominating conventions, a set sum is provided for each party's nominee to conduct the general election campaign. This sum, which totalled about $20 million for each party in 1988, is intended to function as an expenditure ceiling. However, it is estimated that in 1988 both candidates spent about an additional $25 million in so-called 'soft' money, made possible by changes to the law enacted in 1979.[27] This is accomplished by diverting money collected by the parties at the national level to state-level organizations which are not subject to the FECA limits and can spend the money in support of the presidential campaign.[28]

Since public funding began in the 1976 campaigns, no major party nominee has rejected it in the general election campaign. This may in part reflect fear that relying on private funds would be negatively perceived by the media and the public.[29] Public funding of the general election, unlike in the pre-nomination phase, significantly reduces the candidate's fund-raising burden. The other goals achieved through the system are that it reduces the risk of cash-flow problems during the campaign, it reduces overall costs somewhat, and it equalizes to some degree the financial resources of the two candidates during the general election. However, the system is also criticized for blurring the source of private campaign contributions because of the loopholes which encourage evasion.

The system of public financing also furthers the candidate-centred nature of the process. In the nomination phase, all candidates must raise money on their own, and the parties are excluded from spending on behalf of any of the presidential candidates. Following the convention, the party nominee's campaign organization strongly directs the national and state party organizations on their preferred use of 'soft' money, thus reducing the role of the party organizations. On balance, then, the campaign-finance reform laws increase the influence of candidate organizations at the expense of the parties.

One of the primary engines driving the need for money to run campaigns is the high cost of campaigning through the media.[30] The presidency is the only national elective office in the United States, and national media such as television networks and news magazines focus on it. The Kennedy–Nixon election of 1960, in which Kennedy's apparent triumph in the first nationally televised debate was generally viewed as a key to his narrow victory, ushered in an era in which television was seen as a potent force in presidential elections. Other images in the 1960s demonstrated the crucial role of television. Johnson's campaign used a commercial juxtaposition of a young girl picking wild flowers with the image of a thermonuclear atomic explosion, intending to burden his opponent with the image of warmonger. The beating of hundreds of demonstrators by police at the 1968 Democratic convention in Chicago on television was viewed by many political commentators as responsible for dooming the candidacy of party nominee Hubert Humphrey, and fostering the belief that the nominating process needed to be reformed.[31]

Since then, changes in the rules governing presidential elections have increased the role of television even more. The number of delegates chosen by direct primary election rather than by the state parties has been sharply increased, particularly by party reforms enacted since the 1968 convention.[32] The greater use of primaries makes access to voters more crucial (since their votes are now weighed more heavily in the nomination process) and television is the preferred means of communication (since it is the principal news medium used by the public, and is better at reaching the voters than the declining parties). As a result, campaigns and political observers have paid more attention to media campaign reporting.

Media coverage of the nomination process has also changed the set of environmental constraints and incentives on campaigners. One prominent feature of media coverage has been the great emphasis placed on the earliest events in the presidential election calendar, the popular selection of delegates to the national nominating conventions in two of the smaller states in the USA, Iowa and New Hampshire. Since these events take place before the remainder of the states select convention delegates, a disproportionate share of news information about the campaigns comes from these two states. In 1980, for example, one study reported that over a quarter of all coverage of the primary election process by CBS TV and the UPI wire service consisted of reporting on these two states.[33]

In addition, the candidates who do well, or at least better than expected, in these two states receive a disproportionate share of news coverage in the weeks following. The two most striking examples of the 'momentum' gained by doing well in these early states have been Jimmy Carter in 1976, and Gary Hart in 1984. Carter was relatively unknown in national politics before Iowa and New Hampshire, but his campaign was the first to spend large amounts of time and money on these states. After leading the New Hampshire Democratic Party primary with only 30 per cent of the vote, Carter was portrayed by the media as the front runner, the 'man to beat', and given extensive coverage.[34] Similarly, garnering a mere 17 per cent of the vote in the 1984 Iowa Democratic caucuses—just two percentage points ahead of George McGovern—brought Gary Hart the status of the main challenger to frontrunner Walter Mondale, who had won 45 per cent of the vote. In the following week, Hart received more coverage than Mondale, who had beaten him almost three to one.[35]

Media coverage of the nomination process has been criticized for many other reasons. The content of the coverage has come under attack for being both shallow and inconsistent. The charge of shallowness results from the fascination of the media with covering the strategic manœuvres of the campaigns. This is most clearly seen in the extent to which coverage is devoted to the 'horse race'—that is, reporting poll results, campaign strategy, and specu-lation about who is ahead and who will do well in the forthcoming primaries. In Robinson and Sheehan's study of the 1980 coverage, about two-thirds of all CBS and UPI coverage during the nomina-tion phase of the campaign was devoted to 'horse-race' coverage, with the remaining one-third spent covering candidate information and policy issues.[36]

The charge of inconsistency stems largely from the media's unpredictable and quickly changing treatment of candidates, such as Carter and Hart, who do well in the early contests. Journalists try to avoid what they regard as past mistakes in their coverage of the campaign, but are not always able to break out of the requirement to produce news that sells. While the initial burst of news coverage these candidates receive is uniformly positive (and almost exclusively about their newly elevated prospects for win-ning), they may soon be subjected to a strong critical examination of their personal lives and policy stands. The comparison of Carter's experience, in which the media reported very little negative information about him until late in the nomination process, and that of Hart, who was subjected to close scrutiny as soon as he had begun to win votes commensurate with his media coverage, is instructive.[37] The difference stems from the media's need for conflict and drama to 'sell' its product, and consequently to have a competition between at least two contenders to provide some content for this script.[38]

At the same time, the media are capable of learning from past mistakes, at least to some extent. The sharp critical focus brought to bear on Hart in 1984 was in some part due to an effort not to repeat the 'mistake' of the positive coverage given Carter in 1976. According to Larry Bartels, 'A new pattern emerged: unknown candidates who broke out of the pack received very favorable coverage until they showed signs of becoming front-runners; then they were scrutinized much more carefully.'[39] Four years later, the two leaders in the 1988 Iowa party caucuses both complained that the 'momentum' which had been accorded the Iowa winners in previous years was absent for them, another product of the determination of the media not to repeat past excesses in coverage.[40]

But such learning has limitations. There is a tension between the structural needs of the media, particularly the narrow time and cost constraints on television, and the professional pride of journalists who do not wish to be taken advantage of by one or another candidate. This tension will continue to exist, and may be exacerbated by pressure from both directions. Competition by news organizations for audiences, the key to their economic survival, has become more intense as networks and newspapers lose their audiences, in part to other media outlets such as cable TV.[41] Journalists' ability to respond to these pressures is restricted. They have limited time and ability to break outside the twin confines of messages being fed them by the campaigns and the demands of their editors and producers for frequent and up-to-date reportage. Perhaps more importantly, some journalists deny that they have any impact on elections.[42] The tendency of journalists to ignore or minimize their own power may make them more susceptible to the manipulative efforts of campaigns, as campaigns' messages are developed and delivered to take advantage of journalists' needs, schedules, and interests.

Televised presidential debates provide a case in point for the power of journalists and the eagerness of campaign strategists to influence the use of that power. Candidate debates are now an institutionalized feature in American presidential campaigning. In every election since 1976, the two major party candidates have engaged in at least one face-to-face debate, with full coverage on all three national television networks. Advisers prepare candidates for these debates by rehearsing them on points of information, presentation style, quotes and quips, and stock answers to questions for which the answers may be ill-suited.[43] Immediately following the debate, the media are besieged with representatives of each campaign, attempting to claim victory for their candidate.

Campaigns make these efforts because they want the news media to report that their candidate 'won' the debate. Initial public reaction is often somewhat divided, with neither candidate gaining a clear advantage. Yet after a day or so of media coverage proclaiming one of the candidates victorious, public attitudes regarding who 'won' have been shown to shift sharply in that direction.[44] Victory in a debate, however, does not necessarily translate into large shifts in voter preference. Some studies have indicated that, whoever is seen to win, debates primarily serve to reinforce the choices of those who already have a preference.[45]

Yet winning even such a pyrrhic debate 'victory', with marginal effects on voters' choices, is seen by the campaigns as a crucial step in gaining an advantage over their opponent. Campaign managers have no questions about journalists' power. Since they believe that free media can make or break a candidacy, campaigns typically attempt to limit and control media access to their candidate, tightly organize the candidate's schedule, carefully stage their public appearances, and time campaign announcements so as to win maximum exposure and to place their candidate in a favourable light for the media.[46] Two of the most successful models for this kind of activity have been the 1984 Reagan and 1988 Bush presidential campaigns. Both placed experienced campaign strategists and media consultants at the head of a campaign organization with strong central authority. The advantage enjoyed by the Reagan and Bush campaigns over their Democratic opponents was viewed as critical by experts in both parties. This Republican advantage in expertise is now an ongoing feature of presidential campaigns.[47]

Media-conscious presidential campaign strategies are becoming increasingly orientated towards television. But television also now plays a large role in disseminating information to others covering

the campaign, particularly to local news organizations, both electronic and print, and national print media.[48] The ability of a
campaign to do well on national television can have multiplier
effects through the reliance of other media on network news.

This emphasis on television has led campaigners to redouble
their efforts to ensure that the symbols associated with their
candidate are positive. Network news reports often allocate only a
small block of newscast time to campaigns. As a result only a small
amount of verbal information is conveyed, usually reducing a
candidate's speech to a 'sound-bite' of only a few seconds' duration. This limited amount of time prevents explication of even
simple issue positions in anything more than catch phrases, and
places a greater weight on the event's symbolism. The disjuncture
between text and symbol is illustrated by reaction to a report on
CBS News a month before the 1984 presidential election, in which
Lesley Stahl criticized President Reagan for his use of television to
create an image at variance with his policies. During her commentary, the video images projected were exactly those which the
Reagan media team had used to create the impression of a caring
and dynamic President. Contrary to her expectations, the phone
call she received from an official of the Reagan campaign did not
criticize her, but instead thanked her for conveying those positive
visual images, regarding the spoken text as having relatively little
impact on the public.[49] While this incident may overstate the case,
it is indicative of the relative importance allocated to visual images
and verbal content in television news by campaign stategists.

Campaign efforts to control media messages are ultimately aimed
at influencing the public. More and more, campaigns employ a
variety of new technologies to appeal to and gauge the response of
the voters. The most important gauging mechanism is public
opinion research, which consists primarily of telephone polls. In
addition, campaigns may also employ face-to-face interviews lasting upwards of an hour, focus groups (bringing together a small
sample of the public for discussions of candidates, issues, and
campaign strategy), and studies of physiological reactions to advertising messages. These techniques are expensive, and as usual, the
Republican party's greater ability to raise money gives it an edge.

Polling is critical for campaigns. Detailed and accurate information on voters' preferences is a crucial foundation of campaign
strategy, and the pollsters' special ability to gather it has trans-

formed their role in campaigns from the periphery to the centre. This change has taken place in the last thirty years. Louis Harris, who took polls for John F. Kennedy in 1960 was given little opportunity to influence strategy, while pollsters today often act as the primary campaign strategists. Once in office, both Presidents Ronald Reagan and George Bush have worked closely with their polling analysts, a development which has alarmed some observers. Pollsters have replaced mass organizations of activists, either party or candidate, as a means of gathering data on the preferences of the voting public.

Polls are now typically taken every day in the last ten weeks of the campaign, in order to track changes in public opinion in response to campaign developments. This information can then be integrated into subsequent strategy, affecting candidate schedules, the content of campaign messages, the types of advertising, and the allocation of resources to different states. The feedback loop, consisting of the dissemination of a campaign message, gauging public reaction to it, revising strategy based on that reaction, and disseminating a new campaign message, can now be accomplished within three or so days.[50] A campaign without the resources to do this is at a great disadvantage.

Polling is also crucial to the news media, but for different reasons. Reports of poll results constitute one of the key elements in 'horse-race' journalism. Polling data provide 'hard' evidence for news stories on how well the candidates are doing.[51] Throughout the 1960s and early 1970s, the Gallup, Roper, and Harris survey organizations periodically sold national polls to the networks and newspapers. Beginning in the mid-1970s, media organizations began to sponsor, and then conduct, their own polling. This trend has continued, with many local newspapers and television stations now having their own polls, most state-wide, but some national in scope. The latest poll often provides the lead story, and the data from a single poll can be used to provide stories for up to a week. Depending on the news organization's financial resources, polls may be taken bi-weekly, or more frequently as election day draws near. As noted previously, reports on this type of campaign news crowd out reports of campaign activities and issues.[52] One important consequence of this focus on the horse-race is that voters' willingness to vote for their preferred candidate can be dampened by reports from the media placing another candidate atop the standings.[53]

Congressional Elections

Strategies in congressional campaigning differ from those in presidential elections, in large part because the media pay less attention. Most congressional elections get relatively little free coverage, creating a special need to raise enough money to mount a campaign emphasizing heavy media use.[54] Since congressional campaigns are entirely privately funded and there are no caps to spending, fundraising is central to successful campaigning. Understanding the role of money is the key to understanding the congressional campaign environment.

When public funding of presidential elections was enacted in 1974, Congress considered funding congressional elections as well but the measure failed to pass the House. Instead, Congress mandated severe limits on both campaign contributions and expenditures in congressional elections.[55] However, a very significant 1976 Supreme Court decision held that any kind of limits on campaign expenditures (i.e. campaign expenditures, candidate expenditures, or individuals or groups spending 'independently') were unacceptable restrictions of the First Amendment right to free speech.[56] Thus, the combined effect of the legislative and judicial law-making was that costs were not capped while sources of funds were. This policy had the curious effect of stimulating an enormous growth in the numbers and activities of political action committees.

PACs are private groups that solicit funds to distribute to candidates and to conduct campaigns. They began primarily as organizations affiliated with labour unions, such as AFL-CIO's Committee on Political Education (COPE). During the 1960s, other kinds of interests, such as corporations, trade associations, and groups with shared political ideologies, began to form PACs, but the legal status of such groups was not clear. The campaign-finance reforms both clarified the legal status of PACs and created a much greater demand for their services by limiting the direct contributions that individuals could make to parties and candidates. The result was that the number of PACs grew from 113 in 1972 to nearly 4,200 by 1988, and the amount of money they contributed to congressional campaigns rose from $8.5 million in 1971–2 to $130.3 million in 1985–6.[57]

The public and some analysts tend to see PACs as the 'embodiment of special interest politics, rising campaign costs, and corruption'.[58] But analysts such as Larry Sabato and Gary Jacobson argue that PACs simply represent another form of political organization, which should be evaluated according to the traditional democratic norms.[59] They point out that individual contributions continue to be the main source of candidates' funds. For example, in 1986 PACs accounted for only one-third of House and one-fifth of Senate candidate money.[60] Of course, groups who advocate greater regulation of the political process present the same information somewhat differently: for example, Common Cause emphasizes that in 1988 almost half (210/433) of House candidates received 50 per cent or more of campaign funds from PACs.[61]

The increasing competition PACs offer parties for influence over the campaign process has provoked some concern. Critics worry that PACs are 'outside' political forces that are not accountable to voters as parties are, yet still able to affect electoral trends and bring outside influences to local elections. Defenders argue that PACs and their 'cheque-book pluralism' merely create a different distribution of power in politics by enhancing the role of the middle-class donor and may in fact enhance the responsiveness of the political system.[62]

The relationship between parties and PACs is complex, however. They are not mere competitors. There is evidence that both major parties have begun to solicit funds from PACs and channel contributions to needy candidates.[63] On the other hand, political parties and PACs are unlikely to become effective partners. While both support congressional candidates, they have different goals: the party wants to win as many seats as possible (by supporting party nominees in competitive races) whereas PACs seek to maximize access (by supporting likely winners of either party) and ideological change (by supporting candidates whose philosophies agree with theirs).

In addition to concerns about the relationship between PACs and parties in the campaign process, the role of PACs in the complicated campaign finance 'system' inaugurated by the FECA amendments has been widely criticized for negative effects on the governing process. Some analysts argue that broader, national

sources of influence over policy-making are encouraged while
politicians' ties to their local constituencies are weakened. Similarly, they argue that the diminished fund-raising importance of
political parties weakens party cohesion in government and therefore also encourages independent and fragmentary policy-making
by incumbents. Finally, the reforms are believed to encourage
corruption through widespread abuse of loopholes.

But the most commonly voiced criticism is that the incumbent
has an increased advantage in fund-raising, which reduces electoral
competition. The incumbent's ability to raise money, and the
widespread belief that an incumbent is difficult to beat, have played
a major part in the reluctance of potential opponents to challenge
the re-election of officeholders. Potentially strong challengers will
often wait until a scandal touches the incumbent or until the
incumbent's retirement. As a result, the quality of the average
challenger has declined.[64] This lack of competitiveness explains
both the decrease in incumbent defeats and the increasing average
margins by which incumbents win re-election.[65]

The incumbent fund-raising advantage has important implications for the conduct of the campaigns. Congressional candidates
must raise enough money to build an organization able to reach
potential voters, to find out what appeals to them, and to develop
a strategy to maximize the chances of winning.[66] Incumbents have
advantages in all these tasks. Because of their greater financial
resources, incumbents are better able to purchase paid media and
professional campaign services. Because of their positions as elected
representatives, they also have greater exposure in the free media.

However, media strategies in congressional compaigns differ
from those in presidential campaigns. National news media play
virtually no role. The main media outlets in the various states and
House districts vary tremendously, seriously affecting the potential
costs of different media strategies. One extreme is the state of
California with four major media markets of over one million
residents, each with a number of television stations and newspapers. Another extreme is represented by rural congressional
districts whose only media outlets are local newspapers and radio
stations.

For a Senate candidate or a House candidate in a district which
spans several media markets, reaching voters through purchased
media can be an expensive and inefficient tactic. A strategy based

instead on getting favourable free media coverage will be stressed in a campaign 'where the inherent newsworthiness of the race overshadows differences in financial resources, while paid advertisements are more important in well-funded, but relatively unnewsworthy races'.[67] There are limits to each strategy, and deciding which is appropriate is one of the most important questions facing candidates and their consultants. The issue of paid versus free media is particularly relevant to the incumbency advantage. To have any chance of success, challengers must raise enough money for advertising and/or stimulate enough free media to overcome the financial resources and familiarity of their incumbent opponent.

In fact, however, recent research shows that, allowing for inflation, spending by challengers actually declined by 30 per cent between the congressional elections of the 1974–6 period, and the 1984–6 period.[68] These data can be interpreted either as indicating that challenger quality is declining, or that contributors are more reluctant to risk their money supporting challengers. Either interpretation supports the argument that the belief in the incumbency advantage is a factor in the perpetuation of the incumbency advantage, a kind of 'voodoo incumbency' effect or 'false incumbency ideology'.

Regardless of how inflated perceptions of incumbents' advantages might be, the free media resources available to incumbent members of both the House and the Senate on a daily basis are great. Each chamber provides television studios for the members to enable them to produce video spots for use in their districts, sometimes for use in producing campaign advertising. As of 1982, almost half of all congressional press offices produced cable programmes for their home districts.[69] A satellite cable television network, C-Span, provides coverage of the activities of both chambers, including debate on the floor of both House and Senate. Moreover, these free media resources, available only to members of Congress, are provided at taxpayer expense.

Such resources have affected the behaviour of incumbents not only during the campaigning process but throughout their congressional service. C-Span claims to be seen by as many as 38 per cent of the public for at least one hour per month.[70] Its presence in the legislative chambers has stimulated attempts to use the medium for partisan advantage, a re-emphasis on floor debates, efforts by relatively unknown members to enhance their national prestige, and the delivery of ideological appeals to reach national issue constituencies.[71] The video facilities have been used by incumbent legislators to maintain high visibility in the home district by producing material for local television stations. Even when local news programmes do not use the material, the legislator can expect to reach a sizeable percentage of his or her constituents directly through C-Span and local cable public affairs channels, since many local governments require the companies awarded the cable contracts to allocate one or more channels to public affairs and political broadcasts.

Conclusion

This use of electronic communications media blurs the line between campaigning and legislating. While the use of these media undoubtedly increases the level of information held by the viewing constituents, elected representatives make every effort to control the media, in order to appear in the most positive light. The legislator can turn a floor speech into a stirring defence of district interests, or tout his accomplishments in a public affairs programme. The result is that the electronic media have invaded one environment in which concentration on the functioning of the institution of Congress and deliberation about policy was not previously hindered by the glare of television lights. The requirements of campaigning thus gain added influence in the law-making process.

In his important book on the US Congress, David Mayhew used the assumption that members of Congress are 'single-minded seekers after reelection' as a tool to help understand their behaviour.[72] The contrast Mayhew pointed out between the member activities which help to create an appearance of effectiveness for the benefit of the district, and the real work of policy-making (which is not as visible or appealing to the constituents) may be disappearing as communications technology reaches deeper into the working of the House and Senate. The roles of candidate and legislator are less separate, but it is campaigning which has affected legislating, not vice versa. The perpetual campaign is clearly a diversion of legislative energy. It is easier to garner good press for constituency services and symbolic-issue stands than to advocate controversial policies which may be unpopular with a segment of the home constituency. Little incentive exists for those in office to take risks on policy issues, since potential opponents are geared to pounce on mistakes.

Even if this increased use of and access to electronic media does not have negative consequences for the deliberative aspects of policy-making, it puts a powerful set of tools in the hands of incumbents seeking to discourage attempts by potential opponents to defeat them. This should give pause to those who believe that the new campaign technologies are simply supplanting old ways of doing the same things.

In both presidential and congressional campaigns, we must ask whether the vast amounts of time and money spent on campaigning are the best use for these resources. The problem is particularly acute in presidential elections: some candidates have spent over a year campaigning before the first presidential primary. The candidates who emerge from this process are more likely to be those who can handle the physical rigours of long campaigns, but also those who are better at the particular tasks required by our system of campaigning. There is no reason why someone cannot be skilled in both campaigning and governing, but the modern campaign places such a high premium on the former that the latter may become 'crowded out', in a twist of Gresham's Law. The blurring of the lines between the two makes evaluating the latter difficult, if not impossible, for voters and students of government alike.

But by the same token, those who decry the dangers which the American political system faces as a result of these changes in electioneering must clearly specify what the problems are. Incorrect specification of the dysfunctional aspects of the current system can divert attention from more serious problems. The success of any effort to improve the electoral system depends on having a clear understanding of the close interconnections among the components of the campaign environment. The interrelationships among party and legal rules, media, campaign strategists, available technology, fund-raising, and the electorate are complex and tightly drawn. A change in one area will inevitably result in adjustments in other areas. Understanding the likely chain reactions is essential to minimize the degree to which any proposed changes, contrary to the intent of their advocates, may redound to the detriment of the system as a whole.

Notes

1. The term 'American electorate' is misleading if it is understood to imply a single entity. The term is better understood as containing multiple referents, which vary from election to election, over time, and in different locales. Structural features of the American political system, such as the multitude of elective offices at each level of government, often with separate electoral calendars at each level, contribute to the large number of electorates. So do party nomination procedures, which often consist of direct, open primary elections, in which there is no limit to the number of candidates who can run. The result is a profusion of offices and propositions confronting the voter, in some instances running into the hundreds. As a result, levels of turn-out vary by office and election. The highest levels of turn-out are found in the quadrennial general election for President. Voting levels for lower offices—Senators, House Members, Governors—are in turn lower, and local offices and ballot propositions are lower still. One study showed that turn-out averages 55% in presidential elections, 45% in gubernatorial elections, and 25% in mayoral elections. Even in a high turnout presidential election, voters who cast ballots for president often do not complete the lengthy ballot, a phenomenon called 'dropoff'.

2. In recent years this characterization has taken quite a critical turn as elections are increasingly perceived as dominated by 'entrepreneurial', 'professional' candidates rather than party organizations. Examples of this large literature include Alan Ehrenhalt, *The United States of Ambition: Politicians, Power, and the Pursuit of Office* (New York: New York Times Press, 1991); Bruce Cain, John Ferejohn, and Morris Fiorina, *The Personal Vote: Constituency Service and Electoral Independence* (Cambridge, Mass: Harvard University Press, 1987); Richard Fenno, *Homestyle: House Members in Their Districts* (Boston: Little, Brown, 1978); David Mayhew, *Congress: The Electoral Connection* (New Haven, Conn.: Yale University Press, 1974).

3. Leon Epstein, *Political Parties in the American Mold* (Madison, Wis.: University of Wisconsin Press, 1986), ch. 6, 'Parties as Public Utilities', 155–99.

4. V. O. Key, Jr., *Politics, Parties and Pressure Groups*, 3rd edn. (New York: Thomas Y. Crowell, 1952), ch. 11. For more recent analyses of American political parties, see Epstein, *Political Parties*; David Mayhew, *Placing Parties in American Politics: Organization, Electoral Settings, and Government Activity in the Twentieth Century* (Princeton, NJ: Princeton University Press, 1986); Cornelius Cotter, James

Gibson, John Bibby, and Robert Huckshorn, *Party Organizations in American Politics* (New York: Praeger, 1989); and Samuel Eldersveld, *Political Parties in American Society* (New York: Basic Books, 1982).

5. In the electoral college, each state is accorded a number of electoral votes equal to its representation in Congress (i.e. two for its Senators and one for the number of representatives it has according to population). All of a state's electoral votes are cast for the candidate who wins a majority or plurality of the public's vote in the state. If no candidate receives a national majority of the electoral votes, the decision among the top three vote-getters is made by the House of Representatives where each state delegation is assigned one vote and the candidate who receives a majority of these votes is elected.

6. The classic works on state elections are Malcolm E. Jewell and David M. Olson, *American State Political Parties and Elections*, 2nd edn. (Homewood, Ill.: Dorsey Press, 1982); and V. O. Key, Jr., *American State Politics: An Introduction* (New York: Knopf, 1956). For an account of how one important, current national trend transposes to the state level, see David Breaux, 'Specifying the Impact of Incumbency on State Legislative Elections: A District Level Analysis', *American Politics Quarterly*, 18 (1990), 270.

7. Robert J. Dinkin, *Campaigning in America: A History of Election Practices* (New York: Greenwood Press, 1989).

8. See Martin P. Wattenberg, *The Decline of American Political Parties, 1952–1988* (Cambridge, Mass.: Harvard University Press, 1990); Walter De Vries and Lance Tarrance, Jr., *The Ticket Splitter: A New Force in American Politics* (Grand Rapids, Mich.: Eerdmans Publishing Co., 1972); and Angus Campbell and Warren E. Miller, 'The Motivational Basis of Straight and Split Ticket Voting', *American Political Science Review*, 51 (1957), 293–312.

9. Steve Ansolabehere, Roy Behr, and Shanto Iyengar, 'Mass Media and Elections: An Overview', *American Politics Quarterly*, 19 (Jan. 1991), 109–39.

10. Ehrenhalt, *The United States of Ambition*, 22–3.

11. Doris Graber. *Mass Media in American Politics* (Washington, DC: CQ Press, 1990).

12. Dean E. Alger, 'The Media in Elections: Evidence on the Role and the Impact', in Graber, *Media Power in Politics*, 147–60. For some experimental evidence on viewer response to news programmes, see Shanto Iyengar and Donald R. Kinder, *News That Matters* (Chicago: University of Chicago Press, 1987).

13. Nelson W. Polsby and Aaron Wildavsky, *Presidential Elections: Contemporary Strategies of American Electoral Politics*, 7th edn. (New York: Free Press, 1988), 217–18.

14. Larry Sabato, *The Rise of Political Consultants* (New York: Basic Books, 1981).
15. Polsby and Wildavsky, *Presidential Elections*, 45.
16. Authors who have raised this concern include Cain, Ferejohn, and Fiorina, *The Personal Vote*; Gary Jacobson and Sam Kernell, *Strategy and Choice in Congressional Elections*, 2nd edn. (New Haven, Conn.: Yale University Press, 1983); Thomas Mann, *Unsafe at Any Margin* (Washington, DC: American Enterprise Institute, 1978); and Morris Fiorina, *Congress: Keystone of the Washington Establishment* (New Haven, Conn.: Yale University Press, 1977).
17. The literature in this area is voluminous. On declining partisan attachment, see Wattenberg, *The Decline of American Political Parties* The controversy over turnout decline has engaged a number of scholars. See Raymond E. Wolfinger and Steven J. Rosenstone, *Who Votes?* (New Haven, Conn.: Yale University Press, 1980); Walter Dean Burnham, *The Current Crisis in American Politics* (New York: Oxford University Press, 1982); Frances Fox Piven and Richard A. Cloward, *Why Americans Don't Vote* (New York: Pantheon Books, 1989). For evidence regarding residential mobility, see Peverill A. Squire, Raymond E. Wolfinger, and David Glass, 'Residential Mobility and Voter Turnout', *American Political Science Review*, 81 (Mar. 1987), 45-61.
18. Philip E. Converse, 'The Nature of Belief Systems in Mass Publics', in David E. Apter (ed.), *Ideology and Discontent* (New York: Free Press, 1964); W. Russell Neuman, *The Paradox of Mass Politics* (Cambridge, Mass.: Harvard University Press, 1986); Eric R. A. N. Smith, *The Unchanging American Voter* (Berkeley Calif.: University of California Press, 1989).
19. Political scientists are divided on the question of whether these demographic differences have policy implications. One school has emphasized similarities in the opinions of voters and non-voters when polled about candidates or policies under public consideration. Others have argued that the large number of non-voters allows both parties and candidates to ignore the needs of a large portion of the population when crafting policy positions. For an exposition of the two opposing views, see Piven and Cloward, *Why Americans Don't Vote*; R. E. Wolfinger and S. J. Rosenstone, 'The Effects of Registration Laws on Voter Turnout', *American Political Science Review*, 72 (Mar. 1978), 22–45.
20. Sabato, *The Rise of Political Consultants*, 325–6.
21. Polsby and Wildavsky, *Presidential Elections*, 333.
22. Michael J. Robinson and Margaret Sheehan, *Over the Wire and on*

TV; CBS and UPI in Campaign '80 (New York: Russell Sage Foundation, 1983).

23. See Michael M. Gant and Norman R. Luttbeg, *American Electoral Behavior* (Itasca, Ill.: F. E. Peacock, 1991), 219–20, for a complete discussion, including some cautious counter-evidence.

24. However, this restriction does not apply to spending on behalf of candidates by individuals or groups not controlled by the candidates or their organizations.

25. Frank J. Sorauf, *Money in American Elections* (Glenview, Ill.: Scott, Foresman, 1988), 197–201 describes the consequences of poor primary showings, using the illustration of John Glenn, whose 1984 candidacy ran out of money shortly after his losses in early contests. Similarly, Congressman Richard Gephardt withdrew from the race only six weeks after winning the Iowa caucuses, due to his poor showing in other contests, which had eviscerated his previously substantial campaign treasury.

26. Sorauf, *Money in American Elections*, 45–9, has a broad discussion of the difficulties in pinning down this trend using reference to hard data.

27. John H. Kessel, *Presidential Campaign Politics: Coalition Strategies and Citizen Response*, 3rd edn. (Chicago: Dorsey Press, 1988), 150–1.

28. Sorauf, *Money in American Elections*, 320–3. Sorauf cites Elizabeth Drew, *Politics and Money* (New York: Macmillan, 1983), as the source of the term 'soft money'.

29. Even in the nomination phase of the campaign, only one candidate—Republican John Connally in 1980—has rejected public funds, due to the strictures on fund-raising that accompany them. His inability to win more than one delegate despite funds of over $11 million has discouraged others from pursuing that strategy.

30. Graber, *Mass Media in American Politics*, 203–4.

31. For an excellent account of the 1968 conventions, see Theodore H. White, *The Making of the President, 1968* (New York: Atheneum Publishers, 1969).

32. See Byron E. Shafer, *Quiet Revolution: The Struggle for the Democratic Party and the Shaping of Post-Reform Politics* (New York: Russell Sage Foundation, 1983) for an extended account of the first round of what has become a quadrennial controversy. For a discussion of the ongoing debate, see Polsby and Wildavsky, *Presidential Elections*, 238–69.

33. Robinson and Sheehan, *Over the Wire and on TV*.

34. Graber, *Mass Media in American Politics*, 197–202.

35. Gary R. Orren, 'The Nomination Process: Vicissitudes of Candidate

Selection', 53, in Michael Nelson (ed.), *The Elections of 1984* (Washington, DC: CQ Press, 1985); Larry M. Bartels, *Presidential Primaries and The Dynamics of Public Choice* (Princeton, NJ: Princeton University Press, 1988), 35.

36. Robinson and Sheehan, *Over the Wire and on TV*; for a 1984 update, see Michael J. Robinson, 'Where's the Beef? Media and Media Elites in 1984', in Austin Ranney (ed.), *The American Elections of 1984* (Durham, American Enterprise Institute Book published by Duke University Press, 1985), 166–202.

37. Bartels, *Presidential Primaries*, 35–40

38. See Austin Ranney, *Channels of Power* (New York: Basic Books, 1983), 42–63 for a discussion of the structural biases of television news organizations.

39. Bartels, *Presidential Primaries*, 39.

40. Paul Taylor, *See How They Run* (New York: Alfred A. Knopf, 1990), 115–18.

41. Ranney, *Channels of Power*, 160–3.

42. Comment made by John Jacobs at 'What's Wrong with American Political Institutions', conference held at the Institute of Governmental Studies, University of California, Berkeley, 5–7 July 1991. A particularly telling example of this attitude is found in a remark made by Roan Conrad, political editor of NBC News: 'From a newsman's point of view, the news is what happens. The news is what somebody says or does. The news is not a reporter's perception or explanation of what happened; it is simply what happens.' (Quoted in Ranney, *Channels of Power*, 17–18.)

43. See Robinson, 'Where's the Beef?' in Ranney, *The American Elections of 1984*, 196–200; Sidney Kraus, *Televised Presidential Debates and Public Policy* (Hillsdale, NJ: L.Erlbaum Associates, 1988).

44. For one example, see Michael J. Robinson, 'News Media Myths and Realities: What the Network News Did and Didn't Do in the 1984 General Campaign', in Kay Lehman Schlozman (ed.), *Elections in America* (Boston: Allen and Unwin, 1987).

45. F. Christopher Arterton, *Media Politics: The News Strategies of Presidential Campaigns* (Lexington, Mass.: D. C. Heath, 1984), 55.

46. F. Christopher Arterton, 'Campaign Organizations Confront the Media-Political Environment', in Graber, *Media Power in Politics*, 161–9,

47. See Marjorie Randon Hershey, 'The Campaign and the Media', in Gerald M. Pomper *et al.*, *The Election of 1988: Reports and Interpretations* (Chatham, NJ: Chatham House, 1989), 73–102, esp. p. 88, for a discussion of the strategic aspect of the competition between the Bush and Dukakis campaigns.

48. Timothy Crouse, *Boys on the Bus* (New York: Ballantine Books, 1973); see also Paul Abramson, F. Christopher Arterton, and Gary R. Orren, *The Electronic Commonwealth: The Impact of New Media Technologies on Democratic Politics* (New York: Basic Books, 1988), 12–29, for a discussion of the homogenization and pluralism of news media.

49. Martin Schram, 'The Great American Video Game', in Graber, *Media Power in Politics*, 184–92.

50. Abramson, Arterton, and Orren, *The Electronic Commonwealth*, 91–121.

51. Bartels, *Presidential Primaries*, 39–45.

52. Robinson and Sheehan, *Over the Wire and on TV*.

53. Bartels, *Presidential Primaries*.

54. Ansolabehere, Behr, and Iyengar, 'Mass Media and Elections', 109–39.

55. The reforms enacted extensive limits on expenditures by campaigns, personal expenditures by candidates, and independent spending by groups or individuals on behalf of a candidate. There were also strict limits on contributions, which were upheld by the Supreme Court. The limit for individual contributions to candidates was $1,000; the limit for both PAC and party committee contributions was $5,000 per candidate per campaign (so in effect $10,000 per candidate participating in both a primary and general election); and individuals were limited to $25,000 annual limit on total amounts they could contribute. Parties were subject to the same contribution limits as PACs, but state and national parties were allowed to spend additional money on behalf of their candidates (known as 'co-ordinated party spending'). The limits here are indexed in a complicated manner. In House campaigns, the original limit was $10,000; by 1988 inflation made it $23,050. For the Senate, the limit varies with the population of the state but is equal to 2 cents times the voting age population, adjusted for inflation since 1974, with a minimum of $20,000 in 1974 also adjusted; in 1988 the ceiling ranged from about $46,000 in the least populous states to about $940,000 in California, the most populous state. In addition to these reforms, the 1974 FECA amendments created the Federal Election Commission (FEC), an agency to compile and publish records regarding contributions and expenditures as well as to enforce the FECA law generally. For details, see Sorauf, *Money in American Elections*, 34–9.

56. *Buckley v. Valeo*, 424 US 1 (1976).

57. Larry Sabato, *Paying for Elections: The Campaign Finance Thicket* (New York: Priority Press Publications, 1989), 10.

58. Ibid. 17. For a typical critical account of PACs, see R. Kenneth

Godwin, *One Billion Dollars of Influence: The Direct Marketing of Politics* (Chatham, N.J.: Chatham House Publishers, 1988).

59. See Sabato, *Paying for Elections*; and Gary Jacobson, 'Parties and PACs in Congressional Elections', in Lawrence Dodd and Bruce Oppenheimer (eds.), *Congress Reconsidered*, 4th edn. (Washington, DC: Congressional Quarterly Press, 1989), 117–42.

60. Jacobson, 'Parties and PACs', 122.

61. Susan Manes, 'Up for Bid: A Common Cause View', in Margaret Latus Nugent and John Johannes (eds.), *Money, Elections and Democracy: Reforming Congressional Campaign Finance* (Boulder, Colo.: Westview Press, 1990), 17–24.

62. Sorauf, *Money in American Elections*, ch. 4, 'Political Action Committees', 77–120.

63. Larry Sabato, 'PACs and Parties', in Nugent and Johannes, *Money, Elections and Democracy*, 187–204

64. See Gary C. Jacobson, *The Politics of Congressional Elections*, 2nd edn. (Boston: Little, Brown, 1987); and *The Electoral Origins of Divided Government* (Boulder, Colo: Westview Press, 1990).

65. It is worth noting, however, that despite the heavy odds in their favour, some incumbents are defeated, usually by exceptionally good challengers with good financial resources.

66. Ehrenhalt, *United States of Ambition*, 11–17.

67. Ansolabehere, Behr, and Iyengar, 'Mass Media and Elections', 109–39.

68. Alan I. Abramowitz, 'Incumbency, Campaign Spending, and the Decline of Competition in US House Elections', *Journal of Politics*, 53 (Feb. 1991) 34–55.

69. Anne Haskell, 'Live from Capitol Hill', *Washington Journalism Review* (Nov. 1982), 49, cited in Abramson, Arterton, and Orren, *The Electronic Commonwealth*, 52.

70. Michael J. Robinson and Maura Clancy, 'Who Watches C-Span', *C-Span Update*, Special Supplement, 14 January 1985, cited in Abramson, Arterton, and Orren, *The Electronic Commonwealth*, 143.

71. Abramson, Arterton, and Orren, *The Electronic Commonwealth*, 142–6.

72. Mayhew, *Congress: The Electoral Connection*, 5.

References

For a listing of relevant works see the bibliography at the end of Chapter 12.

3

Latin America

ALAN ANGELL, MARIA D'ALVA KINZO, and
DIEGO URBANEJA

Elections in Latin America are held under sharply differing circumstances, ranging from civil war in El Salvador to the peaceful
routines that characterize Venezuela. They may be conducted with
scrupulous attention to legal regulations, as in Costa Rica, or with
flagrant violations of all such codes as in the recent elections in
Haiti. Within the same country, elections in the modern urban
areas may resemble a modern North American campaign while in
the backward rural areas the politics of clientelism and patronage
largely determine and deliver votes. In some countries, parties may
have adopted the techniques of modern electioneering, but without
much change in policies or organization or behaviour. In other
countries, the modernization of electioneering techniques has been
accompanied by the modernization of the overall political system,
with the development of new parties, new policies, and new modes
of political behaviour.

Whatever the differences between the politics and party systems
of Latin American countries, there are some observable general
trends in patterns of electioneering. Compared with the 1950s all
Latin American countries are more urban, more industrialized, and
with a huge increase in access to television. Electoral campaigns
are arguably much more Americanized now than in Europe. The
dominant form of campaigning is on TV; opinion polls are
followed with the interest normally associated with football results;
campaigning emphasizes personalities; and slick TV advertisements
for politicians blend harmoniously with those for consumer products. In one respect elections in Latin America differ from those of
the USA—levels of participation are generally much higher, and
elections generate much greater excitement. Elections in Venezuela
have an atmosphere of public carnival. In Brazil so much campaigning is conducted with musical jingles that an observer might think

he was witnessing a musical competition rather than an electoral contest. These developments contrast with the e.ectoral campaigns of the 1950s in many countries where the core of campaigning was the long and serious set-piece speech of the candidate before a mass public meeting.

Articles dealing with Latin America make disclaimers that not all countries will be covered, and this one is no exception. We will concentrate on elections in Brazil, Chile, and Venezuela, for the good reason that we have individually observed elections in those countries over a number of years. But the three cases also offer interesting parallels and contrasts. Brazil was the only recent military dictatorship to hold regular elections. Admittedly the party system was devised by the regime, and the electoral process was controlled and regulated to serve the government's interests. Yet the very existence of elections which in the urban areas were not distorted by fraud, provided a crucial method of expressing opposition not just to the government but to the political regime. General Pinochet in Chile did not permit elections or party activity, for his intention was a complete restructuring of the political system. However, when there was a free and fair plebiscite in 1988 (as opposed to the questionable ones of 1978 and 1980) it became a verdict on sixteen years of dictatorship. Opposition victory made necessary the holding of competitive elections for President and Congress in 1989. Venezuela before 1958 had, by contrast with Chile, little experience of competitive elections. Since then, however, elections have taken place with clockwork regularity, and parties have been voted in and out of office with almost equal regularity.

Before considering these three cases, some general observations are in order. Latin American political systems are presidential and not parliamentary, and most countries use some form of proportional representation (PR) electoral system. The key election is for the president. In some countries—Colombia and Venezuela are examples—simultaneous presidential and congressional elections deter party fragmentation, and in Uruguay electors must vote for the same party for legislative and executive elections. But most countries have PR electoral systems which ensure the representation of a large number of parties in congress, and staggered elections for President and Congress frequently lead to minority support for the executive in congress. The coexistence of a multi-party system, powerful presidents and staggered elections generate tension and conflict between the President and Congress.

With the return to democracy in several Latin American countries in the last decade, institutional and electoral reform are subjects of debate as countries attempt to devise political systems that do not collapse in the face of social pressure and economic crisis. Elections are currently of great importance, for they are a way for the electorate to demonstrate not just its preference between parties and policies, but also a commitment to the democratic process as such. Rates of electoral participation are generally high, and when they are not the reason may be fear of fraud or of the lack of relevance of the elections. Abstention in Mexico has increased as widespread suspicion of fraud reduced interest in elections. But even Mexico, which for many years controlled elections very closely, has permitted a degree of electoral pluralism. In 1988 the presidential candidate of the official party, the PRI, was elected with the smallest majority (50.36 per cent) in the history of the party. Moreover, for the first time, the regime allowed a member of an opposition party to win an election for a state governorship.

In Colombia, the political pact between the Liberals and Conservatives, first implemented in 1958, alternated the presidency between the parties, and divided Congress equally between them. In these circumstances it is hardly surprising that electoral participation was low, ranging from 68.0 per cent in the first election inaugurating the political agreement in 1958 to a low of 33.4 per cent in 1978. The average turn-out between 1958 to 1986 was 48.5 per cent.[1] There are usually several competing lists of candidates within each of the two major parties. The Colombian electoral system allocates seats according to the Hare quota: seats not allocated by quota are distributed according to the largest remainders. This procedure applies first to the parties, and is then used within the parties to allocate seats between competing lists. This electoral system encourages a party system in which the major parties are divided into a series of factions constituted around a mixture of personal, policy, and regional differences. Political bosses effectively control the process at the local level. Continuing concern with the low level of political participation in Colombia led to two important reforms intended to increase participation: the direct election of mayors by means of a plurality election in a single-seat district, and a primary election within the Liberal Party. The election of a Constituent Assembly in 1991 is also expected to be the prelude to further reforms intended to modernize the party system. Colombia's political system has in fact been remarkably resilient in the face of terrible challenges—first of inter-party violence on a massive scale, then the development of widespread guerrilla activity, then the growth of a huge illegal drugs trade. But there is little doubt that the system of factionalized ill-disciplined parties, however appropriate for an earlier period in the republic's development, is ill suited for the present demands. Hence electoral reform is not merely seeking to improve the system; it may be necessary to the very survival of that system itself.

Even in societies torn by civil strife, such as El Salvador or Peru, elections with genuine, if limited, participation decide who governs. Electors living in areas of those two countries under guerrilla control cannot vote, and sectors of the population who support the guerrillas may choose not to vote, but amongst the remaining population, which constitutes the large majority, elections proceed, if not exactly normally, at least after a fashion; they do reflect changing opinion and provide for alternative governments. Elections may be used as an inducement to persuade guerrilla groups to lay down their arms and compete at the polls. Electoral reform in Colombia is intended to make easier the seating of minority groups in Congress and to attract guerrilla groups into electoral politics. In the late 1980s in some countries which have practically never known competitive elections, such as Paraguay and Haiti, political campaigns were allowed and elections took place. It is true, however, that they were also conducted under conditions that impose serious limits on both parties and candidates, and in Haiti winning an election is no guarantee of assuming office or of remaining there very long.

These are the worst cases. Most countries in Latin America have much longer-established electoral and constitutional traditions: that of Colombia equals many European countries in its almost uninterrupted longevity. Indeed the problem for some republics is not that their elections are too infrequent but that they have too many, with the cost of voter fatigue and boredom, and hence increased abstention.

What explains the recent increase in the importance of elections in Latin America? The collapse of military regimes in a number of countries led to the re-establishment of democracies. But these democracies are still fragile, and elections are a crucial part of the process of consolidation for they serve not only as expressions of popular choice, but as evidence that both the left and the right, whose attachment to democracy in the past has been conditional at best, now accept the rules of pluralistic democracy. The major criticism of the government made by the opposition parties in Mexico is directed, for example, not at its economic policy, but at the lack of democracy in political life, and the absence of safeguards to ensure that elections are free from fraud. Even when the government in Mexico agreed in 1991 after long opposition pressure to draw up a new electoral roll, there were complaints that the government deliberately undercounted the electorate of the capital city where the opposition is strong.

Because of the fragile nature of democracy in a number of countries, and even in Venezuela experience of dictatorship is well within living memory, the legal arrangements for elections assume great importance. It is vital that an independent and impartial regulatory authority should exist and have power. One of the factors that helped to make the 1989 Brazilian presidential elections widely accepted as legitimate was the authority of the Federal Electoral Tribunal which publicly made clear its independence from executive pressure. The same role was played by the Electoral Commission in Chile in the 1988 plebiscite and 1989 elections. One of the factors that casts doubt on the validity of elections in Mexico is the absence of a body with similar authority.

The issues at stake in Latin America are more urgent and ideological than those of Western Europe—a reflection of the economic recession that has affected the region with the debt crisis of the 1980s. Hyperinflation, increasing unemployment, and poverty help to explain why at the forefront of elections in Latin America alternative ideological systems are on offer. The failure of governments to live up to sometimes exaggerated promises helps to explain the sharp fluctuations in electoral results. In Peru, for example, the economy has been in decline for most of the 1980s with the occasional year of ephemeral recovery. Living standards, already low, have been savagely cut as GDP has fallen, and as inflation has risen to dizzy heights: in one twelve-month period in 1988/9 it reached an annual rate of close on 11,000 per cent. In addition a guerrilla war has cost the lives of an estimated 20,000

Peruvians since 1980. It is hardly surprising that outgoing governments have been sweepingly rejected in favour of a very distinct alternative. President Belaunde was elected with 45.4 per cent of the vote in 1980 only to see his party reduced to 6.3 per cent in 1985; and President Alan Garcia, elected with 45.7 per cent in 1985, saw his party fall to 19.1 per cent in 1990, ousted by an almost completely unknown candidate whose appeal seemed to be based largely on the fact that he was unknown, that he was of Japanese origin, and that he was supported by the evangelical Churches.

Peru is an extreme case of electoral volatility. Yet in spite of the economic decline, political uncertainty, and guerrilla conflict, elections are held regularly; they are conducted as fairly as can be expected in the circumstances; and they produce a change of government and of governing ideology. It is no exaggeration to say that the basis of legitimation of the fragile democracy that exists in Peru is founded more than anything else upon regular and competitive elections, and participation is high, given the circumstances— 62 per cent in 1980 and 70 per cent in 1985.

Another reason for the increasing importance of elections in Latin America is that the political right is presently committed to seeking power through elections. In the past the right frequently sought power through support for military intervention. Following the wave of military governments in the 1960s and 1970s, the right tried, though not always successfully, to exercise influence through co-operation with authoritarian governments. With the failure of those governments, and the return to democracy the right has entered the electoral arena. It has done so with some confidence because of its new found belief in neo-liberal ideas, a doctrine that is seen to be in international political ascendancy, and because it sees the left struggling to assemble its own ideology following the collapse of international communism.

The right, with its access to finance and its international links, has further contributed to the modernization of electoral techniques. Television now plays a vital role in election campaigns. Campaign advisers from the USA and elsewhere play an active role in devising campaign strategies, and the tactics of American campaigns—from motor cavalcades to brief and personalized political messages on television—have become widespread. The use of such techniques is widespread across the political spectrum.

In campaigning for the plebiscite in Chile in 1988, President Pinochet sought the advice of British public relations consultants who had advised Mrs Thatcher, and although clearly uneasy with his new role as a candidate for office, spoke on TV in the intimate tones assumed necessary to inspire public confidence. What was remarkable about the campaigning in Chile was the similarity in electioneering techniques used by proponents of very different ideologies. Unfortunately for Pinochet, the opposition campaign was better than that of the government, and it is not unreasonable to argue that the better use of electioneering techniques by the opposition was a powerful factor in explaining their 55 per cent share of the vote.

Electioneering in Brazil

Brazil was unique amongst the Latin American military dictatorships in holding regular elections for Congress, the state legislatures, and municpal offices. But those elections hardly conformed to democratic practices. There was no direct election for the President, who was chosen in theory by an electoral college composed by members of Congress and delegates from the state legislatures, but in practice by a restricted group of senior military officers. Neither were there elections for state governors, for the mayors of the capital cities of the states, nor for cities considered to be 'areas of national security'. The government created and allowed only two parties to operate, a pro-government party ARENA, and an opposition party, the MDB. The government did not hesitate to use intimidation against opposition candidates. After 1973, when a process of controlled liberalization began, the opposition used TV to its advantage in electoral campaigns. The response of the government was to impose further restrictions on the opposition's access to the media, and constant attempts to devise electoral systems that would disadvantage the opposition. But for all these restrictions, the opposition vote continued to grow, especially in the modern urban areas, and this steady growth undermined the military regime's claim to legitimacy, for each election was in effect a plebiscite on the military government.

Restrictions on suffrage have been substantially removed since the return to democracy in 1985. All citizens now have the right to vote: illiterates were enfranchised in 1985, and in accordance with the 1988 Constitution, the age limit for voting has been lowered to 16 (women were given the right to vote in 1932). Voting is compulsory for electors aged between 18 and 70 years. This requirement, and the declaration of election days as public holidays, undoubtedly increases the level of participation in a country with a relatively low level of politicization.[2] But it also helps to explain the high proportion of blank and null ballots—in part indifference to the result, in part a substantial protest vote, in part genuine errors in completing what is a complicated ballot. Blank and null votes amounted to 19 per cent in 1978, 13 per cent in 1982, and 6 per cent in 1985 and in 1989. Abstentions were 18 per cent in 1978, 17 per cent in 1982 and 1985, and 13 per cent in the presidential elections in 1989. In 1990 there was a sharp increase in abstentions, and blank and null voting, because of boredom with elections that had been held every year since 1985 except for 1987, because of increasing criticism of the way that the Congress had been behaving, and because of the excessive number of candidates and a very complicated ballot paper.[3]

Brazil has used a majority voting system as well as proportional representation. Under the new constitution, the President, state governors, and mayors are elected by a run-off ballot between the two leading candidates if neither receives an absolute majority on the first ballot. Federal senators are elected by a simple plurality system, and federal deputies by a system of PR.[4] Candidates are selected by delegates to party conventions. The Workers Party (PT) has begun to experiment with primaries, but normally the choice of candidates is made by the party leadership, though this can be challenged if an aspirant for office controls a large block of party delegates.

To be elected, candidates need to have votes equivalent to the electoral quota; unallocated remaining seats are shared out amongst the winning parties by the D'Hondt system. Most importantly, the system is not based on a predetermined party list order. Rather, the number of individual votes each candidate obtains determines the order in which he or she appears on the party list. This voting system has the advantage of allowing voters, rather than parties, to choose the winning candidates. But it tends to disrupt party organization and discipline in so far as it encourages competition between individual candidates for the same party rather than between parties. At this time in the uncertain political development of Brazil, disciplined and accountable parties could help to strengthen the political system. One can imagine how confusing it is for voters to choose candidates when some party lists contain almost a hundred candidates.[5] It is almost inevitable that many votes are either casual, because of the impossibility of assessing the merits of so many candidates, or based upon personal links with local political bosses whose clientelistic style remains a common device to capture support in the rural areas. In short, as Shugart writes of the Brazilian (and of the similar Colombian electoral system), 'candidates run against members of their own party as much or more than against members of other parties, central party leaders do not determine who will be elected, and members of the assembly seek out 'bailiwicks' wherein they have personal followings cultivated by the provision of services. Such systems thereby hinder the development of campaigns based upon ideology and program.'[6] It is hardly surprising that politicians once elected frequently switch parties. In the Congress elected in 1986 about one-third of the members switched parties in the following three years.

Electoral campaigns begin once the party's convention has nominated candidates—and the convention must be held at least six months before election day. No campaigning is allowed forty-eight hours before and twenty-four hours after election day. Parties have free TV and radio access for two months before the election. Two hours daily at peak evening time are reserved for the parties, who are allotted time proportionate to their representation in the Federal Chamber. No other TV or radio political advertising is permitted. Broadcasting must be transmitted simultaneously on all TV channels or radio stations. This provision has been hotly opposed by the TV companies, but the absence of choice has been quite effective in disseminating political information amongst the largely politically indifferent Brazilian electorate.

Television was important even in the period of military rule. The remarkable performance of the opposition MDB in the 1974 legislative elections was due partly to effective use of the medium.[7] Before 1974, TV campaigning was widely regarded as uninspired and of little importance, consisting mostly of politicians reading long texts promoting their personal qualities. The opposition MDB campaign in 1974 transformed the use of television. Speeches were

cut short and the emphasis was now on criticizing the economic
and social policies of the government. Short films were prepared to
drive home, with vivid images, the message of the opposition.
Perhaps most important of all the opposition MDB came to an
agreement with the TV companies to exchange a continuous
twenty-minute broadcast for twenty clips of 30 seconds each shown
at regular intervals during prime viewing time. The MDB stressed
that it wanted to reach out to the new and undecided voters.

Since 1974 television has been the main instrument used by the
parties to attract voters, or, more precisely, used by candidates to
attract voters. The four leading newspapers in Brazil do not reach
more than 10 per cent of the population, whereas TV is received
by over 90 per cent of urban and 70 per cent of rural households.
Soap operas are hugely popular on Brazilian TV. Since 1982 the
parties have used actors from these series, and popular singers, to
reinforce their popularity. The TV programmes of the Workers'
Party (PT) have been particularly colourful and humorous, even
though some members of the party regarded these tactics as suitable
for selling soap powder but not for promoting a serious left-wing
party. All parties make extensive use of musical songs and jingles
to try to promote party identification in a country where such
identification is very low.

The importance of television in campaigning, and the emphasis
on personal qualities has placed a premium on professional use of
the medium—often to make effective personal attacks on rival
candidates. However, there is one crucial message that must be put
across: that is that the candidate cares about, and even more
important, is capable of doing something about the social and
economic deprivation that affects the great majority of the Brazilian
population, and also of dealing with the corruption that is held to
be endemic in Brazilian politics. Most Brazilian voters are poor.
Even in the most developed state of the country, São Paulo, three-
quarters of the electorate have had education only up to the
elementary level, and have salaries on average less than $US100
per month. Effective political campaigning has to address issues
that affect the majority of voters, especially as compulsory voting
increases the participation of the poor. Candidates are increasingly
making use of opinion polls to assess what particular issues are of
greatest concern.

Campaigning on television is effective only for elections to the presidency, governorships, certain elections for mayors, and the Senate—all elections based on majority voting systems. For the elections for the Federal Chamber and state assemblies, based on PR, campaigning on TV is not possible given the huge number of candidates. This deprives voters of information about candidates at this level, and accounts in part for the higher proportion of blank and null votes. In the second round of the 1989 presidential elections, the debates between the two contenders, Collor de Melo, and the candidate of the left, Ignacio de Silva [Lula], were widely followed and Collor's better performance in the debates was important in convincing undecided voters to vote for him. Collor was helped by the way that the most important TV company, Rede Globo, backed him from the beginning and deliberately reported on the TV debates in a way that favoured Collor.

Public meetings have become less important since the development of TV campaigning, but are still held, especially in the rural interiors of the states. Mass meetings seem to serve largely to provide images of the TV broadcasts, and in the capital cities there is normally only one big public meeting. Meetings have also been displaced by motor cavalcades which certainly make a lot of noise, but whose utility must be doubtful given the resentment they arouse when they cause traffic jams. Telephone canvassing has recently been introduced but is not very common. Doorstep canvassing is less frequent than before, but is still used in the interior of the country and on the outskirts of the big cities. Candidates commonly walk the streets at busy times of the day to try to meet the electorate. Poster advertising is in theory strictly regulated, but in practice the restrictions are ignored.

Details of party finance remain obscure, but costs are very high both because the campaign methods have become more sophisticated and professional, and because candidates are covering a huge territory and electorate. One estimate put the average expenditure of successful candidates for the Congress for São Paulo state in 1986 at over $US600,000.[8] Attempts by the Electoral Court to control expenditure have had little success, partly because most comes from personal funds rather than from the party. Parties do receive some funds from the government, but these cover only a small proportion of total expenditures. Candidates have to raise their own funds, and a great deal comes from companies with contracts with the public sector, hoping to benefit by electing a friendly Congressman or governor.

Public opinion polling has become widespread and important. Given the weakness of party identification in Brazil, a considerable proportion of voters say that they take into account whether a candidate has a chance of winning. In the last month of the campaign three private opinion polls publish their results weekly, and these receive widespread attention and comment. Candidates also make use of private polls, and employ them in their TV propaganda.

The Brazilian electorate is very volatile. The party system in Brazil is weak, and party identification is low. Surveys indicate that only about 30–40 per cent of the population expresses a spontaneous party preference—much lower than the European average, and much lower than in Chile or Venezuela. Organizing national parties in a country as large and diverse as Brazil would be difficult enough in the best of circumstances. But when those circumstances have included a twenty-one-year period of military dictatorship, near hyperinflation, economic recession, a military still powerful in politics, and a young and rapidly growing electorate it is hardly surprising that the electorate of Brazil swings abruptly between parties and between candidates.

Electioneering in Chile

Chile is in many ways a mirror image of Brazil. Unlike Brazil, Chile has a firmly based and long-established party system, and a history of representative government in which very competitive elections were a regular and important feature until interrupted by the military government from 1973 to 1989. Unlike the Brazilian military government, however, Pinochet did not permit any elections until he was constitutionally obliged to hold competitive elections for the presidency and Congress in December 1989 following his defeat in a plebiscite in October 1988.

Elections in Chile before 1973 resembled elections in European countries. They were fought along party lines, with a relatively close association between social class and support for a particular party. The presence of a strong ideological left—the most powerful Communist party in Latin America, and an even more popular and radical Socialist party—was matched by strong ideological parties of the centre and right, most notably the Christian Democratic Party (PDC). Ideological issues were central to elections in which, with one or two exceptions, such as Ibañez in 1952 and to a lesser extent Alessandri in 1958, independent personalities had little electoral impact. TV became important in the 1960s, and played a vital role in the 1970 campaign by showing the initially most popular candidate, the right wing Jorge Alessandri, in a very unfavourable light. Nevertheless the core of party activity was mass public meetings, smaller reunions with local and representative groups, and rallying the party faithful by door-to-door canvassing. The electoral system was a modified version of the D'Hondt PR system, similar to the one used in Finland. Each party presented a list which could include as many candidates as seats, but voters had to cast their single vote for one candidate. The total vote for all candidates on each list decided how many seats each party received, and those were distributed amongst those candidates receiving the highest individual votes. Candidates were challenging not only other parties, but members of their own party on the same list.

The electoral system imposed by Pinochet for the 1989 elections was very different. His government had thought of adopting the British first-past-the-post system, to force Chile into a two-party system. The idea was discarded when it became clear that the right would not necessarily command majority support. The electoral system for the presidency is straightforward. If no candidate receives more than 50 per cent in a national poll then there is a run-off ballot. That was unnecessary in 1989 for the Christian Democratic opposition leader Patricio Aylwin received 55.18 per cent, the right-wing candidate associated with the Pinochet government Hernán Buchi 12.39 per cent, and a right-wing populist businessman Francisco Errázuriz 15.43 per cent.

The system adopted for Congress was designed to ensure that the right, now recognized to be a minority, would secure representation way beyond its share of the poll. In the Senate there are 9 designated Senators, chosen by the outgoing Pinochet government, and 38 elected Senators. In the lower house there are 120 members. Each constituency, whether for Senate or Chamber, returns two members, though each voter has only one vote. Parties are allowed to form alliances to present lists of two candidates per constituency.

If a party alliance gains more than twice the votes of the next most supported list, it takes both seats. If it takes less than that, it returns one member and the next most voted list takes one. Thus, if there are only two lists contesting a constituency, a list with two-thirds of the votes plus one would return two members. If it had one vote less than two-thirds, then it would only return one member, and the minority list with one-third of the votes plus one would return one member. In one of the two Santiago contests for the Senate, a prominent Socialist candidate was not elected even though he came second in the poll with 29.2 per cent of the vote. The second seat went to the leader of a right-wing party identified with the Pinochet government, though he won only 16.4 per cent of the vote.[9] Parties that were not included in one or other of the two major coalitions had no chance of representation in Congress: hence the Communist party, traditionally a powerful block in Congress, elected no representatives. The new government wishes to return to the traditional Chilean PR system. However, it lacks a majority in Congress sufficient to implement this reform.

The major similarity between the elections of 1989 and those before 1973 was the central role played by well-organized pro-grammatic parties. In the case of the opposition, even the parties were the same as before 1973—Christian Democrats, Socialists, Radicals, and Communists. On the right, the major party, National Renewal, had a different name, but there were many continuities both in personnel and policies with the old National Party. The only really new contender was the neo-liberal party, the UDI, closely identified with the policies of the Pinochet government. What was different, compared with elections before 1973, was that the ideological gap between the parties was far narrower, and that the competition was less bitter and sectarian. There was, for example, considerable agreement about economic policy, and almost complete consensus about the need to consolidate democracy.

As in the past, in 1989 mass rallies and canvassing were important. However, there is no doubt that TV played the domi-nant role in the campaign. As in the plebiscite the year before, a fifteen-minute slot each night for three weeks before the election was divided equally between the three presidential candidates. During the day, there was another fifteen-minute period when the parties were able to appeal for congressional votes. There was only one major debate between the two main presidential candidates, but there were many televised interviews with them. The impact of TV on the plebiscite had been dramatic. For fifteen years Chileans had seen nothing but government propaganda on their screens: suddenly the opposition was allowed to put its case. Moreover, it put its case brilliantly, and far better than the government, to an audience which rarely fell below 60 per cent of an attentive electorate. The government could command much greater financial resources than the opposition, and was advised by leading public relations consultants from the USA, and by some of Mrs Thatcher's advisers. But there are limits to what such advisers could do with an unattractive message. There was clear and overwhelming poll evidence both in the plebiscite campaign and in the electoral campaign that the opposition would win by a comfortable margin, and that the TV campaigning brought considerable benefit to the opposition.

Opinion polls were used on a very modest scale before 1973. In the campaigns of 1988 and 1989, however, they were given enormous publicity, partly because in the absence of Congress and a free press, there was no other way in which the electorate could inform itself about public opinion. The press was at least able to publish opinion poll findings, and they had a novelty akin to the opposition TV programmes. Virtually all gave the opposition an advantage over the government both in 1988 and 1989, and played an important role in convincing the electorate that the opposition could win and could form a credible government. The opposition used opinion polls internally to target its message to certain groups, and to change tactics in the light of opinion-poll findings.

Mounting two electoral campaigns in such a short period of time clearly was very expensive. Where did the money come from for an opposition that had been illegal since 1973? The answer is, largely from abroad. Chile received a remarkable amount of international attention, and the Pinochet government was widely condemned while the opposition, much of it in exile, was widely supported. This financial support was absolutely crucial in keeping the opposition alive in the long years of the Pinochet dictatorship, and in financing the campaigns of 1988 and 1989.[10] Much of this support was channelled through church-based groups. In some countries—such as Chile—when parties are banned or controlled, the Church is prepared to use its authority to defend the right to oppose. This was also true in Brazil, where church-based groups were important in the creation of the Workers' Party.

The opposition was worried that voters would believe that the vote was not secret, and that they would be unable to resist the various kinds of pressure employed by the government, especially at the local level, to ensure a vote favourable for the government. The role of the Church was crucial in persuading the electorate to go out and vote, and not to be intimidated by threats or pressure.

Possible fraud by the government was also a constant worry for the opposition. To minimize this, the opposition set up no fewer than three parallel computer systems linked to an intricate network of fax machines. Support came from the USA and elsewhere both for the long-term campaign to register voters, and for computer counting systems on the date of the poll. The US Agency for International Development made a grant of $1.2 million to the Centre for Free Elections (CAPEL) in Costa Rica in December 1987. In turn CAPEL made the grant over to Civitas, a church-linked group in Chile, to campaign for voter registration. At the same time the US Congress approved a $1 million grant to the National Endowment for Democracy to support the activities of the opposition. In the Chilean elections of 1989, the AID made a grant of $470,000 to CAPEL to help the church-sponsored Participa organization do what the Cruzada Civica had done in the plebiscite, that is to encourage the registration and participation of the electorate. At least $US5 million went to Chile from US sources to help prepare the plebiscite and the election. European support for the opposition was on an even greater scale, but had been given to the opposition during the long years of dictatorship. Such support was crucial in keeping the parties viable.

International press coverage of both events was intense, and there is no doubt that the government saw the foreign press and TV as biased against them. Moreover, there were about a thousand observers present at the plebiscite and during the elections, half from various parliaments, and half from a variety of other associations. The presence of these observers was not welcomed by the government, but certainly was by the opposition, who believed that their presence would make fraud more difficult, and would lend much needed encouragement to the opposition, especially at the local level.

In the end, there was little fraud. Over 90 per cent of the total potential electorate was registered to vote, and over 90 per cent of those actually voted. The winning margin was almost identical in both plebiscite and election, with the opposition winning 55 per cent of the vote, to 43 per cent for Pinochet in the plebiscite, and the combined right-wing vote in the election. The government enjoyed so many advantages—years of political propaganda, control over TV, state resources—that at first the opposition's task looked overwhelmingly difficult. But there was a strong desire to return to the tradition of competitive party politics.

Participation has traditionally been high in Chilean elections— usually around 80 per cent—but the plebiscite and the elections were exceptional. Clearly the contests of 1988 and 1989 were special elections, one overtly a plebiscite, and the other still with characteristics of a plebiscite. Yet there are reasons for expecting that elections will continue to attract high levels of interest. Parties in Chile are well organized and disciplined with firm social roots and long historical traditions. There exists a very small anti-party vote. Anti-system parties hardly exist any more as both the extreme left and the extreme right have joined the electoral game. There is agreement across the political spectrum about maintaining the successful economic model. There is less reason than in Brazil to expect wide swings in voter preferences, and in these conditions the techniques of modern electioneering will be important at the margins—but in a multi-party system, which may well return to its traditional PR electoral system, the margin can make all the difference between winning and losing.

Electioneering in Venezuela

Venezuela has a relatively long and uninterrupted electoral history compared with most Latin American countries. Since the fall of the dictatorship of Pérez Jiménez in 1958, there have been seven presidential and congressional elections held at five-year intervals. The Venezuelan electorate has considerable experience of electioneering, and combines enthusiastic support for democracy with increasing scepticism about the electoral promises made by the political parties. Indeed, concern about the firm hold of the two major parties on political life in Venezuela has led to the proposal of electoral reforms aimed at reducing the power of the party leadership by moving from closed to open list forms of PR.[11]

Two major parties dominate the electoral scene, Acción Democrática (AD) and the Comité de Organización Política Electoral Independiente (Copei).[12] Both have an extensive and effective organizational structure that reaches all levels of political, administrative and social organization. Until 1973 there were other important parties, but since then, AD and Copei have shared 80 per cent of the total vote.[13] Moreover, the parties now resemble each other in terms of social and regional support; both are multi-class, national parties, which have moved towards the centre of the political spectrum. The electoral domination of these two parties has created a strong feeling that not to vote for one or the other is a wasted vote.

Electoral campaigns revolve around the work of these two parties which mobilize their huge memberships in a patient process of meetings, conversations, interviews with candidates, and publicity at the local level. The parties mobilize their links with innumerable social and political groups to bring out their vote. With such intensive campaigning it is not surprising that abstention is low. Until 1978 it never reached 10 per cent, and though it has increased with the economic recession of the 1980s its peak was still only 18 per cent in 1988. The vote is compulsory in Venezuela for an electorate whose voting age begins at 18 years.[14] But it is doubtful if this explains the low level of abstention.[15] We would prefer to emphasize the intensity of party electioneering which creates an atmosphere simultaneously of political competition and of political carnival. Elections become a festival of democratic politics and it is difficult for even the most isolated electors to ignore what is happening.

Until 1978 the choice of candidates was a party matter, decided internally. Such decisions could affect party unity, and the AD choice of presidential candiate led to a damaging split in the party in 1968. But in general little public attention was paid to the internal party choice, which was made by a variety of methods from primary elections to different forms of delegate selection. Since 1978, however, and linked to the increasing professionalization of electioneering in Venezuela, pre-candidates for nomination for the presidential elections mount public campaigns to generate support in order to influence the party's choice of candidate. Until

1983, the campaign for nomination, and then the campaign for the presidency, lasted no less than eighteen months, but recent regulations have separated the two campaigns and have ensured that they last no longer than six months in total.[16]

Elections in Venezuela have been conducted regularly and fairly. Four elections of the seven since 1958 have seen the victory of the then opposition party: one of them in 1968 by a tiny margin of 1,083,000 votes to 1,050,000.[17] Governments have the advantage in Venezuela of control over national finances, and there is always the temptation to use public works to manipulate public opinion, or to create a pre-election economic boom. But against that has to be set the decline in support for the government which seems to occur regularly in Venezuela: as one Minister of the Interior lamented publicly, in Venezuela 'governments do not win elections'. Electoral credibility is one of the basic pillars of Venezuelan democracy.

The electoral system has changed since the establishment of democracy in 1958. Until 1973 the President, national Congress, state, and local officials were elected simultaneously. Since then presidential elections have continued to be held every five years, but from 1973 to 1989 municipal councils were elected six months after presidential elections. Since 1989 state governors, mayors, and councillors are elected every three years, separately from presidential and congressional elections; previously state governors were appointed by the President, and the office of mayor did not exist. Presidents are elected by a simple majority. Congressmen and local councillors are elected by a system of PR: the D'Hondt method using closed party lists.[18] The system of closed party lists helped to consolidate democracy in Venezuela by creating strong and disciplined parties. However, the emphasis has now shifted to the need for greater democratic accountability of the parties, and a recent reform means that in future only half of the lower house of Congress will be elected by PR: the rest by a simple majority system. The two Senators returned by each state are elected at present, and will be in the future, by the parties that gain the two largest votes, unless one party has more than double the votes of the next most popular party, in which case it takes both seats.

The Supreme Electoral Council (Consejo Supremo Electoral) has played an important role in guaranteeing fair elections. It is composed of representatives of the five most popular parties in the elections, and the President is an independent, elected by Congress.

It lasts for five years, is in permanent session, and has authority to settle matters of internal party disputes as well. However, there is little fraud in Venezuelan elections, and little use of negative personal attacks beyond the level of rumour and gossip. The most sensitive time in the electoral process is when the votes are counted in the thousands of voting booths all over the country. Small parties that cannot provide representatives at all the polling stations run the risk of having their votes stolen by representatives of the big parties. But the problem is a minor one, limited to rural areas where the absolute number of votes for minor parties is in any case very small. Nevertheless one of the electoral reforms to be adopted is the automatic counting of votes.

It is difficult to generalize about the extent to which elections in Venezuela have been issue orientated. Different elections have revolved around different issues. Those of 1958 and 1963 were about affirming democracy in the face of armed subversion. That of 1968 revolved around the need for a change from the ruling AD government. 1973 saw the emergence of modern electioneering techniques and the personal appeal of the flamboyant AD candidate, Carlos Andrés Pérez. Personal appeal obviously helps a candidate and his party, but has not been sufficient in Venezuela to reverse a generally unfavourable verdict on the party in government. The elections of 1978 and 1983 were basically a judgement on the policies adopted by the relevant government, and confirmed a tendency, clearly apparent in 1988 of both parties to emphasize governing ability rather than differing programmes and ideologies. In 1988 AD won because of its wider organizational base, and because of the personal popularity of its candidate, the former President Carlos Andrés Pérez. However, the adoption of IMF style adjustment policies by the present government—a radical break from previous economic policies—has brought the debate over economic policies and alternatives to the forefront, and these issues are likely to play a more prominent role in future elections.

Since 1973, Venezuelan elections have made intensive use of modern publicity techniques. Until then publicity was relatively simple. In 1973 AD used intensive publicity to convert the image of its candidate, Carlos Andrés Pérez, from that of the sober and unappealing Interior Minister, who had dealt with the guerrilla uprising to that of a more relaxed and attractive personality. Copei also used intensive publicity in this campaign, and thereafter all parties paid close attention to modern methods of political publicity, so that the advantage that AD gained in 1973 was cancelled out. Both parties make extensive use of foreign advisers in these matters, and also seek advice from their international political allies in the Socialist International in the case of AD, and the Christian Democratic International in the case of Copei. By now local politicians have acquired extensive experience, and both parties have effective electoral commands which direct the campaign of the candidates, making such use of external advice as they think appropriate. Both parties make a great effort to have as rapid a system as possible of electoral returns from the polling stations so that they possess their own independent results.

Electoral costs rose gradually from 1958 to 1968, but with the election of 1973 and thereafter, the costs have risen in a dizzy fashion—aided of course by the huge increase in the value of Venezuelan exports with the oil price increases of the 1970s. It is difficult to give accurate figures of electoral expenditures, and figures in US dollars can be misleading as the Venezuelan bolivar has fallen from 4.30 to the US dollar in 1982 to 50 to the dollar by 1991. But in recent years it is generally estimated that the electoral expenditures of each of the two main parties exceed 1,000 million bolivars or 20 million US dollars. The campaigns are financed in three ways. First by quotas from party members, and by commissions that are paid to the party for its good offices in securing public sector contracts. Secondly, from state grants as the Supreme Electoral Council reimburses a part of the costs of parties who gain more than 5 per cent of the vote. Thirdly there is private finance from the wealthy supporters of the party and of the candidate. There is no regulation on financial contributions apart from those coming from the state. This obviously favours the candidates of the two major parties, and there is pressure to limit campaign costs and contributions. But as the two major parties resist this reform it is unlikely to be enacted. Moreover as there is rough equality in the contributions given to each of the two major parties, electoral expenditure does not give one party a significant edge over the other, and the extravagant promises that are made in the campaign are received with increasing scepticism by the electorate.

Electoral campaigns in Venezuela are intense and prolonged. Each candidate will organize huge meetings in the four or five major cities. Candidates make use of TV and radio as much as possible, though the major private TV channels try to be balanced between the candidates (but it is obvious that they have their favourite), and the state TV channels are obliged to give equal treatment to the candidates. Newspapers are inclined to be more partisan, and some have, in the past, made deals with candidates, pledging support in return for favours.

Television debates between candidates have not been important in electoral campaigns, with a couple of exceptions. And neither has there been much use in Venezuela of door-to-door canvassing, telephone canvassing, or mailing of party propaganda. Much more frequent are the innumerable forums of specific groups such as farmers, cattle ranchers, students, businessmen, and so on, where the candidate or his representatives are expected to debate the issues that concern the audience.

Public opinion surveys are intensively used by the parties and have been since 1973. The campaign teams poll constantly to see what issues are held to be important, and what impression the candidate is producing. Such polls have been influential in changing campaign strategy. But the committed or captive vote is very large in Venezuela, and there is little evidence that opinion poll findings have influenced voting behaviour. AD can count on a stable 35 per cent of the vote, and Copei a little less, with 27 per cent. It is true that recent polls show some disenchantment with the major parties, which is hardly surprising given the economic crisis, but the effect so far seems to be that the vote for the major parties is relatively stable, but less enthusiastic. The problem is that there is no credible alternative for the electorate to support.

Electoral behaviour may change in response to the new staggered timetable for elections, and the new electoral system for part of Congress, but there is no doubt that elections will continue to be one of the basic pillars of political legitimacy of the existing regime. One of the firmest political convictions both of the political élite in Venezuela and of the great mass of the electorate is that elections should be free of fraud, and that the results should be respected.

Conclusion

These three cases illustrate how in very different political systems, electioneering has developed in similar fashion. This is hardly surprising. All three countries, and indeed most countries in Latin America, saw important social and economic transformations in the decades after the Second World War. They became much more urbanized, more industrialized, and their populations more educated. In Brazil, for example, the proportion of the population living in cities of over 20,000 inhabitants increased from 20 per cent in 1950 to 55 per cent in 1990. In Chile and Venezuela the proportion of population living in towns is even higher. The Americanization of electioneering is one aspect of the general Americanization of consumer standards in Latin America, even if for many poor Latin Americans such standards represent a dream rather than a reality. But the dream is constantly reinforced by TV, which is now almost as widespread in Latin America as in Europe, at least in terms of viewers.

In the 1950s a great deal of electioneering took place in rural areas, with the candidates as often as not arriving on horseback or in a jeep, addressing a small audience in the presence of the local political boss, who could faithfully deliver votes on election day. Serious issues were debated seriously in campaign meetings in towns, but restricted suffrage and limited access to media, reduced the overall impact of elections on the population. In the 1990s by contrast, elections in Latin America are impossible to ignore, if only because of the noise and litter that accompany campaigning. But the core of electioneering is now conducted on TV with techniques as modern as those in the USA, and with considerably more interest and enthusiasm than elections in that country.

Democracy is still fragile in Latin America, and much depends on the evolution of party and electoral systems. In societies suffering from acute social and economic crisis, as in Peru, the very survival of democracy is at issue in every election, and it is doubtful whether the most modern electioneering techniques would have made a substantial difference to the result in 1985 or 1990. The more settled and legitimate the political system, as in Venezuela, then the greater the importance of modern electoral techniques in influencing political outcomes. Paradoxically, one could argue that electioneering techniques do matter in Brazil, but not because the major issues of democratic consolidation are settled, as in Venezuela, but rather because the party system is so weak and its roots so shallow that publicity and electioneering are necessary for the voters simply to be able to identify the candidates.

Debates on electoral and party reform seem to be taking place in almost every republic. They are linked to another debate: the virtue of the parliamentary as opposed to the existing presidential systems. The argument of those who favour parliamentary systems is that it would help to produce responsible and disciplined parties, and that potential crises would be resolved more quickly than in presidential regimes, where by contrast it is argued, political impasse can lead to regime breakdown. Advocates of parliamentarianism argue that élites in some Latin American countries have adopted institutions and practices that have favoured strong presidents and weak parties and have encouraged personalistic and clientelistic practices.

In opposing dictatorships, opposition parties stressed their commitment to democracy without being specific about the form that democracy would take. Now in power, opposition politicians are finding that issues of electoral and party reform are crucial to the consolidation of those democratic regimes. Substantive political issues rather than questions of presentation and persuasion are likely to be the core of politics in Latin America for some time to come. But parties and politicians across the political spectrum are acutely conscious of the need to influence voters, and the trend towards the adoption of modern electioneering techniques is likely to intensify.

Notes

1. Ronald McDonald and J. Mark Ruhl, *Party Politics and Elections in Latin America* (Boulder, Col. Westview Press 1989), 85. They point out that the actual proportion of eligible voters who do vote may be 10% higher than the official figures because official figures include adults who cannot vote (the armed services), Colombians abroad, and so on. The Colombian electoral system is well described in Matthew Shugart, 'Electoral Systems and Political Reform in Colombia and Venezuela', *Electoral Studies* (Mar. 1992)
2. Electors who do not vote, and who do not justify their absence in the Electoral Tribunal within 30 days (a period of grace which applies only to those who were absent from the city where they were registered to vote) have to pay a fine ranging from 3 to 10% of the legal minimum salary. In addition if one cannot produce the document

proving that one has voted or the legal exemption from voting, it is not possible to apply for a job in the public sector, nor to borrow money from banks and saving associations controlled by the government, nor obtain a passport or identification card, nor be matriculated in a state school.

3. In São Paulo state the percentage of abstention rose from 3.5 to 8.5% between 1985 and 1990, but the percentage of null and blank votes rose from 11.5 to 21.2% for the gubernatorial elections, and an even higher 22.9 to 41.7% for the national Congress.

4. The senatorial mandate lasts for 8 years, but there are elections every four years: once for one-third of the Senate and once for two-thirds. Seats in the lower house and in state assemblies are changed every four years.

5. For example in the last legislative elections in São Paulo state, no less than 610 candidates competed for the state's 60 seats in the Federal Chamber of Deputies, and 1,182 candidates for the 84 seats in the State Assembly.

6. Shugart, 'Electoral Systems and Political Reform'.

7. See Maria D'Alva Kinzo, *Legal Opposition Politics under Authoritarian Rule in Brazil: The Case of the MDB, 1966–1979* (London; Macmillan, 1988).

8. This compares with an estimated $393,000 spent by winning candidates in the 1988 elections for the US House of Representatives.

9. Because of this system, although the opposition alliance came first and second in nine of the senatorial contests, in only two of them did it poll the two-thirds plus one votes necessary to return two candidates. For the right wing alliance this form of discrimination operated only twice.

10. On the elections of 1989 see Alan Angell and Benny Pollack. 'The Chilean Elections of 1989 and the Politics of the Transition to Democracy', *Bulletin of Latin American Research*, 9/1 (1990), 1–23. On the question of international support for the opposition see the chapter on Chile by Alan Angell in Laurence Whitehead (ed.), *International Support for Democracy in Latin America* (forthcoming, 1992). On the general question of foreign funding of political activities see Michael Pinto-Duschinsky, 'Foreign Political Aid: The German Political Foundations and their US Counterparts', *International Affairs*, 67/1 (1991), 33–63

11. For the 1993 congressional elections the plan is to adopt a system similar to the West German model.

12. AD has some two million members, and Copei one million in a population overall of twenty million.

13. AD and Copei usually gain about 40% each of the overall vote: the

principal party of the left, the Movimiento al Socialismo normally averages between 5 and 10%, and other parties of the left a total of 5%; an anti-party independent can count on 2% of the vote, and there are usually a considerable number of insignificant parties.

14. The exception is the Armed Forces who may not vote. But they play an important part in the electoral process, ensuring public order near the polling stations, and overseeing the moving of the ballot boxes to the Supreme Electoral Council.

15. In any case, the sanctions that theoretically exist to encourage voting are rarely applied.

16. However, there is almost incessant electoral activity in Venezuela in the choice of union leaders, professional associations, community associations all of which are influenced to some degree or other by party affiliation (even in beauty contests it is claimed that the parties have their candidates).

17. This election was additionally significant because it was the first one gained by an opposition candidate for the presidency.

18. At present it is not possible to choose between the candidates offered by the party, nor to select different parties for the different bodies being elected at the same time. In effect the party leadership determined who was elected, and as a result parties are very disciplined in Congress for to deviate from the party line is to risk expulsion or to be placed on the list in what amounts to a non-electable position.

References

Angell, Alan, and Pollack, Benny, 'The Chilean Elections of 1989 and the Politics of the Transition to Democracy', *Bulletin of Latin American Research*, 9/1 (1990), 1–23.

Booth, John, and Seligson, Mitchell, *Elections and Democracy in Central America* (Chapel Hill,: University of N. Carolina Press, 1989).

Diamond, Larry, Linz, Juan, and Lipset, Seymour Martin, *Democracy in Developing Countries iv: Latin America* (Boulder, Colo.: Lynne Rienner, 1989).

Drake, Paul, and Silva, Eduardo (eds.), *Elections and Democratization in Latin America* (Center for US–Mexican Studies, University of California, San Diego, Calif., 1986).

Kinzo, Maria D'Alva, *Legal Opposition Politics under Authoritarian Rule in Brazil: The Case of the MDB, 1966–1979* (London: Macmillan, 1988).

Lamounier, Bolívar, *Voto de Desconfiança: Eleições e Mudança Política No Brazil* (Rio de Janeiro: Editora Vozes, 1980).

McDonald, Ronald, and Ruhl, J Mark, *Party Politics and Elections in Latin America* (Boulder, Colo.: Westview Press, 1989).

Martz, John, 'Electoral Campaigning and Latin American Democratization: The GranColombian Experience', *Journal of Inter-American Studies and World Affairs*, 32/1 (Spring 1990), 17–43.

Baloyra, Enrique, *Electoral Mobilization and Public Opinion: The Venezuelan Campaign of 1973* (Chapel Hill, NC: University of N. Carolina Press, 1976).

Weiner, Myron, and Ozbudun, Ergun, *Competitive Elections in Developing Countries* (Washington, DC: American Enterprise Institute, 1987).

Williams, Philip J., 'Elections and Democratization in Nicaragua: The 1990 Elections in Perspective', *Journal of Inter-American Studies and World Affairs*. 32/4 (Winter 1990), 13–34.

4

The United Kingdom

DENNIS KAVANAGH

In the first half of the twentieth century the style of election campaigning in Britain was changed by the extension of the franchise to virtually all adults (by 1928), and developments in party organization. But, in one short burst between 1959 and 1964 there was a transformation, largely because of developments in modern communications. Many of the features of contemporary campaigning arrived—opinion polls, advertising, television, daily press conferences, and serious planning of campaign strategies by party leaders. Elections have changed greatly since the 1950s when Clement Attlee toured the country in a family saloon, driven by his wife, addressing meetings recorded only by the press. Indeed, it takes an effort of mind to remember that until 1959 there was no broadcast coverage of the election campaign. David Butler recalls that

> There was no advertising: no regular press conferences; no serious day-to-day strategies planning by a headquarters committee . . . the politicians muddled through in a very individualistic way to the end. But in 1987 a major role was played by pollsters, media advisers and campaign committees. In this highly self-conscious projection of rival images, everything was timed, phrased and lit for the benefit of television coverage. The 1950 election was more like that of 1880 than that of 1987.[1]

Historically, the style of campaigning in Britain has been shaped by two broad forces:

1. *The legal framework*. There has been remarkably little change in election law. The ground rules are still those largely established by the Corrupt Practices Act (1883) and the Representation of People Act (1918). Strict rules on campaign expenditure at constituency level date back for more than a century. This strict enforcement of limits on election expenses at constituency level limits the

opportunities for innovation, particularly in the use of computers, direct mail, and opinion polling.

2. *The technology of communications.* The most significant development in this respect has been television, although in 1959 over 70 per cent of electors already had television in their homes. The growing importance of television and its saturation coverage of elections have forced the parties to think more seriously about 'packaging' candidates and issues for the medium; and much of the leading politicians' campaign day is geared to television. There have also been growing tensions between the politicians and the broadcasters over who is to set the agenda for the election. Under the terms of their charters the broadcasting media are required to maintain a political balance between the parties and political parties are precluded from buying time on the broadcasting media.

Timing

Election campaigns last three weeks or so between the dissolution of Parliament and polling day, a much shorter period than in the United States. It has been claimed that incumbents have an unfair advantage because of the Prime Minister's right (effectively since Lloyd George in 1918) to choose the most opportune date for the dissolution; he or she is helped in this by opinion-poll readings of public opinion and the government's power to manufacture pre-election economic booms. The Prime Minister can call the election at a time when voters are feeling prosperous and when the government is riding high in the polls. The 1945 general election was the first in Britain to be the subject of an opinion poll when Gallup offered an accurate but little-regarded report of Labour's substantial lead in voting intentions. By 1959, and certainly by 1964, opinion-poll findings of voting intentions were a major influence on a government's decision on when to go to the country. The evidence about the habit of fostering pre-election economic booms is clear (in the form of tax cuts, reductions in interest rates, increases in state benefits, all designed to increase spending power before an election), although it is worth noting that such economic pump-priming may still occur with elections on a fixed calendar.

At times, however, the theoretical advantages to the incumbents of pump-priming and opinion polls have been of no avail. In 1970 and in February 1974 the opinion-poll lead for the government at the outset of the campaign proved fragile and had disappeared by polling day. In 1979 the Labour Prime Minister effectively lost control of the election date when he lost a confidence vote in the House of Commons. Of the twelve dissolutions since 1945 the government has won seven and lost five, and in five elections— 1955, 1959, 1966, 1974 October, and 1983—the governing party increased its share of the vote from the previous election. Of course without control of the timing the government party might have done even worse.[2]

Although the legal life-span of a British Parliament is five years, in the post-war period only the 1945, 1959, and October 1974 Parliaments have actually lasted into their fifth year. The average life of a post-war Parliament has been three and a half years. It is often the case that after the end of the third year an electioneering atmosphere develops. Critics have complained that in this uncertainty governments are tempted to avoid taking measures which may be necessary but unpopular, the civil service marks time, Parliament has little major legislation to consider, and investors and business leaders hold off making decisions.

Expenses

British elections remain inexpensive in comparison with those in many other Western states. Legal limits on spending in the constituencies are uprated regularly to take account of inflation and in 1987 the average maximum expenditure allowed per candidate was in the order of £5,000 and the average expenditure per main party candidate was around £4,000. The strict legal controls have meant that in real terms local spending is only about a quarter of the level in 1945.[3] There are no limits on central expenditure and the two main parties between them spent nearly £13 million in the 1987 election campaign (£8.9 million Conservative and £3.8 million Labour), a figure twice as large as that in the constituencies. The largest single item is press advertising. The spending gap between the Conservative and other parties would probably be even larger but for the controls on local spending and the subsidies in kind (free postage for candidates, free hire of halls for meetings and election broadcasts). The five ten-minute party political broadcasts allocated to each of the Labour, Conservative, and Alliance parties at peak viewing time in 1987 amounted at standard advertising rates to a public subsidy to each party of £7,000,000.

Media

The most significant challenge to and opportunity for campaigners has been the development of the electronic media. The turning point in the relationship between television and politicians was 1959, when the BBC abandoned its self-imposed non-coverage of the election campaign. Before then election coverage was effectively left to the newspapers. A reading of the press in that period shows that it confined itself largely to reports of the tours and speeches of the main figures in the political parties and, in the quality press, constituency reports. There was little discussion of opinion polling, psephology, or election strategy.

In the 1960s the 'balance' in television coverage may have had the effect of reducing press partisanship. Since 1979, however, the tabloid section of the press appears to have become more partisan and more interested in scandals, sensations, and trivia, associated with politics. On the other hand, the coverage in the quality press has become more sophisticated, particularly about opinion polls, party strategies, and electoral behaviour. It is perhaps an acknowledgment of the centralization of the campaign and decline of local campaigning that newspapers contain fewer constituency reports.

While all political parties try to feed favourable lines to newspapers, the Conservatives have more press outlets than Labour. Until 1970 the Conservative Party could rely on the support of newspapers which had 50 per cent of total press readership. But the switch to the Tory camp of the *Sun* (formerly the Labour-supporting *Daily Herald*) in the 1970s has meant that in 1983 the party was supported by papers which had three-quarters and in 1987 two-thirds of total readership.[4]

The typical campaign day for the main parties now starts with a morning press conference, which usually features statements from the party leader or a major front-bench spokesman and then an opportunity is provided for questions. The press conferences were a Labour Party invention in 1959, started by Dick Crossman, in large part to provide occupation for the party's General Secretary, Morgan Phillips. Journalists enjoyed the occasions because they provided them with easy stories and filled in a quiet part of the day. Increasingly, statements by party spokesmen were an opportunity to set the agenda for the day and capture the lunchtime news headlines.

The press has become the main vehicle for party advertising. A key development was the *R. v. Tronoh-Malayan Mines.* (1952) decision which ruled that political advertising was legal as long as it did not refer to a particular candidate. A major press advertising campaign was launched by the Conservatives in 1957 in the run up to the 1959 election. But the parties remained unsure of the legality of such spending during the campaign and not until 1979 did the parties have large-scale press advertising. In the 1987 campaign the Conservatives spent £3.6 million on press advertisements—more than twice Labour's £1.6 million.[5]

Labour leaders have frequently expressed concern about the impact of the crude anti-Labour propaganda carried in some of the tabloids and at the press's ability to influence the political agenda to the party's disadvantage. The relationship can be symbiotic with the lead stories in the press sometimes setting the agenda for television, and the press in turn reporting events covered on television. In 1987 there was a close correspondence between the front-page election stories in the *Daily Mail* and *Daily Express* and the themes launched at that morning's Conservative press conference. Brian Macarthur has demonstrated how lead stories in the press in the 1987 election were developed by television and became major election debates.[6] They covered Labour's plans for taxes, a David Frost interview with Neil Kinnock about Labour's defence policies, and a *TV-am* interview with Denis Healey, in which he lost his temper when questioned about his wife's operation in a private hospital. The coverage of all three operated to the disadvantage of Labour.

On the other hand, sceptics might point to surveys which show that most of the readers of the *Sun* and the *Daily Mail*—the two most Tory-biased papers—voted against the paper's advice in 1987. According to a study by Martin Harrop, the pro-Conservative bias of the press probably is worth 1 per cent of the total vote of Conservatives. This could be important in a close-run election, but it is hardly significant compared with other factors.[7]

Television shapes a party leader's campaign day. Just as morning press conferences are scheduled to catch the midday news programmes, so the leaders' evening speeches are delivered in time for the 9 p.m. and 10 p.m. television news bulletins. Compared to the 1950s and 1960s the party leaders make fewer set-piece rally speeches. Party managers regard activities that are not covered by the media, particularly television, almost as a waste of time. Another consequence is that time has to be found for the major television interviews and for the elaborate preparations on the part of the interviewee.

An American vocabulary is increasingly employed to describe today's media-orientated electioneering. Managers encourage campaign speakers to have good 'sound-bites', succinct statements which can easily be carried by broadcasters, and party leaders' itineraries are carefully planned to provide photo-opportunities. Pictures and images appear to count more than words for the television viewers at home and political argument is strengthened by visual association. A film of Mr Kinnock, for example, visiting a hospital says as much about Labour's concern for the National Health Service as a lengthy policy speech. This approach reached its heights (or depths) when Mrs Thatcher, for the benefit of photographers, spent 13 minutes fondling a new born calf in a field in Norfolk in 1979. If one tries to identify an election in which these trends became marked it was 1979. In that election Mrs Thatcher's campaign advisers, aware that news editors wanted pictures, devised the controlled 'walkabout' to create visual interest. Her visits, for example to a school or an old people's home, were sure to produce photogenic scenes for news editors and press photographers.

Television also provides an enormous amount of news and features programmes on the election campaign. It has increasingly made use of live audiences and, as a way of meeting the requirement for political balance, features party spokesmen in debates and question times before live audiences. It has also 'joined' the rival party campaigns in debate to a much greater extent than in the pre-television era.

There have been claims that the media have helped to make British elections more presidential. It is worth recalling, however, that Gladstone and Lloyd George had a great impact on voters and in the post-war period Winston Churchill and Harold Macmillan were salient figures. The character of the party leader has probably always been a component, though a variable one, of the party's image. We simply lack data on the electoral impact of leaders from the pre-television and pre-survey age. But it is now well documented that in recent general elections over 50 per cent of radio and television coverage of a major political party is devoted to its leader. To a large extent the leader carries the party's message, as conveyed by the television screen. In the 1983 election sound-bites from party leaders accounted for 20 per cent of television coverage of the campaign compared to only 2 per cent in the *Sun* and 3 per cent in *The Times*.[8] Understandably, more attention is given by party managers to 'packaging' or presenting the leader. Among the highlights of the campaign are the party leader's lengthy interviews with professional interviewers on different channels. (Interviewers like Brian Walden, Sir Robin Day, Sir Alastair Burnet, and David and Jonathan Dimbleby have become campaign figures in their own right.) The growth of the tabloid press from the 1970s, and its more personalized treatment of politics, has probably also increased public interest in the personalities of party leaders. An analysis of election coverage in *The Times* from the 1950s to the 1980s shows a steady rise in the number of stories about the Prime Minister, with a sharp increase in the last decade. There has also been an increase in coverage of the main opposition party leader.

Party leaders in Britain, however, have not been popular figures. Between 1955 and 1966 the combined Gallup average rates of approval for the Labour and Conservative party leaders fluctuated narrowly around 100 per cent. For the subsequent parliaments, however, the approval ratings have ranged from an average of 72 per cent (in the 1979 Parliament) to 87 per cent (the 1974 Parliament). According to one study party leaders do 'have effects on the party balance when (the image of the leaders) are preponderantly positive or negative'.[9] But surveys show that votes are determined more by issues and party loyalty than by attitudes to the leader. In 1970 Mr Wilson was more popular than Mr Heath and in 1979 Mr Callaghan was more popular than Mrs Thatcher, but Labour still lost both elections decisively. Even without a change in party leaders the poll ratings for political parties fluctuate widely. In spite of her election successes Mrs Thatcher was not much liked by the electorate. She trailed various Labour leaders when voters were asked to rate her as a 'caring' or 'likeable' person but regularly outscored them on the qualities of strength, determination, decisiveness, and ability in a crisis.

Opinion Polls

Another major change has been the development of opinion polling. Until 1959, when three other organizations appeared, Gallup virtually had the field in political polling to itself. Editors quickly realized that publishing the findings of opinion polls was an efficient way of advertising a newspaper. Polls often make the lead story in the sponsoring newspaper and, if released early enough, may figure in the previous evening's television news bulletin. Since 1970 there has been a steady increase in the number of polls, polling organizations, and types of polls—quicky, issue, constituency, regional, and personality. In 1983 there were 49 nation-wide polls and in 1987 83, most of them sponsored by the press. The code of conduct drawn up by the pollsters in 1969 has done much to improve election commentary and analysis and today many of the quality newspapers have specialist reporters on opinion polls. The private polls conducted by parties are used to test themes and slogans, identify target voters and their concerns and assist the presentation of policies. Labour began private polling on a modest scale in 1959 with Mark Abrams. The Conservatives started in 1966 with Harris (originally Opinion Research Centre) and have remained with them since. Private and public survey research has also been important since the 1987 general-election defeat in educating Labour leaders into an awareness of the barriers existing between the party and the electorate.

Some politicians express concern about the effects on voters of opinion polls, yet there is no evidence of a regular bandwagon effect; since 1964 the average eve-of-poll forecast of the polls has understated the lead of the winning party only once—in 1987. Even if the polls do not dominate the election campaigns they affect the perceptions of the politicians and morale of political parties, and influence government party managers in choosing the date of the election. As Ivor Crewe observes, opinion polls have largely replaced the views of party activists and canvass returns as a barometer of the popular mood for party leaders and campaign strategists.[10] It is now almost inconceivable to imagine discussion of the impact or the progress of an election campaign without the evidence of polls. Party leaders would be even freer to make outrageous claims about their prospects were it not for the availability of public-opinion polls. Assessment of the rise of the Alliance in the 1983 election, and of the poor performances of Michael Foot and Roy Jenkins in that contest were all coloured by the findings of opinion polls. The claims in a 'rogue' poll that Labour was gaining on the Conservatives a week before polling day in 1987 caused panic in the City and in Mrs Thatcher's office. Opinion polls are even more influential in by-elections, particularly for tactical voting.

The sums of money involved on polling by the main political party are rather modest. In the last Parliament Labour spent some £80,000 annually on private polls, the Conservatives £100,000 annually. In the 1987 campaign Labour spent £120,000 on polling, the Conservatives some £200,000. In the 1987 Parliament the Conservatives have significantly expanded such expenditure to fund a study of the electorate's voting, using as an adviser to the project Dick Wirthlin—pollster for Ronald Reagan.

Public Relations

The party managers have become increasingly concerned to control and plan their election campaigns. In deciding on the date of an election the governing party strategists try to anticipate the release of economic statistics; they take account of the findings of opinion polls, both public and private; and in 1983 and 1987 they drew on analyses of the May local elections. Conservative strategists met in January 1987 to plan the forthcoming election campaign in some detail. A comprehensive 'War Book' nominated speakers and themes for the daily press conferences, and contained advice on how to handle sensitive issues, plans for each day of the leaders' campaign, and so on. Labour similarly planned Neil Kinnock's campaign well in advance and sought to have him filmed in background locations which were identified with a new modern Labour Party. There was no such detailed advanced planning in the 1950s, not least because of the modest role of television.

Strategists also increasingly talk of 'targeting' particular sections of the electorate—families, C2s, home-owners, pensioners, shareholders, voters in marginal seats, and so on with mail, election broadcasts, and rallies—and about the 'pacing' of campaigns, finishing strongly, and fighting on 'our agenda'. Labour usually wants to fight on 'its' issues of schools, health, jobs, and fairness, issues on which it usually leads the Conservatives. The Conservatives want to fight on their strong issues of defence, industrial relations, leadership, and law and order. A party's chosen issue for the day will be launched at the morning press conference by the appropriate party spokesman, featured in an afternoon walkabout or visit, and again in an evening rally. In this way, the party tries to set the agenda for the media. Given the leaders' calculation that the election agenda is set through the media, one can readily understand the mounting tension between the media and politicians.

The chief gainers from the new politics have been public relations advisers, advertisers, and opinion pollsters. Labour and Conservative party managers have come to view the electorate as a market and employed the skills of these professionals to research the values of the voters and to present and promote the parties' message. As in the United States the campaign advisers counsel the politicians that, having started the campaign day with a theme, they should not 'kill' it by raising another issue later in the day. The party's communications directors act as 'spin doctors' who seek to guide the media in interpreting opinion polls and campaign events. In trying to achieve a disciplined communications programme, and to eliminate the unexpected, party leaders are increasingly coached for major television interviews and appear more interested in delivering prepared statements than handling hostile questions and embarrassing topics.[11] Between 1985 and 1990 Mr Kinnock relied heavily on the communication skills of Peter Mandelson and the Shadow Communications Agency of advertising people. Mrs Thatcher was supported by a team of speech writers (long-standing members were the playwright Sir Ronald Millar and journalist John O'Sullivan), advertising and public relations advisers (Sir Tim Bell, from advertising, and Sir Gordon Reece, a former television producer). Mrs Thatcher's advisers were particularly concerned to have low key unchallenging interviews with the likes of disc jockey Jimmy Young or chat show host Terry Wogan (whose programmes have large audiences) rather than encounters with the heavyweight political interviewers. These trends have produced a centralization of the campaign decision-making. Under Mr Wilson and Mr Callaghan this occurred largely because of their distrust of the Labour Party's National Executive Committee, which in the 1970s had a substantial left wing presence and was suspected of leaking. Under Mr Kinnock more and more campaign decisions were made from his office and his personality loomed large in Labour's 1987 campaign.

A greater role for advertising has also been noticeable over the past thirty years. In 1957 the Conservative Party caused some surprise by employing the agency Colman, Prentis and Varley to handle their advertising. In spite of the clear election victory in 1959 there were critics of advertising within the party. Labour leaders were even more emphatic in their rejection. A Labour leader in the House of Commons in 1960 condemned the Conservatives for introducing 'something into our political life which is alien to our British democracy'.[12] But by 1962 Labour was employing professional public-relations helpers. Harold Wilson took note of John Kennedy's media techniques in the 1960 presidential election, particularly the use of phrases and paragraphs which were designed for television coverage.[13] For the 1979 election and subsequent campaigns the Conservatives again employed an advertising agency—Saatchi and Saatchi—which was particularly provocative in its knocking campaign posters. The agency handled the total communications programme, covering party political broadcasts, press advertisements, posters, and themes. In 1986 it staged and designed the party's Annual Conference and suggested themes for the speeches of ministers to relate to the conference logo, *The Next Move Forward*.

Persistent left–right divisions over policy and a complex party structure have made the Labour Party a difficult client for an advertising agency. Many in the party have been distrustful of public relations and 'selling' of policies and the party has lacked the money to employ a full-time agency. After 1983 the new Communications and Campaigns Director, Peter Mandelson, was determined to employ modern communication methods and recruited a Shadow Communications Agency, drawn from Labour sympathizers in the public-relations world. The agency dealt with all aspects of communications—design, speech writing, research, copy writing, and arts direction—as well as advertising. It helped to stage-manage conferences and television and press addresses by

Mr Kinnock and other front-bench spokesmen took place against carefully devised backdrops. It provided a patriotic red rose as a logo. Labour party political broadcasts and leaflets were professionally designed; the party sought and gained endorsements from pop and sports stars; leaders appeared on TV chat shows and Mr Kinnock even took part in a pop-song video.[14]

It is not clear how much all this matters. Clearly a campaign run as badly as Labour's was in 1983 can hurt a party. But although Labour's 1987 campaign delighted the media professionals and party managers and the Conservative one was widely criticized, the Conservatives had the same lead over Labour on polling day as at the beginning of the campaign. More telling perhaps, was the collapse after the 1987 election of the Social Democrats, a party in whose creation market researchers played a key role. When faced with a survey finding that only 1 per cent of voters admitted to being influenced by advertising in 1987, party managers usually claim that the expenditure is good for the morale of party workers and that, anyway, they have to spend to keep up with the other parties.

Local Campaigning

Most of these trends have by-passed the campaign in the constituencies. It is usual for many candidates to feel redundant while the national campaign is being transmitted on the television screen. The Labour MP, Austin Mitchell, complained that he was engaged in an 'arcane irrelevance, a background noise which distracts from the decisive national campaign coming over on the box.'[15] According to Gallup in 1987 only 6 per cent of voters were canvassed or personally contacted by the parties on polling day and only 3 per cent attended an outdoor meeting. Figure 4.1. charts the steady decline in local-party activity. Three-party politics in 1983 and 1987 has contributed to a slight recovery in the activity level. Much local campaign effort was devoted to identifying the candidate with his party. Much of this was rendered unnecessary by the Representation of the People Act (1969) which allowed the candidate to mention his party on the ballot form. One indicator of effective local organization may be that a party has a full-time agent. Thirty years ago most Conservative constituency associa-

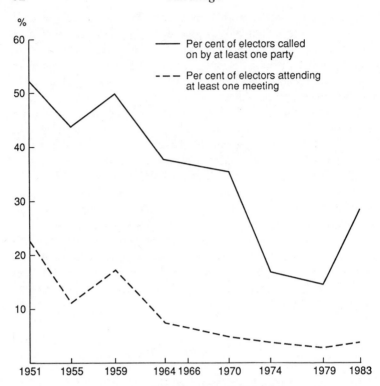

FIG. 4.1   *Local activity in British campaigns*
Source: Gallup, quoted in Harrop and Miller, *Elections and Voters*, 232.

tions had one; today less than half do. In 1950 Labour had 296
agents, in 1987 only 68. As noted, the limits on local expenditure
effectively preclude local candidates from using local opinion
polling or extensive advertising.

   Good local party organization and a high level of campaign
activity can be useful (*a*) in marginal seats (but these are declining
in number anyway), (*b*) where the organization of one party is
efficient and that of the main opposition is weak, and (*c*) where the
turn-out is low, so increasing the value of the votes cast.[16] The
organization can also be decisive in by-elections. Recent research
shows that an MP defending a seat can win on average about 750
votes, essentially built up as a result of his or her constituency
services and greater media attention. Liberal MPs have been

particularly effective in building up personal support for themselves and the fact that there are so few of them in the House of Commons virtually guarantees them a high profile.[17] But the size of this personal vote is not as large as that for incumbents in the United States. Another area in which good organization can pay off is in postal votes. There were 780,000 valid ballots cast in 1987 (2 per cent of the total vote) and the Conservatives probably gained five seats from their greater efficiency in this exercise.

Kevin Swaddle has pointed to the opportunities which the development of computers provides for constituency electioneering, and for removing the need for clerical chores.[18] Computerized mail can be sent to specialized targets of seats or of voters and computerized canvass data can also be used for locating supporters on election day. Legislation in 1985 obliged local authorities to supply parties with electoral registers on computer tape. But for the moment, the comprehensive use of direct mail lies in the future.

There is some evidence that the electorate has become more volatile. Certainly the amount of wavering during elections seems to have increased. Ivor Crewe (1987) has reported that the average change in each party's share of the vote between the first week of the campaign and polling day until the 1970 election was 2 per cent. This steadily increased until it reached 5.3 per cent in 1983.[19] In the 1979 Parliament the Conservative, Labour, and Alliance support, according to opinion polls, varied between 25 and 50 per cent. During the February 1974 election campaign Liberal support surged from 11 per cent to 19 per cent and over the campaign period in the 1983 election Alliance support surged from 18 to 26 per cent. There have also been huge shifts in party support at by-elections, particularly to the benefit of third parties. Tactical voting seems to have increased and voters have had more credible third parties to vote for.

The growth of such 'floating' has been encouraged by a weakening of party loyalties. Strong party identification with the Labour and Conservative parties has virtually halved since 1964. One can only speculate about the causes of the diminution in the solidity of party loyalty: disillusion with the performance of all governments in a period of national decline must offer part of the explanation, but it may also have something to do with the spread of education, greater social mobility, and greater exposure to television, which is committed to presenting 'balanced' programmes on politics. The weakening of their 'stabilizing' forces of social class and party loyalty increases the scope for short-term factors associated with the campaign—issues, personalities, and events—to shift votes.

Conclusion

The main campaigning changes in the past thirty years have been at national level and have been a working-out of trends apparent in the early 1960s. Elections are more leader-centred, increasingly stage-managed for the media, particularly television, and a greater role is played by public relations advisers, advertisers, and opinion pollsters. Some observers regret these developments, particularly the packaging and selling of politicians, and the way that broadcasts and print journals co-operate with politicians in publicizing media events, occasions specially staged by party managers to generate coverage. Over thirty years ago Aneurin Bevan accused opinion pollsters of taking the poetry out of politics. Writing about the 1964 general election, the distinguished political correspondent of *The Times*, David Wood, complained of the risk

that we are moving towards the day when market research, opinion poll findings, techniques of motivational persuasion and public relations, and even the analyses of political scientists will be crudely and cold-bloodedly used to govern party strategies in government.[20]

Near the end of his career in 1979, he deplored the poor job the media did in coping with the new style of electioneering. Pictures were killing off words and the press were now the 'spears in a Shakespearian play who march on and off looking like an army'.

But the process has not gone as far as in the United States. Political parties in Britain are still more programmatic and aware of their traditions. Legislation restricts the use of money and access to television and limits the scope for local candidates to run as figures separate from their parties. There is also a positive side to the developments in political communications. Policies and themes are better researched and politicians and policies are more attractively presented.

Notes

1. D. Butler, *British General Elections Since 1945* (Oxford: Blackwell, 1990), 2.
2. See Dennis Kavanagh, 'The Timing of Elections: The British Case', in I. Crewe and M. Harrop (eds.), *Political Communications: The British General Election Campaign of 1987* (Cambridge: Cambridge University Press, 1989).
3. M. Pinto-Duschinsky, *British Political Finance 1830–1980* (Washington, DC: American Enterprise Institute, 1981).
4. B. MacArthur, 'The National Press', in Crewe and Harrop, *Political Communications* (1989), 95.
5. M. Harrop, 'Political Marketing', *Parliamentary Affairs*, 43/3 (1990), 277–91.
6. MacArthur, 'The National Press'.
7. M. Harrop, 'Press Coverage of Post-War British Elections', in Crewe and Harrop, *Political Communications: The General Election of 1983* (Cambridge: Cambridge University Press, 1986).
8. H. Semetko, J. Blumler, M. Gurevitch, and D. Weaver, *The Formation of Campaign Agendas* (Hillsdale, NJ: L. Erlbaum Associates, 1991).
9. D. Butler and D. Stokes, *Political Change in Britain*, 2nd edn. (London: Macmillan, 1974), 357–68.
10. I. Crewe, 'Saturation Polling, the Media and the 1983 Election', in Crewe and Harrop, *Political Communications* (1986), 233.
11. R. Day, 'Interviewing Politicians', ibid.
12. R. Rose, *Influencing Voters* (London: Faber, 1967).
13. M. Cockerell, *Live From No. 10* (London: Faber, 1988).
14. D. Butler and D. Kavanagh, *The British General Election of 1987* (London: Macmillan, 1988), 62–6.
15. A. Mitchell, 'Taking it Personally', *New Society*, 5 June 1987.
16. D. Kavanagh, *Constituency Electioneering* (London: Longman, 1970).
17. See the Appendix by J. Curtice and M. Steed in Butler and Kavanagh, *The General Election of 1987*, 333–5.
18. K. Swaddle, 'Ancient and Modern: Innovations in Electioneering at the Constituency Level', in Crewe and Harrop, *Political Communications* (1989).
19. I. Crewe, 'The Campaign Confusion', *New Society*, 8 May 1987.
20. *The Times*, 22 Apr. 1965.

References

Butler, D., *British General Elections Since 1945* (Oxford: Blackwell, 1990).

—— and Kavanagh, D., *The British General Election of 1987* (London: Macmillan, 1988).

—— and Stokes, D., *Political Change in Britain*, 2nd edn. (London: Macmillan, 1974).

Cockerell, M., *Live From No. 10* (London: Faber, 1988).

Crewe, I., 'Saturation Polling, the Media and the 1983 Election', in I. Crewe and M. Harrop (eds.), *Political Communications: The British General Election Campaign of 1983* (Cambridge: Cambridge University Press, 1986).

—— 'The Campaign Confusion', *New Society*, 8 May 1987.

—— and Harrop, M., *Political Communications: The British General Election Campaign of 1987* (Cambridge: Cambridge University Press, 1989).

Day, R., 'Interviewing Politicians', in I. Crewe and M. Harrop (eds.), *Political Communications: The British General Election Campaign of 1987* (Cambridge: Cambridge University Press, 1989).

Harrop, M., 'Press Coverage of Post-War British Elections', in I. Crewe and M. Harrop (eds.), *Political Communications: The British General Election Campaign of 1983* (Cambridge: Cambridge University Press, 1986).

—— 'Political Marketing', *Parliamentary Affairs*, 43/3 (1990), 277–91.

—— and Miller, W., *Elections and Voters* (London: Macmillan, 1987).

Kavanagh, D., *Constituency Electioneering* (London: Longman, 1970).

—— 'The Timing of Elections: The British Case', in I. Crewe and M. Harrop (eds.), *Political Communications: The British General Election Campaign of 1987* (Cambridge: Cambridge University Press, 1989).

MacArthur, B., 'The National Press', in I. Crewe and M. Harrop (eds.), *Political Communications: The British General Election Campaign of 1987* (Cambridge: Cambridge University Press, 1989).

Mitchell, A., 'Taking it Personally', *New Society*, 5 June 1987.

Pinto-Duschinsky, M., *British Political Finance 1830–1980* (Washington, DC: American Enterprise Institute, 1981).

Rose, R., *Influencing Voters* (London: Faber, 1967).

Semetko, H., Blumler, J., Gurevitch, M., and Weaver, D., *The Formation of Campaign Agendas: A Comparative Analysis of Party and Media Roles in Recent American and British Elections* (Hillside, NJ: L. Erlbaum, 1991).

Swaddle, K., 'Ancient and Modern: Innovations in Electioneering at the Constituency Level', in I. Crewe and M. Harrop (eds.), *Political Communications: The British General Election Campaign of 1987* (Cambridge: Cambridge University Press, 1989).

5

Australia and New Zealand

COLIN A. HUGHES

The political systems of Australia and New Zealand are 'noted for their general similarity',[1] yet in the electoral sphere there are significant variations. Size is an obvious difference likely to influence electioneering: Australia's national electorate is five times as numerous as New Zealand's and spread over almost thirty times the area. But both are highly urbanized societies whose rural constituencies are a minority interest which has declined in importance for most of the century. Australia has compulsory voting, both have compulsory enrolment. But turn-out figures in New Zealand are not very much below the Australian level.

For decades both conducted 'traditional' election campaigns which were dominated by live performances before live audiences and by the print media; such campaigns were conducted on a decentralized basis by armies of party members who needed quite modest amounts of money for what they had to do. By the 1990s both had experienced a revolutionary change; they now conducted campaigns which were highly centralized, transmitted into electors' homes by the electronic media and computer-prepared mail, and driven by advertising executives and pollsters who required huge sums of money. Even such routine tasks as still survived from the old style campaign, like the 'letter-box stuffing' of pamphlets and hand-bills, might have to be paid for rather than undertaken by party-faithful volunteers. A politician's campaign tour now comprises visits to local radio stations to take part in 'talk-back' shows and being available for 'photo-opportunities' and delivering 'one-liners' for the evening's television news reports, instead of hour-long or longer set speeches to supporters and opponents in rented halls or on street corners.

People and ideas move regularly between the two countries. Political fashions, especially those imported from the United States of America, catch on in both at about the same time and are overtaken by the next novelty about the same time. Politicians of the same persuasion, left or right, sometimes help one another. Thus regular cross-fertilization reinforces the common historical and socio-economic foundations of their politics, whilst commentators and analysts pick over the same trends and praise or condemn the way the political world is going.

The Australian party system took its present configuration eighty years ago on the merger of the two middle-class parties which grew out of the factional politics that prevailed in the second half of the nineteenth century. Their 'Fusion' ended twenty years during which the rapid growth of the first mass party, the Australian Labor Party (ALP), reshaped political debate and the nature of election campaigns. Nation, party, and ideology-orientated motivations replaced personal loyalties and parochial interests in electoral choices.

The ALP drew its support from the trade unions which had formed a party to pursue their economic objectives in the political arena, and their manpower and discipline in election campaigns challenged the older parties. In some colonies proper cadre parties were already in the field; in other colonies, still an organizational lap back, there were comparable proto-party formations. All defensively improved their organizations and modified their campaign techniques to the new era of the mass party.

A mass electorate of adult males had existed in Australia for more than half a century, but in absolute numbers populations were still small and thinly scattered. Individual constituencies contained at most a few thousand electors and might have no more than a few hundred, so there was still some scope for personal influence. The only mass medium, the newspapers, was just as fragmented geographically; those with the largest circulations, published in the state capitals, had limited impact beyond those cities and minimal distribution outside their own state. The established press was generally anti-Labor, but the costs of establishing a new newspaper were modest and radical and Labor journals were plentiful. The press reported what was said in manifestos and at campaign meetings and wrote strong editorials; they did very little to personalize contests between either local candidates or the party leaders.

Since 1910 the population has grown so that the national

electorate of 1990 is more than five times as large as that of 1903 (by which time women had been enfranchised in all states). Newspapers remain state-based and orientated, with the two exceptions having very modest circulations. Although the Labor-connected papers have long since disappeared, since the early 1970s editorial support for and reporting bias towards the ALP can occur. Radio and television networking in both the public and private sectors produced the first truly national media and incidentally saturated the local audience remarkably quickly. Increased affluence has extended the boundaries of the middle class, and the manual working class in primary industry—agricultural, pastoral, and mining—and manufacturing has been decimated.

Nevertheless, changes to the Australian party system have been minor. About the end of the First World War rural interests created the Country Party which, after a moment's hesitation, settled into almost permanent coalescence (Sartori's term) with the party produced by the Fusion—the latter being known successively as Liberal (1909), National (1917), United Australia (1931), then Liberal again (1944). The appearance of the Country Party was probably the greatest upheaval. All three of the major parties have split on occasion, and the breakaway elements have operated as minor parties for a time. But whilst such minor parties might win up to 10 per cent or, very rarely, more of the national vote, winning seats was possible only for the upper house, the Senate, where proportional representation operated from 1949 onwards. Usually they duplicated the party structures and campaign practices of the major party from which they had seceded, the one exception being the Australian Democrats, who have tried to implement the values of participatory democracy.

The path of New Zealand party history is similar but turned the same corners slightly later. Adult male suffrage came two decades later, a two-party system still emerged from the factions about 1890, but the New Zealand Labour party (which favoured the English spelling of Labour over the American version preferred by the ALP) was not established until 1916 and did not achieve national office until 1935, again roughly two decades later. That development forced the merger of the United, previously known as Liberal, and Reform parties into the National party. There was one long-surviving minor party, Social Credit under various names, but more recently other minor parties have come and gone faster than their Australian equivalents. Since the beginning of the century the New Zealand electorate, too, has grown fivefold; its newspapers remain relatively parochial and its electronic media nationally orientated—like the Australian.

Those two elections, 1910 in Australia and 1935 in New Zealand, re-drew the electoral map horizontally, as to which constituencies would normally be safe for either side and which marginal, and vertically as to socio-economic alignments. The patterns endured remarkably well but the possibility that these lines are starting to dissolve is now a concern. Both countries' two-party systems have been remarkably stable and self-adjusting. In New Zealand, at the fourteen general elections from 1938 to 1978, the National vote never fell below 40 per cent and went over 50 per cent only twice, while the Labour vote fell below 40 per cent once and went over 50 per cent twice. In Australia, examining the primary vote before distribution of preferences, at the twenty-seven general elections from 1910 to 1975, the anti-Labor party or coalition vote fell below 40 per cent only once (in 1943 when the United Australia Party had disintegrated) and polled better than 50 per cent nine times, the ALP fell below 40 per cent twice (both times after the party had split) and polled better than 50 per cent only four times. Although the electoral pendulum remained to the right of centre most of the time, its arc was confined to a small sector and party strategies concentrated, though not exclusively, on the battle there.

There was one difference of pace in the post-alignment period between the two countries which concerned the party of the right's response to the successful mass organization already achieved by the party of the left. In New Zealand the new National Party created a new-look mass party with extraordinary speed. By the next election in 1938 it had over 1,000 branches with a membership estimated at 100,000 when the national enrolment was just under one million.[2] But in Australia none of the first three versions of the anti-Labor party managed to establish as effective a mass organization and it was not until the late 1940s when the second Liberal Party was formed out of the remnants of the United Australia Party that such a grass-roots structure was finally established. Nevertheless, in both countries each party ran much the same sort of campaign with similar success. Organizational achievement did not bring the New Zealand National Party to office until the fourth election after it had rebuilt. The Australian Liberal Party won the second election after its reformation—but with an extra ingredient in its campaign techniques.

The exceptional feature of Australian electoral life, one it has shared with few other countries, has been compulsory voting. Introduced in 1924 and coupled with the earlier introduction of compulsory enrolment in 1911, responsibility for one of the most demanding and labour-intensive activities required of political parties passed to the state. Consequently Australian parties, even when they qualified for the label 'mass' could get by with fewer members and at a lower level of activity and expenditure than most democratic parties.[3] It was still possible for some parts of the federal structure adopted by each of the Australian national parties to have extremely healthy numbers; for example, the South Australian branch of the Liberals, which had reabsorbed the local Country Party, had 350 branches and 50,000 members in a total electorate of 450,000. But other state branches had much smaller memberships proportionate to population without apparent ill-effects on their electoral performance.

'Traditional' campaigning methods changed little over time. And, it should be added, although interest today is in the new techniques, and their impact on the political process,[4] a lot of 'traditional' campaigning still goes on at every election. Old habits die hard; rank-and-file members know these methods, believe they work, and resist proposals that they be scrapped. Party operators may allow, even at times encourage, practices which they believe to be inefficient to continue because they do not cost very much and keep the grass roots happy and occupied.

The account of Australian electioneering just after the Second World War written by a recent visitor, Louise Overacker,[5] closely resembles the accounts of elections another decade on in both Australia and New Zealand written by local political scientists[6] and describes practices which might be observed in later elections.

The one campaign that broke new ground, but then was not repeated for decades, the Liberal *tour de force* of 1949, took place after she had left Australia. The campaign was unusually well funded, as business interests in Australia and London mobilized to get rid of an ALP government bent on socialist experiments such as nationalizing the privately owned banks. The campaign period was also unusually long, with planning and early advertising starting less than halfway through the life of the parliament. It made good use of radio, the only electronic medium then available, through saturation of time and imaginative dramatization of political material. It had a big idea which it pursued consistently, and it was masterminded by an advertising executive who had been enticed away from the ALP.[7] But it failed to become the norm, and two decades later many of its elements had to be imported from the United States for a fresh start with the ALP's 1972 campaign.

Traditional campaigns were short, lasting less than a month, preceded by another month of preparation though candidates were likely to have been chosen ('pre-selected') earlier than that. Australian Prime Ministers often called an early election, New Zealand did not, but their campaign timetables were similar. The formal start was the Policy Speech, delivered at some length before a large audience by the party's parliamentary leader. At the first federal election in 1901 one of the two serious candidates for the Australian prime ministership had provided a policy speech, the other had not,[8] and subsequently it had become an essential feature of the campaign, providing most of the ammunition for the rest of the campaign and containing such mandate as might later be claimed by the winner. Live radio carried it immediately and at peak listening time to a large part of the electorate, and it dominated the news pages the following day. It was usually accompanied by a longer, more detailed and extensive account of party policy which might be called a manifesto; that could be quarried by journalists and party speakers for more variety than the policy speech's time limits allowed.

Thereafter the campaign proceeded with innumerable meetings on street corners and in halls large and small, addressed by party leaders, by visiting MPs, and by local candidates and party officers. Overacker observed that party managers and journalists agreed that attendance at meetings had fallen off with the advent of radio,[9] but meetings were still thought necessary.

Print still played a large part: leaflets and handbills were in profusion, as were posters though these were very small in size for Australian federal elections as a wartime paper-saving regulation had lingered on for no apparent good reason. Even more important was the volume of material that appeared in the newspapers, as paid advertising and in reports of speeches and campaign activities.

Radio had made its debut as a major force in the 1931 campaign won easily by Lyons's United Australia Party, which combined the previous National Party and some ex-ALP politicians including Lyons himself, under the slogan 'Tune in with Britain' where Ramsay Macdonald had just executed a similar manœuvre. Australia's broadcasting system was a mixture of private sector, which sold time for spot commercials, and public sector, which provided free time for more substantial broadcasts. There was a statutory prohibition of political broadcasting after midnight on the Wednesday preceding the poll on Saturday, giving two days in which the press could continue to purvey partisan politics but radio might not. In New Zealand the public sector was predominant, and the advertising component consequently diminished. The other medium that was predominantly entertainment but could carry political messages, film, mattered much less, though there were advertising slides at the local cinema and the occasional propaganda film was made—by the Australian Nationals for the 1925 election and by New Zealand Labour for the 1938 election, for example.

Despite the legal obligation on all electors to enrol and to get themselves to the polling place of their choice within their constituency, Australian parties still invested considerable manpower in house-to-house canvassing, especially by the candidate personally, and in 'letter-box stuffing', distribution of several leaflets through the campaign which gave branch members and their families something meaningful to do. Similarly on polling day, though there was some provision by the parties of transport to the polls for elderly persons, most manpower went into distributing how-to-vote cards at the entrances to polling places and, for the more politically aware, scrutineering. The how-to-vote card was essential in Australia because, though the electorate was literate and reasonably well informed by other means, the absence of party affiliations from the ballot-paper and the need to number candidates consecutively and correctly to comply with the requirements of the alternative vote (or single transferable vote when and where that was used) made assistance in the voting compartment very necessary.

Campaign expenditure was modest so the fact that the statutory maxima and disclosure provisions were ineffectual[10] mattered little. A substantial proportion of the money was raised and spent locally, within each constituency. State headquarters helped the weakest constituencies and sometimes stronger local branches sent their surplus enthusiasts to help; the stronger state organizations might send money to another state where, for example, the party had been out of office a long while and its usual supporters had tightened their purse-strings. Overall though, a national election was a collection of state and local contests, held together only by the shopping list of promises contained in the policy speeches, the personalities of the alternative Prime Ministers and a handful of front-benchers who achieved recognition, and the nature of the times and the issues generated thereby and reflected in the mass media.

The New Zealand scene was much the same though the smaller scale encouraged a more intensive cover of the country and visits to more smaller centres by the party leader. Thus at the 1957 election, the veteran Labour leader, Walter Nash, opened with his policy speech in Auckland Town Hall:

The broadcast was regarded as being as important as the rest of the campaign put together. Labour officials and supporters in Auckland and throughout the country agreed that Mr Nash was in fine form and thought his speech much the best of the opening broadcasts. Many were exultant and believed that the election was won then and there, while all thought the party's prospects had been greatly enhanced.[11]

He then set off to tour the country, addressing 'twenty-three major meetings and several other lunch-hour and workplace gatherings' including one heroic day in which he spoke to 5,000 people including three successive evening meetings. All told he spoke to more than 20,000, only three of his audiences were below 500, and one of those poor houses was attributable to the local flooding.[12]

Alongside statistics for speeches can be set the numbers of major print items: at that 1957 election a grand total of 1.6 million, up from the previous election's 1.4 million, of which a condensed version of the party's manifesto accounted for 600,000 and a welfare pamphlet covering health, education, and social security another 600,000,[13] one for every household. The New Zealand electorate by then numbered one and a quarter million. It might be noted that the contemporary cost of posting such a pamphlet to every household was $A5,000, a modest sum today but then about 5 per cent of Labour's entire election budget. In addition to local press advertising at the constituency level, the Labour Party produced fifteen different newspaper ads for general use.

After Overacker's pioneering account, in the 1950s elections (and by-elections) were reported in case-studies of rural,[14] inner city,[15] and outer suburban[16] constituencies in Australia, and urban[17] constituencies in New Zealand. Constituency case-studies are almost always written about close contests, and possibly they give a misleading impression of vigorous good health in the branches and of effective and purposeful campaigns. Because campaigns were so decentralized, considerable resources were wasted in safe seats where the strongest branches with the most money were to be found.

At the national level, or state level when it was a state election in Australia, the parties' leaders tried to pursue rational strategies which should have meant focusing on swinging voters in marginal seats, but sometimes failed to do when the syndical interests which had created the party cast too much of a shadow. Chronicling the 1958 Australian election, Rawson commented that although the ALP's commitment to internal democracy ought to have meant that its rank-and-file members would have a relatively large share in preparing election policies, the organization limitations of the central party organs threw much more responsibility on to the party leaders and the party's advertising agency. After a central fund, controlled by the leader and one or two other senior party figures as trustees, had been established in 1940 it became the means of raising money independently of party channels, that is mainly from business, and directing it to a central spending point, the party's advertising agency. But there remained problems of co-ordinating material produced centrally with subnational tactics, and of getting the agency's estimates of the effectiveness of issues and campaign themes accepted by the party leaders. The Liberal Party, with much stronger national and state secretariats, was able to plan and co-ordinate more effectively.[18]

Whilst on the subject of organizational strength, in the 1950s the ALP experienced the trauma of the 'Split', the secession of a substantial number of right-wing, predominantly Catholic supporters and some members of parliament. They set up the Democratic Labour Party (DLP) and sought to keep the ALP from office until it mended its ways along the lines the DLP proposed. Such high drama, coupled with plots and counter-plots to take control of particular local branches or state headquarters, probably stimulated membership and sustained enthusiasm for traditional campaign activities.

New Zealand politics was spared such a blood-letting in the 1950s and, according to one subsequent analyst, the New Zealand Labour Party went into a long-term and 'dramatic decline in party membership, the number of branches, the commitment of branch office-holders, meeting activity, and fund raising at the primary level'.[19] That assessment needs to be set against a contemporary account of the 1956 election focused on the Labour Representation Committees (LRCs), the bodies above the local branches within the party structure on which ordinary branch members and affiliated trade unionists were represented proportionate to their number in the area covered, which found:

Local organisations varied greatly from place to place according to the personalities involved and the financial state of the LRC. The four metropolitan LRCs all possess paid secretaries (who are also trade union secretaries) and some of the provincial LRC's, for example Napier, appointed a full-time organiser for the duration of the campaign. There is no doubt that efficiency is enhanced if this can be done, but not all LRC's think it necessary or can afford it. The ability and enthusiasm of a few key people appears to be the main ingredients in good local organisation, and if an LRC has this it usually has a good branch structure as well. Generally, the enthusiasm of branch members was impressive, and was greater than in 1954.[20]

The extent and implications of the decline Gustafson identified deserve brief attention because of recent concerns about the apparent reappearance of such phenomena in association with, and possibly as a consequence of, the newest techniques of electioneering and post-ideological positions. Membership declined, branches disappeared or were reduced in size, meetings became infrequent. The nature of grass-roots activity changed, to concentrate on fundraising and campaigning at the expense of local and community affairs and membership recruitment, and perceptions of the Labour Party itself changed to its being merely an election-winning machine. The older loyalists retired and were not replaced; the electorate changed and Labour could no longer rely on instinctive loyalties. Education pushed the younger and abler members of the working class into new contacts and allegiances. More widespread ownership of automobiles, the advent of television and later closing of hotel bars enticed supporters away from humdrum party activities.

Television in particular, Gustafson thought, undermined traditional relationships by

reducing the self-educative and propaganda roles of party branches. Activists learn more about what is going on in their own country and in the world by watching television than by attending a branch meeting, although there is a residual feeling, if the local MP is to give a report to the branch, that members are being given confidential, inside information. Television has also become the major means by which party leaders influence the public directly, replacing party activists 'gossiping the gospel' to their friends and workmates.[21]

Viewers became saturated with politics and cynical from over-exposure to politicians on television, but the government of the day retained an advantage as the more newsworthy source. Urban growth and redevelopment fractured old networks, and the active and stable branches of the inner-city areas, now depopulated by commercial uses and cut up by new roads to bring suburban workers in to the Central Business District, were not replaced by equally healthy branches in the outer suburbs. Disruption of political networks was aggravated by frequent redistribution of electoral boundaries.

The 1957 election had been won narrowly by the New Zealand Labour Party, 41 : 39. Its victory was immediately followed by a foreign exchange and economic crisis which revived memories of austerities under the only previous Labour government, which had seen the country through the latter part of the Depression and the Second World War. Austin Mitchell's account of the 1960 campaign records a run-down in Labour's resources and effectiveness since 1957, and remarks on the good use to which the National Party had begun to put opinion polls whilst Labour continued to rely 'on a curious blend of occasional conversations with the "man in the street" (or the pub) and an assumed insight into the mind of "the people"'.[22]

Gustafson's account of Labour's problems at this time is of more than a mere run-down, for he adds to Mitchell's version a steep rise in membership dissatisfaction over the government's performance evidenced in 'more letters of protest from branch and electorate secretaries . . . to Head Office than in all the rest of the period

1945–72 put together'[23] and a scarcity of activists to work at the election. Not only did Labour lose the 1960 election and remain out of office for twelve years, but the events that weakened its performance at the election opened the way to a transformation of the party some years later. With the party's next defeat in 1975, again after a single term of office, there was another, faster cycle of decline and revival, but with less impact on party membership.[24]

It would appear that whilst the so-called Americanization of electioneering undoubtedly has been having, and will continue to have, a major impact on the political process in both Australia and New Zealand, there are good reasons to be cautious about assessing its effect on party organization, and grass-roots vitality in particular. Some of the problems were apparent long before the latest campaign techniques took over. But it is also possible that bouts of grass-roots malaise, previously caused by social changes and the frustrations of office, might become fatal when the trauma of the latest campaign techniques is added.

To this point attention has been paid primarily to the two labour parties. The parties of the right, Liberal and Country in Australia, National in New Zealand, may have deserved the accusation that their commitment to mass organization and democratic principle was not genuine, that they were really cadre parties of the moderately successful middle class and rural notables masquerading behind an extensive branch structure and huge membership. If so, they put up a remarkably good performance.

Aimer described the Liberal branches of Victoria as 'close-knit, socially homogeneous middle-class structures' and 'small groups of active party supporters embedded in a larger apathetic membership' for whom participation in party politics was 'largely a social activity . . . a gathering of old friends as well as a political meeting'.[25] Elections were so frequent—general election campaigns in two out of every three years—that the branches lived with election planning and preparation. Whilst planning tended to be centralized and the content of the campaign was settled at the state level, electioneering itself was left largely to local initiative:

Within the framework of tactics and policies laid down by the party's leaders . . . each candidate wages his own campaign, using as far as possible the resources of the party organisation in his electorate. Electorate committees are thus responsible for such details as the printing and distribution of the candidate's manifesto and how-to-vote cards (the order

of voting preferences having been determined by the party leaders),
arranging the candidate's meetings throughout the electorate, and advertising in the local press or by means of radio and television scatters. The
candidate and his local machine are free to decide what type of campaign
best suits the candidate, given the nature of the electorate and the money
and helpers available. It is not, therefore, because electorates are lacking
in autonomy that the techniques of campaigning within them are nearly
uniform; it is the result of tradition-bound practices combined with
centralised control over the political content of the party campaign.[26]

Aitkin emphasizes the role the campaign plays in reinforcing party
commitment for the New South Wales Country Party, the only
occasion when loyalties can be publicly reaffirmed, though again
the frequency of elections gave ample opportunity. As with the
Victorian Liberals, there were levels of responsibility and action:
the leaders plan the overall campaign, determine policies, and
allocate central funds; at the constituency level there are 'local
issues and tactics, the candidate and his image, and local advertising and skirmishing'.[27] But given the diversity of rural electorates,
there was potential for more tension between the levels. State-wide,
or federal, advertising had to be general and non-parochial; local
activists wanted to spend what they regarded as their money on
local issues. Sometimes things could go awry, as when a party
advertisement claiming credit for lifting the price of butter
appeared in non-dairying constituencies as well.[28]

The 1972 elections in both countries not only produced the
return of the labour parties to office after long spells in the
wilderness and with a reforming zeal and new leadership; they also
changed the style of electioneering to more centralized control and
professionalism, coupled with a readiness to learn from experience
at previous elections and by-elections. In Australia the Dawson
(1966), Corio (1967), and Capricornia (1967) by-elections and in
New Zealand the Marlborough by-election (1970) gave the
national leader a winner's reputation and sharpened techniques in
ideal conditions with the deployment of resources possible only at
a by-election.

In New Zealand Labour planned to ensure that the desired level
of activity could be sustained throughout the four weeks of the
campaign. Targeted marginal seats were given an overseeing
Special Assistance to Selected Electorates committee of senior

politicians to dispatch reinforcements and keep the local organizations up to standard. Party organizers

were told to supplement and build upon the Party's nation-wide advertising campaign and to take advantage of points made by the leaders and
generally to dove-tail advertising and promotion efforts into the big
campaign. Wherever possible, candidates were to speak on the subject that
the Party's advertisements were featuring in the newspapers that day.
Candidates were given an outline of the national advertising theme
schedule—the environment on Wednesday, 8 November, cost of living on
Saturday, 14 November, and so on. . . . Background material and advice
was issued progressively until by campaign's end a candidate would have
received a stack of paper four inches high. When Labour MPs addressed
meetings the local candidate went with him to see how such notes could
be used.[29]

However, preparing the party's manifesto, commenced in 1970
with the 1969 version as a basis and run through party conference
and post-conference committees, went so slowly that the text was
available for candidates only at the weekend before the campaign
started.

Similarly the National Party's campaign was a mix of old and
new. Prime Minister Marshall delivered his policy speech extending
over two hours in a provincial town hall; the first hour was to be
televised, the balance not, and he sought to cover two-thirds of
policy topics in the one speech. The Broadcasting Commission's
network failed, and most of the telecast was lost. Thereafter it was
still a whistle-stop tour of the country, still drawing large crowds
to hall meetings, but with demonstrators rather than hecklers as
the speaker's hazard.

One aspect of the changing connections between politics and the
media was illustrated at Christchurch Town Hall where twenty
demonstrators in a crowd of 1,300 at a National meeting provoked
the chairman into calling on police to take 'appropriate action'.
The police picked the demonstrators off, photographed them
outside the hall, and put them into a patrol wagon. Journalists
who went to observe this were spoken to sharply by the police, and
the Prime Minister then unwisely told his audience that they could
expect press reports of police brutality the following day.[30]

In Australia the ALP experimented even more. There had already
been a successful state campaign, in South Australia, based on
extensive market research and a television advertising campaign

concentrated on a larger-than-life party leader. Federally the ALP had done well in 1969 and could have reasonable expectations for 1972 given the signs of disrepair in the coalition government. A group of ALP supporters financed, at a cost of $5,000, a special survey to identify problems with negative components in the leader's public image. Steps were then taken to reshape the image; for example, he went down less well with women voters so a special effort was made with talk-back radio which has a high proportion of women listeners.

Another special donation financed a mini-campaign a year before the election so that the release of a series of policies would attract news reports at no further cost to the party. It would also allow those new policies which needed time to get across more scope than they would have if hoarded for the policy speech—though there were costs as new policy launches outside the campaign itself were much more at risk of receiving public criticism from within the party as indeed proved to be the case.[31]

A full-time campaign director was appointed a year before the election had to be held, compared to three months' preparation for the 1969 election, and the national budget target was set at five times 1969's—$250,000—though in fact $140,000 had been raised in 1969 and $300,000 would be raised in 1972. A further $250,000–300,000 was raised at the state level to be spent by the state branches and another $200,000 raised in the constituencies and spent on their activities, so overall the ALP campaign cost at least $800,000. At least $125,000 of the money raised nationally went to the state branches to support their activities, but Blewett reports complaints that federal fund-raising was tapping business and trade-union donations which had previously gone to the state branches.

The ALP's 1972 campaign marks the start of the transitional period in electioneering, the main features of which were chronicled in detail in the series of election studies edited by Penniman.[32] Whilst the ALP campaign was still under way, market research and advertising firms had begun to press their new wares on the Liberal Party,[33] and from the other side of the Tasman Sea the New Zealand Labour Party took a close interest in what the ALP was doing[34] in addition to developing a number of the new techniques independently.

Features which would continue in all subsequent elections in both countries were: longer campaigns which were divided into periods during which different techniques were used and different emphases given; higher levels of expenditure and therefore more vigorous fund-raising; more central control over the day-by-day presentation of policies and handling of issues; more professionalism; substantial use of polling to test the acceptability of policies, identify issues, monitor performance through the campaign, select target audiences and marginal seats which could be won over by approaches tailored to their concerns. In New Zealand restricted access to the electronic media meant that half the budget still went on newspaper advertising and only 10 per cent on films for television. In Australia just over 10 per cent went to the press and possibly half to television. By the 1990 election the ALP was spending 70 per cent of its national media budget of $6 million on television, the Liberals 50 per cent of their $4.5 million; with radio accounting for another 10 per cent for each, the press had 20 per cent of Labor's expenditure, and 35 per cent of the Liberals'.

One parallel development should be mentioned. In 1941 the first Australian polling organization was started in association with a newspaper chain; it remained unique for thirty years. In 1970–1 two more were started, again linked to other newspaper chains, and then another.[35] In New Zealand the first polling organization came in 1968, and a second in 1972 although its findings were not for the public until 1978.[36] The polls' measurement of shifts of opinion and assessments of leaders and policies fed into the campaign where they could be matched against data from polls commissioned by the parties and kept confidential although the latter usually pursued more subtle ideas by different means. More importantly they could influence those electors who were aware of their findings, for example by inducing a band-wagon effect.[37]

The growing role of polling introduces the latest phase in electioneering which is dominated by 'tracking and targeting':

Tracking refers to the use of public opinion polls and other research methods to monitor changing attitudes in the population. Targeting is the use of TV advertisements to aim political messages at electorally strategic parts of the population. Separately, each half of this relationship is like a blunt scissors blade: advertising without research can be words into the ether, intuitive gambles that the public is paying attention; research without advertising can be a dry accumulation of statistics unchallenged by the demands of actually communicating with people. But together they add up to a method of political campaigning.

Tracking gives the Party ears to listen to the electorate; targeting is the voice with which it replies. Tracking suggests the strategy of the campaign; targeting is its practical implementation.[38]

In one respect the circle has been completed. The parties once more need information about the attitudes and loyalties of individual electors, the sort of thing that canvassers used to collect at the local level though now it may be collected over the telephone by party workers at headquarters or employees of the party's polling organization under the guise of polling. That information may also be deduced from socio-economic and other characteristics of the electors extracted from data banks and mailing lists acquired by the party for the purpose. It drives not only the television advertisements that Mills mentions, but returns to print as well in the personalized approach of the computer-produced letter addressed to the targeted elector or household. It allows campaign messages to be shaped and streamed, as in Labour's 1987 campaign in New Zealand:

Labour's early qualitative polls (in-depth interviews exploring respondents' attitudes) allowed them to create an overall positive campaign mood designed to placate its traditional supporters. Later, tracking polls and marginal electorate surveys enabled Labour to forge an ancillary set of specific issue appeals, targeted to key groups of deserters and converts, and to identify a 'hit list' of crucial marginal electorates for additional funds and organisational attention.[39]

The parties also need information about their opponents' campaign to fine-tune their own activities and to capitalize promptly on any gaffes which can be spotted. Extensive media-monitoring on line to campaign headquarters gives, hour by hour, information about the progress of the campaign; fax links with candidates at the constituency level enable immediate responses to new developments and a closely orchestrated compliance with the grand design of the campaign.

Cutting across the selection of techniques is the shift in appeals from the shopping lists of specific promises, public works, welfare payments, legislative and policy specifics, which used to be directed at identifiable targets—farmers, old-age pensioners, parents with school-age children, predicated, it used to be said, on the accountant model of electors: electors would note and add up each cash benefit, strike a balance, and decide to vote for the party offering the larger return. The small group discussions which have become the staple of the parties' commissioned research shift emphasis by probing 'not just the purely rational, cognitive manifestations of opinion but of the more shadowy area where values, emotions and feelings are dominant: the swampy landscape in which opinions are really generated'.[40] The most recent changes in information technology have impacts far beyond politics, of course, but in the political realm their influence extends to allowing party leaders to disregard traditional pressure-group allies and their own rank-and-file as unrepresentative of the widest opinions which determine elections, to build factions rather than coalitions (Polsby's terms), and to avoid grappling with the difficult problems by favouring soft, popular issues.

Atkinson reports a New Zealand episode which nicely illustrates the problems of such conversions. The National Party imported a computerized fund-raising and political intelligence system from the United States, 'Hannibal'.

The most vociferous complaints came from the stronger, better-organised electorates. It was here that National's volunteer army of supporters most resented Hannibal's short-circuiting of the existing chain of command between local party leaders and members; a chain of command based on personal contacts and channelled through efficiently-run electorate organisations. They worried that if Hannibal made grass roots activists feel either over-solicited or obsolescent, National's position as, per capita, one of the largest mass membership political parties in the democratic world, might be threatened. Feelings ran high enough to precipitate the ousting of National party Secretary-General, Max Bradford, but Hannibal remained in place. Bradford had seen the future correctly. With mass marketing and computer mailing, the emphasis of the Party was changing from vote-getting to money-making, and the new focus called for a smaller, better-heeled membership.[41]

Party leaders riding the tiger have been examining ways of dismounting or at least controlling the beast: how to revive meaningful branch activities, how to reduce the ever increasing demand for money to pay for television advertising—and avoid the dangers of corruption and undue influence that go with desperate financial problems, how to avoid the fragmentation of the electorate among increasingly militant interest groups, how to avoid the trivialization of politics by television's need for small doses of image. No signs of consensus on which problems are most serious, or what can be done, have appeared.

Notes

1. Clive Bean, 'Electoral Law, Electoral Behaviour and Electoral Outcomes: Australia and New Zealand Compared', *Journal of Commonwealth and Comparative Politics*, 24/1 (1986), 57–73.

2. Robert Chapman, 'From Labour to National', in W. H. Oliver (ed.), *The Oxford History of New Zealand* (Wellington: Oxford University Press, 1981), 333–68; R. S. Milne, *Political Parties in New Zealand* (Oxford: Clarendon Press, 1966), 204–6.

3. Arnold J. Heidenheimer, 'Comparative Party Finance', *Journal of Politics*, 25/3 (1963), 798.

4. Stephen Mills, *The New Machine Men* (Melbourne: Penguin, 1986). David Denemark, 'Electoral Instability and the Modern Campaign: New Zealand Labour in 1987', *Australian Journal of Political Science*, 26/2 (1991), 250–76.

5. Louise Overacker, *The Australian Party System* (New Haven, Conn.: Yale University Press, 1952), 271–86.

6. D. W. Rawson, *Australia Votes* (Melbourne: Melbourne University Press, 1961). R. M. Chapman, W. K. Jackson, and A. V. Mitchell, *New Zealand Politics in Action* (Wellington: Oxford University Press, 1962). Austin Mitchell, *Waitaki Votes: A Study of a New Zealand By-election, 1962* (Dunedin: University of Otago Press, 1962).

7. Mills, *The New Machine Men*.

8. Gavin Souter, *Acts of Parliament* (Melbourne: Melbourne University Press, 1988), 32–3.

9. Overacker, *The Australian Party System*, 272.

10. Colin A. Hughes, 'Australia', *Journal of Politics*, 25/3 (1963), 646–63; id., 'Control of Election Expenses: Australia', *Parliamentarian*, 50/4 (1969), 285–92.

11. Bruce Brown, 'The Labour Campaign', *Political Science*, 10/1 (1958), 15.

12. Ibid. 16.

13. Ibid. 19.

14. Henry Mayer and Joan Rydon, *The Gwydir By-election 1953* (Canberra: Australian National University, 1954). D. W. Rawson, and Susan M. Holtzinger, *Politics in Eden-Monaro* (Melbourne: Heinemann, 1958).

15. P. B. Westerway, 'The Election in Parkes', in Rawson, *Australia Votes*; Colin A. Hughes and B. A. Knox, 'The Election in Brisbane', ibid. 197–217.

16. Creighton Burns, *Parties and People* (Melbourne: Melbourne University Press, 1961).

17. R. H. Brookes, 'Wellington Central: The Field and the Battle', *Political Science*, 10/2 (1958), 15–29. Austin Mitchell, 'The Voter and the Election: Dunedin Central', in Chapman, Jackson, and Mitchell, *New Zealand Politics in Action*.

18. Rawson, *Australia Votes*, 75–9.

19. Barry Gustafson, *Social Change and Party Reorganization* (London: Sage, 1976), 9–22.

20. Brown, 'The Labour Campaign', 20.

21. Gustafson, *Social Change and Party Reorganization*, 17.

22. Mitchell, 'The Voter and the Election: Dunedin Central', 86.

23. Gustafson, *Social Change and Party Reorganization*, 21.

24. Jack Vowles, 'Ends, Means, and for Whom?', in Jonathan Boston and Martin Holland (eds.), *The Fourth Labour Government* (Auckland: Oxford University Press, 1987), 23–4.

25. Peter Aimer, *Politics, Power and Persuasion* (Melbourne: James Bennett, 1974), 60, 61.

26. Ibid. 158–9.

27. Don Aitkin, *The Country Party in New South Wales* (Canberra: Australian National University Press, 1972), 247.

28. Ibid. 249.

29. Brian Lockstone and Warren Page, *Landslide '72* (Dunedin: John McIndoe, 1973), 27–8.

30. Ibid. 50–2.

31. Neal Blewett, 'Labor 1968–72', in Henry Mayer (ed.), *Labor to Power* (Sydney: Angus and Robertson, 1973), 8.

32. Howard R. Penniman (ed.), *Australia at the Polls: The National Elections of 1975* (Washington, DC: American Enterprise Institute, 1977); id. (ed.), *The Australian National Elections of 1977* (Washington, DC: American Enterprise Institute, 1979); id. (ed.), *Australia at the Polls: The National Elections of 1980 and 1983* (Washington, DC: American Enterprise Institute, 1983); id. (ed.), *New Zealand at the Polls: The General Election of 1978* (Washington, DC: American Enterprise Institute, 1980).

33. Mills, *The New Machine Men*, 97–8.

34. Jim Eagles and Colin James, *The Making of a New Zealand Prime Minister* (Melbourne: Cheshire, 1973), 105–6.

35. Terence W. Beed, 'Opinion Polling and the Elections', in Penniman, *Australia at the Polls: The National Elections of 1975*, 211–15.

36. Brian Murphy, 'Polling and the Election', in Penniman, *New Zealand at the Polls: The General Election of 1978*, 168– }0.
37. Mills, *The New Machine Men*, 126–7.
38. Ibid. 8.
39. Denemark, 'Electoral Instability and the Modern Campaign: New Zealand Labour in 1987', 264.
40. Mills, *The New Machine Men*, 77.
41. Joe Atkinson, 'Mass Communications, Economic Liberalisation and the New Mediators', *Political Science*, 41/2 (1989), 93–4.

References

Atkinson, Joe, 'Mass Communications, Economic Liberalisation and the New Mediators', *Political Science*, 41/2 (1989), 85–108.

Bean, Clive, 'Electoral Law, Electoral Behaviour and Electoral Outcomes: Australia and New Zealand Compared', *Journal of Commonwealth & Comparative Politics*, 24/1 (1986), 57–73.

—— McAllister, Ian, and Warhurst, John, *The Greening of Australian Politics: The 1990 Federal Election* (Melbourne: Longman Cheshire. 1990).

Chapman, R. M., Jackson, W. K., and Mitchell, A. V., *New Zealand Politics in Action* (Wellington: Oxford University Press, 1962).

Denemark, David, 'Electoral Instability and the Modern Campaign: New Zealand Labour in 1987', *Australian Journal of Political Science*, 26/2 (1991), 250–76.

Eagles, Jim, and James, Colin, *The Making of a New Zealand Prime Minister* (Melbourne: Cheshire, 1973).

Gustafson, Barry, *Social Change and Party Reorganization* (London: Sage, 1976).

McAllister, Ian, and Warhurst, John (eds.), *Australia Votes: The 1987 Federal Election* (Melbourne: Longman Cheshire, 1988).

McLeay, Elizabeth (ed.), *The 1990 General Election: Perspectives of Political Change in New Zealand* (Wellington: Department of Politics, Victoria University of Wellington, Occasional Paper No. 3, forthcoming).

Mayer, Henry (ed.), *Labor to Power* (Sydney: Angus and Robertson, 1973).

Mills, Stephen, *The New Machine Men* (Melbourne: Penguin, 1986).

Penniman, Howard R. (ed.), *Australia at the Polls: The National Elections of 1975* (Washington, DC: American Enterprise Institute, 1977).

—— *The Australian National Elections of 1977* (Washington, DC: American Enterprise Institute, 1979).

—— *Australia at the Polls: The National Elections of 1980 and 1983* (Washington, DC: American Enterprise Institute, 1983).

—— *New Zealand at the Polls: The General Election of 1978* (Washington, DC: American Enterprise Institute, 1980).

Rawson, D. W., *Australia Votes* (Melbourne: Melbourne University Press, 1961).

Roberts, Nigel, 'The New Zealand General Election of 1990' *Political Science*, 43/1 (1991), 1–19.

6

India

JAMES MANOR

Electioneering has changed considerably in India since the first exercise of universal suffrage in 1952, but this owes far less to legal or technological changes than to changes in the political system. It is mainly attributable to political awakening within the electorate and to decay within political institutions.[1]

India's parliamentary and electoral systems bear a strong resemblance to those of Britain. Elections to the Lok Sabha, the dominant lower house of India's parliament, must in normal circumstances be held within five years of the previous election (although by act of parliament during the State of Emergency declared in mid-1975, six years were allowed to elapse between the 1971 and 1977 polls). The same is true of elections to the state legislatures in this federal system.

Seats are won by candidates gaining a plurality on the first ballot. Those receiving less than one-sixth of the votes lose their deposit, but deposits are so small that the number of candidates has grown to vast proportions (from 1,985 in 1962 to 6,158 in 1989). Usually, however, only two or three candidates attract large numbers of votes in any contest. Just over one-fifth of the seats are reserved for candidates from the Scheduled Castes ('ex'-untouchables) or Scheduled Tribes, although the electorate in those constituencies is the entire population over 18 and not just members of those disadvantaged communities.

During the first two general elections in 1952 and 1957, voters were given a small slip of paper (or two or three slips in multi-member constituencies) to be placed in one of several boxes marked with the symbol of various parties and candidates. This process was cumbersome and open to some abuse, so since 1962 the voter has marked a single ballot paper, placing it in a single sealed box. This change has had little impact on campaigning. (Voting machines were used in a small number of constituencies in 1989, but plans to deploy them more widely were scrapped after a court case decided that they were not compatible with the constitutional provision for 'ballot-papers'. A promised constitutional amendment has not yet been passed.)

The agency controlling the conduct of elections has always been the national Election Commission, a largely autonomous body presided over by an Election Commissioner who is appointed by India's President. The President occupies a position similar to that of Britain's monarch and must act on the advice of the Prime Minister, but this did not lead to concern over the impartiality of the Commission until the 1989 election. On that occasion, two additional commissioners were inserted just before the campaign and opposition groups feared that at least one of them might assist the ruling Congress-I Party. In the event, however, the man in question turned out to be energetically fair. In early 1991, fresh anxiety arose about possible pro-Congress-I sympathies of the newly appointed Election Commissioner, and two leaders of the party of the Hindu right were briefly arrested for demanding his dismissal. His aggressive role during the 1991 campaign aroused considerable controversy. But the Commission was even-handed on previous occasions, and it would be difficult for a single partisan figure at the apex of this enormous system to affect the result. Election Commissioners are also appointed in each state and Union Territory, from among senior civil servants, and their impartiality has also been widely acknowledged.

There are two things to say about the length of election campaigns—one simple and one complex. First, the process by which votes are cast and counted has taken far less time at recent elections than it did at the first two elections in 1952 and 1957. They required, respectively, four months and nineteen days. That prolonged the period during which electioneering occurred. More recently, the norm has been three days for national elections and usually one or two for state elections. (In 1991, polling was scheduled for 20, 24, and 26 May, but the assassination of Rajiv Gandhi on 21 May caused the final two days of polling to be postponed until 12 and 15 June).

The duration of campaigns prior to polling is a more complicated matter. The length of official campaigns never varies: three weeks from the day on which candidate lists are finalized by the Election

Commission until forty-eight hours before polling concludes. (Campaigning in that final two days and the provision of transport to voters are both illegal, but much discreet mobilizing and ferrying of voters actually takes place.) There are, however, significant variations in the length of actual campaigns, and (to say something slightly different) in the amount of time that elapses between the announcement that an election is required and the polling days. These variations are largely explained by the eagerness or disinclination of incumbent governments to expedite the process and the preparedness of the Election Commission.

The shortest national election campaign—less than six weeks—occurred in December 1984, when the ruling Congress-I wanted to move quickly while the memory of the assassination of Indira Gandhi remained fresh in voters' minds, since this was rightly expected to boost the party's prospects. Such speed was possible because the Election Commission had already made preparations for an election which had to take place by the middle of the following month. The longest delay occurred between August 1979 and the first week of 1980, mainly because the Election Commission had not anticipated a mid-term poll and was legally bound to complete a time-consuming revision of the electoral rolls. Both of these extreme examples are drawn from recent, indeed from successive elections. As this suggests, there has been no marked trend toward shorter or longer campaigns.

Approximately seven in ten Indians live in villages and constituencies are large—with near to a million voters for most parliamentary seats and over 100,000 for most state assembly seats. A typical assembly constituency might contain at least 100 villages, with many times that in parliamentary races, and they are often reached only by poor roads or mere tracks. Campaigning is thus a punishing business, with activists from major parties attempting to conduct house-to-house canvassing in most villages, and candidates seeking to visit nearly all villages in their bailiwicks. A large proportion of the electorate is reached in most elections. A study of the 1967 election in the state of Gujarat found that 29 per cent of voters had a high degree of exposure to the campaign, 37 per cent a medium degree, and 35 per cent a low degree.[2] The growth of the electorate and, more crucially, the decay of most party organizations since then has probably resulted in a decline in the extent of such contact, but not a radical decline.

All India Radio—which monopolizes the air waves within India—is thought by most politicians to have only a limited impact, and the telecasts from the government television monopoly, Doordarshan, in 1984, 1989, and 1991 appear (as we shall see) not to have determined many contests. The major, privately owned newspapers have rightly been seen by voters as more balanced—and party newspapers more diverse—than the electronic media since the latter were turned into partisan instruments by ruling parties in New Delhi in the mid-1970s. But only about one-third of the electorate is literate and press distribution to remote rural areas is far less reliable than in urban centres. Most politicians believe that the main impact of the press occurs prior to election campaigns, when they contribute to an impression that incumbent state and national governments are or are not governing effectively. Most politicians therefore conclude that their best hope during campaigns is to concentrate on gruelling efforts at mass contact.[3]

This takes several forms. Party manifestos are liberally distributed, as are election posters and handbills containing photographs of leaders and the election symbols of parties which are so important with such a high proportion of illiterates. (Indeed, ballots contain the symbols, but not the names of parties, alongside candidates' names.) Party symbols are painted ubiquitously on walls, while party flags, caps, and badges are displayed, and arches are constructed over roads bedecked in party colours. Loudspeakers—fixed and mobile—pound out partisan messages (live and recorded), slides and short films are shown in cinemas, and audio recordings by artists and political leaders are distributed. Public meetings are held, often attended by gaudy, noisy processions including dancers.

Candidates and sometimes more prominent leaders offer speeches calling attention to the achievements or misdeeds of incumbents, offering promises for the future, and stressing the candidate's commitment to the common good and his or her opponent's disregard thereof. Activists working for a candidate often stress less high-minded themes—his or her membership in and service to a caste or community, specific promises to a local area or group, the allegedly vile doings of opponents. They also distribute money and gifts, both to ordinary voters and—more generously—to leaders of important caste or religious groups or to important organized interests.[4]

We shall see presently how the messages which politicians seek to convey, the means by which they are conveyed, and the role of money have changed during campaigns, in response to the awakening within the electorate and the decay of institutions, especially parties. We shall also see how the role of prominent national and state leaders has changed somewhat in response to these things. But the preoccupation of politicians with mass contact has remained intense.

Electioneering in India has changed hardly at all as a result of changes in election laws or rules. Few such changes have been made, and those which have occurred have not had much impact on campaigning. The move to a single ballot paper between the 1957 and 1962 elections streamlined the polling process, but had little effect on electioneering. The subsequent use of numbered counterfoils on ballots and successive changes in policy on whether the vote tally for every polling station should be separately recorded have potential implications for popular fears about the secrecy of the ballot. But campaigning has not changed as a consequence. The one change which might have made a difference, restrictions on the donations which candidates can receive and on the amounts that they can spend, are, as we shall see, widely and openly flouted.

Advances in the 'technology' of electioneering have had only a slightly greater impact. The list of such advances which have not made a difference is at least as long as those which have. Telephone canvassing is of little use since only a tiny and unrepresentative slice of the electorate has telephones. Fax machines are used only minimally—indeed, this writer has never seen one even in the state headquarters of the well-funded Congress-I Party. Direct mail is more or less unheard of. Only three 'technological' innovations are worth noting. They all arrived fully on the scene during the 1980s, and each has had a more limited impact than in the industrialized democracies. They are (*a*) finely tuned series of newspaper advertisements, (*b*) accurate opinion polling, and (*c*) television and video cassette recorders. Advice from overseas has seldom, if ever, been sought.

The Congress-I Party has been the main deployer of series of newspaper advertisements, expensively designed by leading advertising agencies. They have used them only since 1984. The 1984 series looked impressive to the 5 per cent of the electorate that reads English since it was based on an English pun. Each day a new slogan would emerge, 'Give Order a Hand', 'Give Efficiency a Hand', etc.—the hand being the election symbol of the party. But the pun translated poorly or not at all into indigenous languages, and these advertisements made little difference in the result which was as good as determined on the day Mrs Gandhi was murdered. In 1989, a similar series was abandoned half-way through the campaign in favour of aggressive negative advertisements against the opposition, but neither saved the Congress-I from electoral embarrassment. The opposition made modest use of these techniques in 1989—carefully exploiting photographs of locally popular leaders in different regions (they did the same with their election posters which were more important than advertisements in the press). But they were constrained both by limited funds and by their belief that such advertisements had little impact.[5] So while parties, especially the Congress-I during Rajiv Gandhi's time as leader, have used admen and leading journalists as consultants and employed full-time workers to a far greater extent than in the 1970s, when such things were extreme rarities, their influence has been limited.

India has long had opinion polls, but, until the 1980s, enough of them turned out to be famously wrong and politicians were loath to trust them. They preferred to rely on information provided by their own party organizations. When organizational decay undermined those sources, Indira and Rajiv Gandhi and some regional leaders turned to reports by police and intelligence services, although these were also usually unreliable because these services found it difficult to break with their habit of telling the leader what she or he wanted to hear.

By 1980, however, certain pollsters had become patently reliable. A poll by Bashiruddin Ahmed on the eve of that election was highly accurate, and polls by Prannoy Roy and Ashok Lahiri were similarly impressive. The latter team produced still more accurate predictions in 1984. Since then pollsters have had far more credibility, although some have remained unreliable. One result is that parties—especially moneyed parties, which mainly means the Congress-I—occasionally commission polls from teams using these more reliable techniques, as have India's burgeoning newsmagazines. But considerable mistrust persists. Many leaders of the Congress-I were, for example, extremely fearful of a general election in March 1991, despite one poll indicating that they would win a solid parliamentary majority.[6] Pollsters have still not fully 'arrived' in India.

India's national television network, Doordarshan, did not reach large numbers of people until the 1984 election. The central government, which controls the system, claimed that around 70 per cent of the population could receive television signals at that time, but investigations by this writer in numerous state capitals indicated that so few of the low-power transmitters were functional that the actual figure was roughly 30 per cent. By the next election, in 1989, the vast majority of Indians could receive telecasts—either on privately owned sets or on sets made available to village communities by the government.

We badly need research into the influence of television, but it appears that Doordarshan broadcasts, which in both campaigns were intensely partisan in favour of the ruling Congress-I Party, had only a modest impact. In 1984, viewers were offered frequent reminders of the assassination and funeral of Indira Gandhi, and of her son's dignified bereavement and effort to carry on as Prime Minister in her absence. But partly because so few were reached by telecasts, and mainly because the assassination was in any case widely and vividly understood by everyone, Doordarshan's coverage appears to have swung relatively few votes. The Congress-I performed no better in areas which received television signals than in areas which did not. Debates among party leaders have never occurred in India, either on television or radio. Disputes among opposition parties over time allocations prevented them from taking up offers of radio broadcasts in Nehru's day, although both opposition and Congress-I leaders made brief and highly inept television presentations in 1984. In 1991, major parties were offered only unappealing late night timings for brief election telecasts.

In 1989, Doordarshan's hugely partisan reports were disregarded by most voters who had grown discontented with Congress-I rule, and who had access to alternative views from newspapers and from the campaigns of opposition parties. Varying regional and local factors provided a much more convincing explanation for the varying performances of the Congress-I Party in different regions than did the consistently pro-Congress telecasts all across the subcontinent. By 1989, voters had experienced a decade and a half of heavily biased broadcasts on All India Radio which had frequently failed to persuade them to re-elect incumbents. Most of them plainly concluded that the still more partisan reports on television should be treated with similar scepticism.

Indeed, telecasts on the air waves appear to have had less impact than the showings at public meetings of campaign video cassettes on the mobile televisions sets with 100-inch screens which all major parties used. This device was used on a truly vast scale in 1989 and 1991, and it gave much more exposure to senior leaders of parties than they have ever received before. But there are good reasons to doubt whether this decided many contests. The parties with more money could afford more video cassette recorders and tapes, but the tendency of the electorate to choose impecunious opposition parties and candidates over well-funded incumbents was as noticeable in 1989 as on most previous occasions since the mid-1970s.

If so few of the changes in campaigning in recent Indian elections can be traced to legal or technological change, where does the explanation lie? It is bound up with the two main themes in India's recent political history, awakening and decay.[7]

The political awakening is a process by which individuals and groups develop a fuller understanding of the workings and possibilities of democratic politics, and become more active in seeking to participate in it. They increasingly understand that elected politicians are supposed to respond to felt needs, and when this does not happen, voters have become more inclined to punish them for it. People increasingly see that their caste, class, occupational group, region, locality, etc., can co-operate or compete with other such interests. Social groups have grown more assertive, both toward other groups (so that social conflict has quickened) and within the political process more generally.

This awakening began earlier and has gone further among more prosperous and literate groups, but it has occurred among the poor and illiterate as well. Even the most oppressed groups have grown less willing to accept advice or instructions from richer neighbours about how to vote, as they did at early elections. As they crystallize into coherent actors in the political process, these groups become less willing to tolerate tokenism and to re-elect representatives who offer only tokens.

The awakening has made India a more genuine democracy, but it has also made it a more difficult country to govern. Incumbent legislators find it harder to achieve re-election. So do ruling parties at the national and state levels. This has caused the norms to change at elections. Until the late 1960s, incumbent governments usually gained re-election. Since the early 1970s, they have often been ousted. This means that the dominance which the Congress Party enjoyed in the first two decades after Indian independence is no longer sustainable. Every Indian state has now had at least one (and usually more than one) spell of non-Congress rule, and at the national level, power changed hands at four of the five elections between 1977 and 1991.

The second major change in recent times, political decay, is a decline in the capacity of political institutions to respond creatively or even adequately to the discontents and aspirations of social groups.[8] Both the formal institutions of state and political parties have undergone serious decay since the late 1960s. This has occurred for two main reasons. First, institutions have tended to stagnate and ossify as managers and operatives have become lazy, complacent, or corrupt, or as older, committed activists have retired or died. Second and more importantly, certain leaders have undermined the autonomy, power, and corporate character of institutions, by denying them resources and by disregarding rules and principles by which they had long functioned.

Chief among these leaders was Indira Gandhi. She perceived herself to be threatened not only between 1966 and 1971 when she actually faced serious challenges from state-level leaders of her party, but also after 1971, when their power had been broken. Up to the early 1970s, she tended to fortify institutions in which she had strength—such as parliament and certain agencies within her party—at the expense of others where she was less influential. Thereafter, she mounted a more generalized assault on institutions, in the interests of personal and, eventually, of dynastic rule. Prominent among the institutions that suffered damage in the process was her party, which she viewed less as an instrument of government or of achieving re-election than as an encumbrance and a threat.

She radically centralized power within both the government and the party, on the assumption that this would make her stronger and enable her to homogenize the heterogeneous regions of India. This strengthened her hand in certain ways, but in the main, it produced the opposite results to those which she intended. In such a complex system, those who stand at the apex make their influence penetrate downward better by means of compromise with those at lower levels than by diktat. Mrs Gandhi soon found herself heading a government and a party of 'yes-men', which cut her off from frank reports on conditions in the regions and thus from influence over much that occurred there. Partly as a result, the various regions tended to diverge and become more, not less heterogeneous. By giving preference to those who offered the most abject professions of loyalty, whatever their background, she allowed corrupt and even criminal elements to play an increasingly large role in her party and to wreak serious damage on formal political institutions. This decay was occurring at the very time when the political awakening was making India a more difficult country to govern. The combination produced numerous changes—not least in electioneering.

At the first four national elections, images and government performance tended to outweigh the importance of issues. This was partly explained by the fact that the dominant Congress Party sought to appeal to every conceivable interest—every religious group, high castes and low, urban and rural dwellers, industrialists and workers, etc.—and therefore naturally downplayed ideological details and issues. But its leader in the first three of those elections, Jawaharlal Nehru, still emphasized his enthusiasm for land reform and his opposition to caste or religious or linguistic parochialism. These issues did not weigh as heavily in campaigns as might have been wished, however, because his mostly conservative party activists at and below the state level sought to promote linguistically homogeneous states and to thwart land reform and most other social reforms. What mattered most was Congress's image as the force that had won independence and then developed the organizational capacity to deliver goods and services to the more prosperous and influential social groups, while offering tokens to the rest. It also helped that Nehru appealed both to those who wanted stability and to those who desired change. It was thus left to the more ideologically orientated opposition parties on the right and left to raise issues, to which Congress was well able to respond until 1967, when it found it harder to please everyone and lost ground.

Thereafter, issues—or at least slogans and vague themes—grew in importance, mainly because Congress under Indira Gandhi raised them. Her indiscriminate borrowings from left and then right suggested little commitment to principle. In 1971, she played the progressive, proposing to 'abolish poverty'. After losing in 1977 amid the reaction against her Emergency, she appealed for order in 1980, calling for 'a government that works'. By 1982 in certain states, she was manipulating Hindu resentments of minorities—a theme that she would have used in 1984 had she not been murdered. That theme was then taken up by her son and it helped carry him to victory in that year.[9] Other parties denied Congress victory with appeals to issues—in 1977 with a call to save democracy, and in 1989 with denunciations of the Bofors bribery scandal and Rajiv Gandhi's tendency to change direction on most important issues.

It would, however, be wrong to say simply that issues or themes have predominated at recent elections. Two further things need to be stressed. First, new types of issues have proved effective. In part, this is a result of the tendency since 1971 for state and national elections to take place at different times. In that year, Mrs Gandhi intentionally de-linked elections at the two levels—which had previously tended to occur simultaneously. She did so in order to seek an endorsement of her national leadership and certain India-wide issues which she was raising, and to undercut her rivals whose main power bases were in individual states. Before 1971 both state and national issues had had significant influence on voters. Since then national issues and personalities have usually predominated in national elections and (to Mrs Gandhi's chagrin) state issues and personalities in state elections, although when national-level concerns fail to preoccupy voters as in 1991, concerns and events at the state level can strongly influence voting patterns in national elections. Both of these sets of issues have outweighed international issues, which have never been pre-eminent in Indian elections.

Recently, another new type or set of issues has become influential—issues which play upon people's anxieties, resentments, and their sense of victimization. Examples include the competing appeals in 1991 to the resentments of disadvantaged castes and of the Hindu majority. But they also include the exploitation of anti-Sikh feeling in 1984 by the Congress-I and appeals to regional groups' grievances against New Delhi in several states through the 1980s. These feelings—which seldom figured before the 1980s—

have become important precisely because the electorate has been awakening to greater discernment about and impatience with state and national governments, at a time when political decay has undermined governments' capacity to respond adequately. This incapacity has caused many social groups to become exasperated and turn inward, to batten on parochial identities and resentments of other groups, and thus to come increasingly into conflict with those groups, so that appeals to resentments of other castes or religious or interest groups resonate powerfully. This marks a major change from the situation prior to the 1980s.

Second, promises at elections often count for as much as issues, and for far more than they did before the 1980s. The classic campaign document in this vein is the Congress-I manifesto for the 1984 election. It consisted almost entirely of denunciations of the Janata Party's poor record in power between 1977 and 1980, and of promises of future largess to a vast array of interests. The curious thing about this was that almost no reference was made to the achievements of the incumbent Congress-I government between 1980 and 1984. Party leaders privately stated that they took this line because they feared that decay within the party had prevented it from achieving much since 1980. They were also concerned because opposition parties had made huge promises to various interests which the Congress-I had to match or top.

This view has become common in recent years among many incumbent ruling parties at state and national levels. Campaigns have often taken on an auction room frenzy, as one party offers to reserve a certain portion of jobs or resources for a given group, only to revise its bid upward when a rival party outbids it, and so on. Such extravagant promises often cannot be fulfilled after the election, and this eventually intensifies the frustrations of voters and compounds the already huge difficulties of incumbents. This process has sometimes been reversed by state governments that perform well, but not many have done so.

The decay of political institutions, especially of parties, has had a considerable impact on the role of personalities in Indian elections. Three things are worth noting here. First, the types of personalities that have lately tended to achieve importance differ from those which predominated before the mid-1970s or so. Second, the rate at which personalities wax and wane has increased since the mid-1970s. Finally, the importance of personalities has increased as the strength of institutions has ebbed, but the increase is far less marked than we might expect and the Indian press would have us believe.

Let us consider the first two of these points together. Nehru loomed large in Congress campaigns during his lifetime, as did many of the party's leaders at the state level, but they were seen differently from most of their recent counterparts. They were rightly regarded as formidably competent managers, custodians of political machines that could deliver goods and services to those interests that were politically aware, prosperous, and numerically strong. They were considered to be more impressive than exciting, mainly because they presided over an impressive set of institutions—including most crucially, the Congress organization.

They also tended to remain in prominent roles for extended periods. More recently, especially since the mid-1970s, we have witnessed much more volatility. Personalities have tended to emerge quite suddenly from obscurity, to make an impact for a time, and then to fall precipitously from grace. This is explained partly by Mrs Gandhi's habit of raising up relative unknowns (since, as her creatures, they would be beholden to her) and then undermining and eventually dropping them, lest they become threats. It is also explained by the awakening electorate's habit of ousting various ruling parties, because their organizational incapacities had earned popular disdain.

Indian journalists and some scholars have lately tended to stress the importance of charisma in election campaigns, but this is almost entirely unjustified. Two state-level leaders—the film-star Chief Ministers of the southern states of Tamil Nadu and Andhra Pradesh—can be regarded as genuinely 'charismatic' figures. But this word cannot be applied with confidence to anyone else—including Indira and Rajiv Gandhi. Consider, for example, the impact the Gandhis' alleged charisma made in the Karnataka state election of 1983. Congress Party leaders in that state realized in mid-campaign that they were in danger of losing, and they urgently requested Mrs Gandhi and her son to save the day by showing themselves in over thirty key constituencies. The Gandhis obliged, only to see their party defeated in every one of the constituencies that they visited. The most appropriate adjective to describe the new type of personality in recent Indian elections is not 'charismatic', but 'notorious'—given the increased salience of corrupt and criminal elements in politics.

Indeed, it is surprising—given the decay that has occurred—that so few gaudy personalities have succeeded and that personalities in general have had so little impact in elections. We badly need research on this, but it appears that the electorate is too sophisticated and too concerned with concrete performance and non-performance by incumbent governments to be distracted by personalities for very long. Voters are sometimes willing to put impressive personalities in power, especially if they are the only alternative to discredited incumbents. But if they perform poorly, they are frequently ousted, as the film star Rama Rao discovered in 1989. The reason that his Tamil counterpart, the late M. G. Ramachandran, never lost an election was because in addition to charisma, he had a semi-efficient party machine through which to govern and campaign.

Candidate selection is a hugely complex topic, which can only be briefly summarized here.[10] Important changes have occurred both in the manner in which candidates are chosen and in the types of persons that obtain party tickets. In the period up to 1967, when the Congress Party was both dominant within the political system and democratic in its internal processes, the preferences of regional and subregional units of the party usually carried considerable weight in the selection process. In that period, Congress offered modest representation to religious minorities and disadvantaged castes, but most candidates tended to come from the landed groups which dominate rural society. Since the early 1970s, both of these things have changed. The high command at the national level has frequently imposed its will upon lower levels of the party—often on the dubious advice of police and intelligence officials—even if (as was usually the case) it had little understanding of the subtleties of regional social and political realities. Candidates lists (of both the Congress and other parties—especially parties of the centre) have also usually given more adequate representation to minorities and less prosperous groups, in recognition that such groups have become impatient with tokenism.

At the same time, however, the process of selection has become far more contentious within centrist parties which have suffered decay. Factional conflict often leads to embarrassing incidents. At the 1989 election, for example, the Congress leader in Karnataka had to sleep in a different hotel in the state capital every night of the crucial selection week, to avoid being besieged by elements within his party. An elder statesman of the party in Andhra Pradesh had to be rescued by police from a mob of Congressmen angered by the rejection of men from their faction—and so it goes on. In many states, corrupt and criminal elements have also gained increasing numbers of tickets within the Congress and other centrist parties.

Some (though far less) of this has also been occurring within the parties of the left and the Hindu right. They had little hope of victory in early elections, and therefore tended to select candidates mainly for their loyalty and ideological rectitude. As they have developed regional power bases in more recent times, they have paid more heed to the electability of potential candidates. In early 1991, the Hindu revivalist Bharatiya Janata Party formally announced that it would bend more often to 'electoral compulsions', which meant choosing some candidates because of their membership in a locally influential caste or their access to resources.[11]

Parties also frequently choose candidates in order to complicate things for their opponents. This takes two forms. First, they select particularly formidable candidates to confront especially popular or effective leaders of other parties, in order to tie such people down to their constituencies. Second, they often arrange for people to stand as 'independents' who are from the same caste or interest group as rival candidates, in order to split the votes of the groups that support those opponents.

A related aspect of Indian campaigns is the tendency of members of a party or electoral alliance to undermine the campaigns of candidates whom they are supposed to support. It can take two forms: direct sabotage and passivity or an exodus of activists to another constituency. The first of these almost always occurs when one faction within a party has a candidate from a rival faction imposed upon it. If activists dislike their party's nominee even more than his or her rival, or if intra-party conflicts are more important to them than competition with the opposition, they may work for the rival candidate and even indulge in dirty tricks against their own nominee. The second set of practices can arise in similar circumstances, but they are more common when more than one party form an alliance. If activists find that the alliance candidate in their constituency is from another party, they often remain inactive or decamp for a nearby constituency where a member of their party is standing. Both of these types of activity (or inactivity) can alter electoral outcomes in close contests.

Both practices have also increased as the years have passed. This is especially true of sabotage, as political decay has caused factional conflict (mainly within centrist parties, and especially within Congress) to increase both in quantity and in intensity.[12] The second set of activities has also increased since 1967 as inter-party alliances have become quite common.

The amounts of money spent during Indian election campaigns have increased enormously since the early 1970s when the process of escalation began in earnest, but the same cannot be said about the influence of money on elections. Indeed, poorly funded parties have defeated richer rivals far more often since the early 1970s than before. This takes some explaining.

First, it should be emphasized that while most parties have increased election spending, the main force behind the huge growth in expenditure has been the Congress Party led by Indira and Rajiv Gandhi. That party has probably outspent all of its rivals combined, at every state and national election since 1971—usually on a vast scale—although the well-funded Bharatiya Janata Party in 1991 may be an exception to this. At the 1984 general election, for example, the Congress-I probably spent $90 million on its campaign, including $18 million on posters alone. This was more than ten times the amount spent by all of the other parties together.[13] Indeed, the Congress-I spent twice as much on posters as all of its rivals spent on their entire campaigns. And yet, this disparity in spending does little to explain the victory of the Congress-I in that election. Most political analysts agree that the assassination of Indira Gandhi a few weeks before polling virtually assured the party of victory, and that it need not have spent anything like this amount. In numerous other state and national elections, similar disparities in spending have not saved the Congress-I from frequent defeats and occasional humiliation.

If election spending is of such dubious value, why do parties indulge in it? In part, this is because elections have become more competitive. Until 1967, the Congress Party enjoyed such dominance in all national and most state elections that neither it nor its rivals saw much point in vast election outlays. Since then, the very real possibility that Congress might be defeated has encouraged all parties—not least Congress—to spend as freely as they can.

A more important factor, however, is the decay which has badly afflicted many parties. It has greatly eroded their capacity to gather and disseminate information, and to operate in a disciplined and effective manner, both as instruments of government and in election campaigns. Corruption and intra-party factional strife often seriously damage parties' election prospects. Leading politicians, sensing this, naturally feel anxious and see increased election expenditure as a means of compensating.

Decay has also entailed a greater willingness among both leaders and party activists—again, especially in the Congress—to engage in dubious or illegal doings in order to raise huge election war chests. In Nehru's day, both he and most of his state Chief Ministers declined to engage in illicit 'fund-raising' on the massive scale of recent times, not only because they felt little need for such money, but also because they felt morally bound to restrain themselves. This has changed. It is seldom acknowledged in public but widely conceded in private by politicians that parties which control national or state governments systematically skim off percentages of certain state expenditures and extract kickbacks and other 'donations' from wealthy (and not-so-wealthy) interests who desire concessions from the authorities. Parties which have ruled in New Delhi have also been widely and reliably reported to take enormous payments from foreign arms suppliers. Finally, when 'fund-raising' is highly centralized—as it has been, especially where state-level politicians are often rewarded for lavish tributary payments to persons at the apex of the party's national organization—it becomes particularly attractive to those persons at the apex, since it gives them immense resources with which to dominate their parties.

Candidates routinely spend far more than the unrealistically low legal limits—up to Rs. 150,000 (£4,000 at 1991 exchange rates) in a parliamentary contest and Rs. 50,000 in a state assembly contest, with certain regional variations. They are helped in this by the fact that parties are permitted to spend unlimited amounts to assist their candidates, as long as the candidate or his or her agent does not authorize this.[14] But vast overspending is so widespread a practice that few people bother to take refuge behind this provision. They simply understate their expenditure in reports to the Election Commission.

Election violence is a subject that, in the Indian case, needs to be addressed. Violence had received enormous attention from the international press at the Indian elections of 1989 and 1991, even before the assassination of Rajiv Gandhi while campaigning. Indeed, it has tended to attract more attention than the election result and its implications. This is unfortunate. It is true that election violence has reached serious proportions in recent years.[15] But we need to ask whether the use or the threat of violence has interfered much with electioneering, and whether it has altered results in many constituencies. The answer to the first question is 'very little', and to the second is 'hardly at all'. This has usually been true even in states plagued by terrorist violence—witness, for example, the 1985 state election in Punjab where a very competitive campaign evoked a remarkably high turn-out.

The 1991 election may have marked a change from the pattern in previous years in that the period preceding polling witnessed substantial violence whereas in 1980, 1984, and 1989 most of the violence occurred on polling days. That is to say that during the 1980s, campaigning (which concludes just prior to polling day) was seldom significantly curtailed as a result of ructions or intimidation. It is too early to speak authoritatively about 1991, so let us consider the polling day violence of the 1980s.

It tended to consist of attempts either to frighten particular groups of voters—usually poor, low caste people—away from polling stations, or to seize polling stations and ballot boxes in order to stuff or destroy boxes. These things rarely succeeded in changing the results of elections to state legislatures, and no convincing evidence has been produced to show that even one parliamentary contest was decided by such tactics.

There are several reasons for this. First, the police (and in turbulent regions, the army and/or paramilitary forces) have usually provided a significant counterweight to such doings, although they have sometimes acquiesced or assisted. Second, such incidents usually became known, either through a vigilant press, protests by victimized groups and parties, or reports by bureaucrats who operated the polling stations. And when they became known, the Election Commission usually ordered a re-poll amid a heavy police presence soon thereafter. Finally, even when attempts to interfere with polling succeeded, there was little hope of altering the result in large state assembly constituencies, and almost no hope of doing so in enormous parliamentary constituencies. In either case, violence on a vast scale would be required, and there are too many checks on violence to permit that to happen. There are exceptions to this. Congress Party toughs, with some police complicity, probably succeeded in intimidating enough Communist voters in certain parts of Calcutta in 1972 to affect some assembly results. But exceptions are very rare.

Violence around election time is a matter of legitimate and grave concern to those who wish Indian democracy well. But despite the ill-informed and well nigh hysterical reactions in the international press to the murder of Rajiv Gandhi, we should not presume that India is about to disintegrate, that its lively democracy is about to self-destruct, or even that violence alters many electoral results. (It is worth stressing that Rajiv Gandhi's murder does not constitute an example of 'election violence'. He appears to have been killed by non-Indians for reasons that had nothing to do with the election that he was fighting. They simply took advantage of his exposure during the campaign.)

Rigging, mainly involving perversions of vote counting, is also an extreme rarity. Prominent Indian figures with access to confidential information now concede, privately and sometimes openly, that rigging occurred in early elections in the sensitive border state of Kashmir in the 1950s and 1960s, to disguise pro-Pakistan sentiment there. But no other credible allegations of rigging have emerged in recent times.

Electioneering has changed less over the last three decades in India than in most and perhaps all of the other countries examined in this volume. There have been fewer changes in election law than in most other nations, and those changes which have occurred have had relatively little impact on campaigning. Technological advances have arrived in India more tardily and have often failed to reach the high levels that are common in industrialized democracies. Even the great changes within India's political system—the popular awakening and institutional decay—have failed to alter electioneering dramatically, mainly because a large majority of voters are still illiterate and widely dispersed across a huge landscape in small, inaccessible rural settlements, and because the electorate is so vast.

Finally, a word of caution is in order. It may appear, from our preoccupation with electioneering, that the doings of party leaders and activists during campaigns exercise a decisive influence at elections. In India at least, this may not be true—or to be more precise, it may seldom have been true. Events which occurred before (often long before) an election campaign, as well as the condition of contending parties and the reputations of candidates which were the result of accumulated actions and omissions prior to campaigns, appear to have counted far more heavily than electioneering in determining electoral outcomes.

It is difficult, for example, to imagine that during the heyday of the Congress Party's dominance up to the late 1960s, a poor campaign by the Congress or a brilliant campaign by an opponent turned voters against it very often. Similarly, in the years since the mid-1970s, when a sophisticated and impatient electorate has repeatedly punished incumbent national and state governments that failed to be responsive and effective in the delivery of goods and services, it is difficult to believe that campaigns lasting only a few weeks have altered many election verdicts.[16] This does not mean that campaigns are unworthy of study, but they need to be kept in perspective.

Notes

1. The author has conducted research on the last six of India's ten general elections, that is, since the 1971 election. He is grateful to W. H. Morris-Jones and B. D. Graham for discussions of the first four elections.

2. N. D. Palmer, *Elections and Political Development: The South Asian Experience* (Durham, NC: Duke University Press, 1975), 126. He is drawing upon an unpublished manuscript by D. N. Pathak and K. D. Desai, 'A Study of Political Behaviour in Gujarat . . .' (Ahmedabad, 1970). Other comments in this paragraph are derived from P. R. Brass, *The New Cambridge History of India: The Politics of India since Independence* (Cambridge: Cambridge University Press, 1990), 83–5.

3. These comments and many others in this chapter are based on this writer's discussions with politicians at the state level and below in numerous regions of India at general elections between 1971 and 1989, and at several state elections in that period.

4. This is fully set out in Y. Atal, *Local Communities and National*

Politics (New Delhi, 1971), 189–90. It is summarized in more detail than is possible here in Palmer, *Elections and Political Development*, 131–3.

5. Interviews with senior Janata Dal party organizers in New Delhi and Bangalore, November 1989.

6. *Hindu*, 7 Mar. 1991.

7. I have described these processes in detail on several previous occasions. See e.g. J. Manor, 'The Electoral Process amid Awakening and Decay: Reflections on the Indian General Election of 1980', in P. Lyon and J. Manor (eds.), *Transfer and Transformation: Political Institutions in the New Commonwealth* (Leicester University Press, 1983), 81–116.

8. The concept was developed in S. P. Huntington, *Political Order in Changing Societies* (New Haven, Conn.: Yale University Press, 1968).

9. J. Manor, 'Parties and the Party System', in A. Kohli (ed.), *India's Democracy: A Study of Changing State–Society Relations* (Princeton, NJ: Princeton University Press, 1988), 80–7.

10. For fuller discussions of these matters, see R. L. Hardgrave and S. A. Kochanek, *India: Government and Politics in a Developing Nation*, 4th edn. (San Diego: Harcourt Brace Jovanovich, 1986), 282–7; Palmer, *Elections and Political Development*, 115–25; S. A. Kochanek, *The Congress Party of India: The Dynamics of One-Party Democracy* (Princeton, NJ: Princeton University Press, 1968); and W. H. Morris-Jones, 'Candidate Selection: The Ordeal of the Indian National Congress, 1966–1967', in M. S. Rajan (ed.), *Studies in Politics: National and International* (New Delhi, 1971).

11. *Times of India*, 20 Jan. 1991.

12. See e.g., the early trend noted in R. Sisson, *The Congress Party in Rajasthan: Political Integration and Institution Building in an Indian State* (Berkeley, Calif.: University of California Press, 1972), 238–40 and 250–1.

13. Hardgrave and Kochanek, *India*, 286.

14. Ibid. 289.

15. See e.g. ibid. 296–8 and K. Nayar, 'Curbing Violence at Polls', *India Abroad*, 22 Mar. 1985. The violence at the 1989 and 1991 elections surpassed what they discuss.

16. There is conflicting evidence on this. Norman Palmer devoted more attention to it than anyone else, and his own uncertainties are clear from a comparison of pp. 127 and 137–9 of his *Elections and Political Development*.

References

Ahmed, B., and Eldersveld, S. J., *Citizens and Politics: Mass Political Behavior in India* (University of Chicago Press, 1978).

Bhalla, R. P., *Elections in India (1950–1972)* (New Delhi: S. Chand, 1973).

Blair, H. W., *Voting, Caste, Community, Society* (New Delhi; Young Asia Publications 1979).

Bose, S., and Singh, V. B., *State Elections in India: Data Handbook on Vidhan Sabha Elections*, 5 vols. (New Delhi: Sage, 1987–8).

Brass, P. R., 'Congress, the Lok Dal and the Middle Peasant Castes: An Analysis of the 1977 and 1980 Parliamentary Elections in Uttar Pradesh', *Pacific Affairs* (Spring, 1981), 5–41.

—— 'Indian Election Studies', *South Asia* (Sept. 1978), 91–108.

Butler, D., Roy, P., and Lahiri, A., *India Decides*, 2nd edn. (New Delhi: India Today, 1991).

Dasgupta, B., and Morris-Jones, W. H., *Patterns and Trends in Indian Politics: An Ecological Analysis of Aggregate Data on Society and Elections* (New Delhi: Allied Publications, 1975).

Elkins, D. J., *Electoral Participation in a South Asian Context* (New Delhi: Vikas, 1975).

Field, J. O., *Consolidating Democracy: Politicization and Partisanship in India* (New Delhi: Manohar Book Service, 1980).

—— and Weiner, M. (eds.), *Studies in Electoral Politics in the Indian States*, 4 vols. (New Delhi: Manohar Book Sevice, 1974–7).

Graham, B. D., 'The Candidate-Selection Policies of the Indian National Congress, 1952–69', *Journal of Commonwealth and Comparative Politics* (July, 1986), 197–218.

—— 'Electoral Symbols and Party Identification in Indian Politics', in P. Lyon and J. Manor (eds.), *Transfer and Transformation: Political Institutions in the New Commonwealth* (Leicester University Press, 1983), 71–86.

Kochanek, S. A., *The Congress Party of India: The Dynamics of One-Party Democracy* (Princeton NJ; Princeton University Press, 1968).

—— 'Mrs Gandhi's Pyramid: The New Congress', in H. C. Hart (ed.), *Indira Gandhi's India: A Political System Reappraised* (Boulder, Colo.: Westview Press, 1976), 93–124.

Kothari, R., 'The Congress "System" in India', *Asian Survey* (Dec. 1964), 161–73.

—— (ed.), *Party Systems and Election Studies* (New Delhi, 1967).

Manor, J., 'The Electoral Process amid Awakening and Decay: Reflections on the Indian General Election of 1980', in P. Lyon and J. Manor (eds.),

Transfer and Transformation: Political Institutions in the New Commonwealth (Leicester University Press, 1983), 87–116.

—— 'Parties and the Party System' in A. Kohli (ed.), *India's Democracy: A Study of Changing State–Society Relations* (Princeton, NJ: Princeton University Press, 1988).

—— 'Party Decay and Political Crisis in India', *Washington Quarterly* (Summer, 1981), 25–40.

Morris-Jones, W. H., 'Parliament and Dominant Party: Indian Experience', in his *Politics Mainly Indian* (Madras: Orient Longman 1978), 196–212.

Palmer, N. D., *Elections and Political Development: The South Asian Experience* (Durham, NC: Duke University Press, 1975).

Sheth, D. L. (ed.), *Citizens and Parties: Aspects of Competitive Politics in India* (Bombay: South Asia Books, 1975).

Weiner, M., *India at the Polls: The Parliamentary Elections of 1977* (Washington, DC: American Enterprise Institute, 1978).

—— *India at the Polls 1980: A Study of the Parliamentary Elections* (Washington, DC: American Enterprise Institute, 1978).

7

France

JEAN CHARLOT and MONICA CHARLOT

Electioneering in France changed fundamentally with the inception in 1965 of the direct election of the President of the Republic by the people. Since then a wider use of referendums, which until the Fifth Republic were rare and only used for narrowly constitutional issues, together with the coming of European elections have added two other types of national elections to that of the election of the President. These elections, in which the whole of France constitutes one single constituency, involve each party's national leaders to a much greater extent than general or local elections.

The presidential election has, however, coloured all the other types of elections, making them into tests of the President's popularity. Each general election, for instance, is now seen as an occasion to give or refuse a parliamentary majority to the President of the Republic. Should it be refused and should the President be forced into a system of 'cohabitation' his personal power will be diminished and so will that of his party.

Personalization has gradually increased under the Fifth Republic and the pressure in favour of making elections more national occurred at a time when the new means of campaigning—television broadcasting, opinion polling, the rationalization of tactics and strategies—were developing in France (where they emerged later than in most other Western democracies).

The Élysée Effect

Under the Fourth Republic (1946–58) power at the national level was only democratically won or lost at general elections, held every five years. The Fifth Republic introduced both referendums (held at irregular intervals) and presidential elections (held every seven

TABLE 7.1. *Frequency of elections at which the Executive is challenged, from Fourth to Fifth Republics*

	Number of cases	Average frequency
Fourth Republic (1946–58)		
Parliamentary elections		
1946, 1951, 1956[a]	3	4 years
Fourth Republic (up to 1988)		
Parliamentary elections		
1958, 1962,[a] 1967, 1968,[a] 1973,		
1978, 1981,[a] 1986, 1988[a]	9	3 years 4 months
Referendums		
1958, 1961, Apr. 1962, Oct. 1962,		
1969[b] 1972,[c] 1988[c]	7	4 years 4 months
Presidential elections		
1965,[d] 1969[e] 1974[f] 1981, 1988	5	6 years
SUBTOTAL (excluding referendums)	14	2 years 1 month
TOTAL	21[g]	1 year 3 months

[a] Early election, following a dissolution.
[b] The Noes won: General de Gaulle resigned from the presidency of the Republic.
[c] Referendum on which the President of the Republic did not ask for a vote of confidence and could have stayed in power even if the Noes had won the day, but they did not.
[d] First presidential election fought with direct universal suffrage.
[e] Early election, due to the resignation of General de Gaulle.
[f] Early election, following Georges Pompidou's death.
[g] Without including European elections (1979, 1984, 1989), which bear no influence on the attribution of central government functions, without including local elections also more numerous than under the Fourth Republic since the institution of regional elections (in 1986), which complete the set of municipal (communes) and cantonal (departments) elections.

years). It thus increased the frequency of elections and the control over the Executive. The very nature of electioneering was modified by the major role which was rapidly attributed to the presidential election.

The frequency of elections was greatly increased under the Fifth Republic (Table 7.1). First a new use of the referendum was introduced. It could be called on the initiative of the President of the Republic with the understanding—under the presidency of General de Gaulle—that it was an opportunity for the people to show their confidence in the President. This meant that if the voters did not agree with the President's proposal he was in honour bound to resign—which de Gaulle himself did after the electorate's negative reply to the referendum of April 1969. Secondly, in October 1962 a revision of the constitution laid down that the President would henceforth be directly elected by universal suffrage. The first President of France under the 1958 constitution had been elected by local councillors and parliamentarians. The first election under the new rules took place in December 1965. Thirdly, the President of the Republic could, under the 1958 constitution, dissolve the National Assembly more easily—and effectively did so more often. The length of a parliament was in theory five years but in actual practice it was reduced to three. In addition de Gaulle's resignation before the end of his mandate and Georges Pompidou's death before the end of his, reduced presidential mandates on average between 1965 and 1988 from seven years to six. Thus national elections which were held on average once every forty-eight months under the Fourth Republic were held in the first thirty years of the Fifth Republic every fifteen months if referendums are taken into account, every twenty-five months if they are not.

One might have expected the frequency of consultation to increase non-voting (Table 7.2). But this has not been the case. Abstention in presidential elections has been on average 18.2 per cent on the first ballot, 17.9 per cent only on the second ballot, whereas under the Fourth Republic at general elections (which were then the only national elections) abstention was on average 19.6 per cent. The presidential election on one occasion enabled even France to establish the record of the lowest level of abstention in its electoral history: in 1974, at the second ballot when Giscard d'Estaing and Mitterrand fought one another only 12.6 per cent abstained. The only presidential election in which the number of abstentions at the second ballot was high—31.1 per cent—was that of 1969. But this can be explained by the fact that all the candidates of the left had been eliminated at the first ballot. The two remaining candidates were Georges Pompidou and Alain Poher, a Gaullist and a centrist, dubbed by the Communist Party as 'Tweedledum and Tweedledee' (*bonnet blanc et blanc bonnet*).

The presidential election mobilizes voters more than other elections for two major reasons: it is a personalized election, and it is a national election. It thus has greater unity and simplicity. France

TABLE 7.2 *Non-voting in the Fourth and Fifth Republics* (percentages with reference to the electorate)

	Percentage of non-voting		
Types of elections	lowest	average	highest
Fourth Republic			
Parliamentary elections (3 cases)	17.2 (1956)	19.6	21.9 (1946)
Fifth Republic (up to and including 1988)			
Presidential elections (5 cases)			
First ballot	15.2 (1965)	18.2	22.4 (1969)
Second ballot	12.6 (1974)	17.9	31.1 (1969)
Parliamentary elections (9 cases)			
First ballot[a]	16.7 (1978)	23.7	34.3 (1988)
Referendums (7 cases)	15.1 (1958)	29.6	62.4 (1988)

[a] Statistics on second ballots are not comparable: they constitute neither all nor even the same constituencies from one election to the next. In addition in 1986 the election was fought on a PR system with only one ballot.

is one constituency, the electors choose a single individual. Each candidate is allowed equal television time, each voter knows that his ballot will not be wasted. The dramatic nature of the second ballot is all the greater as there are only two candidates. Electors are all the more easily mobilized when, as in 1974, the opinion polls give voting intentions as 50:50. Philippe Braud offers a psychoanalytical interpretation of the presidential election. It is a ritual homage to democracy, a festive occasion for all and sundry.[1] The state is no longer a faceless monster.

During the election campaign every elector is pandered to. Distinctions are forgotten and all are treated with the same solicitude. The revolutionary values of freedom and equality are celebrated and the election has undoubtedly a symbolic and ritualistic role. Nevertheless its major function is the allocation of political power.[2]

The President, once he is elected, can dissolve the National Assembly and bring about a general election which his party has every chance of winning. The reverse is not true. The party which wins the general election does not have the constitutional power to force the President to resign. Thus it was that the RPR-UDF majority under Jacques Chirac in the 1986 elections was obliged to 'cohabit' with the Socialist President François Mitterrand until the end of his mandate in 1988.

It is not easy to distinguish the respective weight, in a presidential election, of the candidates and their parties. For de Gaulle the presidential election was a matter of candidates making a direct appeal, independently of the parties, to the people. Many specialists are struck today by 'the return of the parties'. General de Gaulle himself had in fact become aware of this during the first presidential election of 1965.

I suggested to the country that we change the Constitution in 1958 ... with the intention ... of putting an end to the rule of the parties ... We created confessionals to try and push back the devil! But if the devil is in the confessional that changes everything!

Despite the direct nature of the election of the President of the Republic an attempt was being made, de Gaulle claimed, 'to put the State back into the hands of the parties'.[3]

Over the years the influence of the parties has steadily increased. Since the death of Pompidou major candidates have not put themselves up for election on their own but have sought the backing of a political party. It has become more and more rare to find candidates supported by several different parties on the first ballot. The tendency now is for each party to nominate its own candidate.

At the beginning of the Fifth Republic the candidate was not only stronger than the party; his existence led to the creation of the party in several cases. The Gaullist party—UNR—was created to support the already powerful de Gaulle. While he was in power it served him unconditionally. After his departure he remained the constant reference. Although the party became the RPR and managed to survive the General's death and remain one of the major French parties it still measures its ideas and actions against the yardstick of Gaullism.[4]

Valéry Giscard d'Estaing created Giscardism and a Giscardian party then came into being. But it was responsible neither for his presidential victory in 1974 nor his defeat in 1981. Similarly the Socialist Party owes more to François Mitterrand than he owes to it. François Mitterrand remodelled the party and brought it to power in his wake in 1981 and again in 1988.

During the period 1965–74 major presidential candidates were capable of mobilizing wide support at the first ballot. De Gaulle in 1965, Pompidou in 1969, Giscard in 1974, Mitterrand in 1965 and 1974, each attracted support on the first ballot clearly beyond that of his own party. Since 1981 things have changed and the influence of the parties can clearly be seen by the fact that each party—whether major or minor presents its own candidate. The Communist Party supported Georges Marchais, then André Lajoinie; the Socialist Party, François Mitterrand; the UDF Giscard, then Raymond Barre; the RPR Jacques Chirac; the Greens Brice Lalonde, then Antoine Waechter, the National Front in 1988 Jean-Marie Le Pen. Sometimes factions within parties even put up their own candidates: Michel Debré was the candidate of the old guard of the RPR in 1981, Pierre Juquin was the candidate of the renovators of the Communist Party in 1988. The presidential election has thus become the occasion for parties and sometimes factions within them to stand up and be counted.

It was in 1981 that for the first time a major presidential candidate—François Mitterrand—asked for an official nomination, that of the Socialist Party. General de Gaulle, Georges Pompidou, and Valéry Giscard d'Estaing had all put their names forward without enlisting the support of their parties beforehand. Their aim was to cast the net for votes as widely as possible—they were in a sense catch-all candidates who believed that too strong a party link might in fact operate to their disadvantage.

The agreement signed in April 1991 by the Gaullist party (RPR) with the Giscardian UDF for the organization of open primary elections on the American model to decide which candidate should obtain the investiture of the UPF. (UDF-RPR Alliance) at the first ballot of the next presidential election marks the culmination of the process of appropriation of the election by the parties. Raymond Barre is undoubtedly right when he says that this system of primaries is contrary to de Gaulle's idea of what a presidential election should be. But primaries could well lead to a decline in the power of political parties as they have done in the United States.

The presidential election has been captured by the political parties but they have also been transformed by it. They have been obliged to presidentialize themselves, as it were, and in so doing their very nature has changed. First, each party now has to put itself behind a presidential candidate and even if the parties choose their candidates, once chosen they have a latitude of action which goes far beyond the letter of the party constitution and sometimes goes quite against the party's traditions. Secondly, the presidential election has forced the parties to adopt strategies of alliance which means they have to make concessions to allied parties.

So although the parties dominate the presidential election they are also dominated by it. The parties may have made a comeback but the parties that have come back are very different from those de Gaulle criticized with such vehemence.

Although France has gone from the Fourth to the Fifth Republic the party system has remained virtually unchanged. France still has a multi-party system with five or six major parties. Three of them are potential governing parties—the Social Party (PS), the Gaullist party (RPR), and the regrouping of the Giscardian parties (UDF). And they are all slightly stronger electorally than their equivalents under the Fourth Republic. There has been a great change in the strength of the extremist parties. The Communist Party has declined dramatically and the breakthrough of the National Front and the emergence of the Greens have not compensated for this. Now only one vote in five goes to an extremist party whereas one in two did under the Fourth Republic.

The party system under the Fifth Republic remains unstable. Factions struggle within the Socialist Party and RPR and the Giscardian-centrist grouping (UDF) is fragile. It is not the party system which gives stability to the government, it is the constraints imposed by the constitution which have simplified and rendered more efficient the weak and divided French parties.[5]

In order to go through to the second ballot a presidential candidate must come first or second on the first ballot. Today only the PS, RPR, or UDF candidate can hope to do so. No party, not even the PS, which is the strongest of the three, can hope to have its candidate elected on the second ballot unless voters transfer from other parties. In 1981 the Socialists obtained 25.8 per cent of the votes cast at the first ballot of the presidential election, in 1988 34.1 per cent. In the general elections of 1981, 1986, and 1988 the party obtained respectively 36.0, 30.8, and 34.7 per cent of the votes cast. So the leader is far from the 50 per cent level necessary to win and must find outside his normal party support the 16.2 per cent of additional voters. The RPR and UDF can together count on 36–42 per cent of the votes. If they remain divided they each have roughly half of this total. But they lose a not insubstantial proportion of votes between the two ballots. In short, alliances are inevitable. In an election in which a single person is elected there is a tendency for votes to be concentrated on the candidate of the strongest party and his nearest rival.

It is the candidates of the three major parties who decide on programmes and alliances, tactics and strategy. Their parties allow them freedom of movement so long as their presidential credibility is maintained.

The strategy of the candidate is necessarily different from the one his party would have adopted if it had followed its natural bent. This can lead to frustration and conflict. Hugues Portelli says of the Socialist Party:

As early as 1971 the rules of the constitution [of the Socialist Party] were no longer applied: the central committee [*comité directeur*], the parliament of the party, has no more effective power than the National Assembly under the Fifth Republic; the executive committee which is theoretically the government of the party, saw its powers absorbed by the secretariat as the government has been by the President of the Republic.[6]

Power was in fact increasingly in the hands of parallel structures created by the party leader to help him achieve power. It was on his own programmes—the 110 proposals in 1981 (ratified by the Socialist Party) and his 'letter to all the French' in 1988—that François Mitterrand was first elected and the re-elected. His programmes moved, moreover, further and further away from the utopias of the 1972 Socialist Party Programme with its pledges to workers' control, nationalization, planification, and the end of capitalism. Party activists began to question their socialist identity and their future.

Alliances too were forged by François Mitterrand in 1988 as in 1981. In 1988 the watchword was 'overtures' (*l'ouverture*) and the emphasis was placed for tactical reasons on the alliance with the centre. This would not have been the choice of the party faithful: 'Their preferences are 84% for an alliance with the ecologists, then 55% for an alliance with the Communist Party. 46% are in favour of an alliance with the centre, 45% against.'[7]

Such problems are not restricted to the Socialist Party although an activist-centred party is more alien to presidentialization than a party with a charismatic tradition like the Gaullist party (RPR) or a party of notables like the UDF. Within the UDF certain subgroups such as the CDS or the PR disagree with Giscard's tactics and would have preferred not to unite with the RPR. Those who oppose Jacques Chirac within the RPR—Charles Pasqua and Philippe Seguin—disapprove of his search for an alliance with the UDF. The critics in both parties think that they have or will come off worst in the negotiation and that the sacrifices made are too great. The candidates see them as necessary to the furtherance of their aims.

The Motivations of Voters

The relative importance in voters' choices of the presidential candidate and the political party is all the more difficult to assess as it is complicated by the increasing tendency of electors to vote on issues.

An exit poll by IFRES on the occasion of the first ballot of the presidential election on 24 April 1988 threw light on the relative weight of the three major influences on electoral choice—issues, parties, and candidates. The question put was 'in voting for this candidate what counted most for you: his personal qualities, his past political action, a sizeable part of his programme, his party, or something else?' The results were clear (Table 7.3)—electors vote more for the candidate (45 per cent) than for his programme (23 per cent) or his party (17 per cent). This does not of course mean that because the vote is personalized it is apolitical: 16 per cent of voters voted for a candidate because of his political past. Moreover, the qualities that were considered when choosing a candidate were those usually linked to political action. Nevertheless the presidential election has rooted political choice more clearly in the candidates than in political parties. When the replies to what influenced their votes were crossed with the various candidates they voted for, a clear divide could be seen between the 'credible' candidates—Mitterrand, Chirac, Barre, who had some hope of winning—and the others. The personalization was most powerful for the credible candidates—64 per cent for J. Chirac, 62 per cent for R. Barre, 54 per cent for F. Mitterrand—and least powerful for the minor candidates—10 per cent for J. M. Le Pen, 8 per cent for A. Waechter, 16 per cent for A. Lajoinie. What came as a surprise was that the division between credible candidates and minor

TABLE 7.3   *The motivations of voters: Presidential election, first ballot,*
24 April 1988 (IFRES) (%)[a]

| | The candidate | | | | | | |
	his personal qualities	his past political acts	Issues	His party	Other	DK	Total
All	29	16	23	17	14	1	(100)
Voting for							
Mitterrand	32	22	8	24	13	1	(100)
Chirac	42	22	12	16	7	1	(100)
Barre	45	17	19	8	10	1	(100)
Le Pen	7	3	61	7	20	2	(100)
Lajoinie	8	8	39	36	8	1	(100)
Waechter	6	2	48	16	27	1	(100)
TOTAL LEFT[c]	27	19	15	24	14	1	(100)
TOTAL RIGHT	33	15	28	11	12	1	(100)

[a] *Exit Poll*, 24 Apr. 1988, sample: 4,109 persons.
[b] Candidates with more than 2% of valid votes.
[c] Total Left = Mitterrand + Lajoinie + Juquin + Laguiller + Boussel; Total
Right = Chirac + Barre + Le Pen. Waechter (Green Party) is considered to be
neither left nor right.

candidates was more relevant than the left–right divide. Personalization was important for 46 per cent of those voting for candidates
of the left, and 48 per cent of those voting for the right.

The most powerful influence towards voting for the minor
candidates was issue-voting: 61 per cent of Le Pen's voters (as
against an average of 23 per cent of all voters) chose him because
of an 'important proposal' he had in their opinion put forward in
his programme (for 61 per cent of Le Pen's voters the proposal
concerned immigration); 48 per cent of Waechter's voters also
explained their vote by the capital importance of a single political
issue (the environment or health); the same is true of 38 per cent
of Lajoinie's electorate. Here voters were particularly sensitive to
the unemployment issue. These figures contrast with the very
marginal importance of issues for those voting for F. Mitterrand (8
per cent of his electorate on the first ballot), J. Chirac (12 per cent)
or R. Barre (19 per cent).

The third variable—the party label—is only notably above

average (17 per cent) in the case of communist voters (36 per cent) and to a lesser degree socialist voters (24 per cent). This means there is still a slight difference between voters for left and right. Both vote principally for the candidate but when this is not the case the party is more important on the left, a major issue on the right.

The Élysée effect on the French political system has been not only to personify power at the top of each party but also to increase the importance of candidates at the expense of political issues and political parties. The French political system can now be seen as a hierarchy of elected monarchs: the President, the President of the Regional Councils, the Presidents of the Departmental Councils, and the Mayors. Electioneeering has changed all the more as the technological evolution of the means of electoral persuasion has reinforced the institutional constraints created by the passage, in 1958, from a parliamentary Republic dominated and handicapped by numerous weak parties to a semi-presidential Republic dominated by the direct election of the President.

Local Elections

There has in France been a tendency for the differences between types of elections to be less clearly marked than in other political systems. Although in recent years the old political practice of a single person holding several mandates has been severely restricted it is still alive. Two mandates can still be held at the same time—Jacques Chirac is for instance mayor of Paris and deputy for the Corrèze, Valéry Giscard d'Estaing is a Member of the European Parliament and a local representative of the Auvergne, Pierre Mauroy is deputy for Lille and the mayor of the town. The result of this practice is that there are not élites at different levels but a single national élite.

Another practice which tends to reduce differences between elections is that of holding different types of elections on the same day or within a very short period of time. On 16 March 1986 the first direct regional elections (1,840 regional counsellors in twenty-two metropolitan regions and four overseas regions) were coupled with the general election. The result was that no clear regional identity was manifest.[8] The dual election campaign—for the general election and the regional election—stifled the voice of the regions. The parties and the media centred all their efforts on the general election. General election behaviour structured regional election behaviour to a very great extent. Partisan voting was identical in both elections for 89 per cent of the Communist and Socialist voters; for 87 per of those voting RPR and UDF where they presented a common *liste*; for slightly less—75–80 per cent— where they were rivals; for 79 per cent of those voting for the National Front.[9]

In municipal elections on account of the enormous number of communes—36,000 of which 34,000 are in fact rural villages— the candidates, the issues, and hence the election campaigns depend on the size of the unit. If there are less than 9,000 inhabitants political labels are not of major importance and indeed often remain uncertain. If the candidate is from the commune, can communicate, and is seen as a good manager he stands a good chance of being elected. As the size of the commune increases so politics become more important. But the sitting mayors, whatever their party, are very difficult to beat and there is much more stability here than elsewhere. The only hope of winning against the sitting mayor is to divide the coalition supporting him and to sink a great deal of money in a campaign with no guarantee of success. In cases deemed important by the parties—the attempt to remove Jacques Chirac from Paris by the Socialists, or Pierre Mauroy from Lille by the right—municipal campaigns are mounted using all the modern electioneering techniques. It is significant that in both the instances cited they failed.

New Campaign Techniques

The development of television and of opinion polls was contemporaneous with the presidentialization of elections in France.

In 1958 when the Fifth Republic came into being less than 10 per cent of French households had television sets. In 1965 came the first presidential election and the first significant television election campaign. 40 per cent of households were able to follow in their own homes the confrontation of de Gaulle, Mitterrand, and Lecanuet. General de Gaulle who had refused to use his

TABLE 7.4. *Means of information used by voters during election campaigns, France, 1958–1988*

Referendum parliamentary election (1958)[a]	Presidential election (1974)[b]	Parliamentary election (1978)[b]	Presidential election (1981)[b]	Presidential election (1988)[c]
press	television	television	television	television
radio (and TV)	press	press	press	press
posters	radio	radio	radio	radio
private conversations	private conversations	private conversations	private conversations	private conversations
the hustings	the hustings	opinion polls	opinion polls	opinion polls
	posters	posters	the hustings	the hustings
	leaflets	leaflets	leaflets	leaflets
		the hustings	posters	posters

[a] IFOP, *Sondages*[4] (1960).
[b] R. Cayrol, in D. Gaxie (ed.), *Explication du vote: bilan des études électorales en France* (Paris: Fondation National des Sciences Politiques, 1985), 386.
[c] SOFRES, *L'État de l'opinion* (1989), 221.

television time on the first ballot was not elected at the first ballot and had to stand again at the second.

Television from 1965 onwards was the principal ground of party struggles both at and between elections. Party leaders and candidates prepared themselves for it assiduously.[10] For the voter television rapidly came to be seen as the prime source of information when deciding how to vote (Table 7.4). In 1988 a Sofres poll found that 62 per cent of voters thought television among the most useful sources as against 37 per cent the press, 30 per cent the radio, 20 per cent private conversations, 12 per cent opinion polls, 6 per cent the hustings, 4 per cent posters, and 4 per cent leaflets. Television was seen as particularly useful in that it enabled the voter actually to see the politicians and form an opinion as to their personalities and also kept the voter up to date with regard to the issues of the day. The newspapers on the other hand were particularly appreciated when it came to finding arguments to combat other people's ideas.[11]

Although television progressively dominated the election this did not mean an increase in inequality between the parties. On the contrary since the use of television was regulated and given free it was in fact a source of greater democratization. During general election campaigns time was allocated equally to the majority and to the opposition—with the parties in each camp deciding how it was to be distributed. For presidential elections an equal amount of time was given to each candidate.

The predominance of television has meant that the other media plan their campaign with one eye on television, thus increasing its importance. The newspapers announce in advance what is going to be broadcast. After the event, they publish extensive polls on the effects of television. Only *Le Monde* occasionally makes television news headlines. Hustings are organized so that the television will be present and major speeches and even statements within them are carefully timed so that they can be got into the major news programme at 8 p.m. One striking development concerns the use politicians make of the radio during the free party-political broadcasts. There used to be specific broadcasts for radio and television. Today the radio programme is simply the sound-track of the television programme.

The effect of the dominance of television has been to personalize all campaigns and to make them national—even those for local elections. The individual candidates in the constituencies have become less important in general elections than the party leaders and in local elections it is the national alliances that capture attention. The argument that all this has made political choice dependent on 'showbiz' rather than on reflection is not very convincing. The major effect of more national campaigning would seem to have been a greater interest in politics and a greater mobilization of voters.

One of the major innovations that television has brought is the confrontation of candidates and an adversarial style of campaigning. On 10 May 1974 at 8.30 p.m., nine days before the second ballot of the presidential election, the first television duel was organized between the two remaining candidates Giscard and Mitterrand. 81 per cent of voters followed it. Since then these second-ballot television duels have remained the focal point of every presidential campaign.

Electioneering in France gives a lesser role to activists than in many other systems. Possibly because the parties are weaker and party membership very small. The growing sophistication and professionalization of electioneering has made this less of a problem.

As for opinion polls it was not until 1965 and their third relaunch in France that they began to play a part in elections. Opinion polling first appeared in France in 1938 when the academic Jean Stoetzel, on returning from America, had created the Institut Français d'Opinion Publique (IFOP). One of its first polls had been on the Munich Agreement. IFOP could in 1938 have informed French political leaders of the state of public opinion. They would have seen that 'cowardly relief' was not universal (37 per cent of the French thought the Munich Agreement 'harmful', while 57 per cent were in favour of it) and more important still that 70 per cent of the French were in favour of preventing Hitler 'if necessary by force' from taking the free town of Danzig. But the political élites at this time did not understand what polls were and how they worked. The second birth of the polls in France came after the Liberation in 1944–5. The American authorities, who were familiar with opinion polling, commissioned IFOP to carry out a series of polls on the morale of the French. General de Gaulle, the head of the provisional government had done the same at the suggestion of André Malraux, who had convinced the General's entourage that polls were like medicine—'less scientific than they claim but more scientific than anything else'.[12] But the majority of the voters still knew nothing about opinion polls. It was finally not until the first ballot at the presidential election of 1965 when IFOP announced that General de Gaulle would be forced to a second ballot that the opinion polls were seen by the French as useful indicators of what the electorate thought and how it would vote. In its last poll on voting intentions, published in *France Soir* on the eve of the election, IFOP predicted General de Gaulle would have 43 per cent of the votes cast (and not the 50 per cent necessary to be re-elected at the first ballot). He obtained 43.76 per cent of the votes on 5 December. On the morning of 6 December the Minister of Information, Alain Peyrefitte, telephoned the Director of the IFOP. 'It was not', he said, 'a success for the General but it was a triumph for the opinion polls.'[13] At this time a single institute— IFOP—had a monopoly of political polls in France. Today at least eight private institutes of public opinion regularly carry out political surveys: IFOP (1938), SOFRES (1963), BVA (1970), IPSOS (1975), Harris France (1976), IFRES (1979), Faits et Opinions (1980),

CSA (1985). Each year they publish 500–600 surveys, without counting the private polling they do for the government and the parties, for presidential candidates, and for other political figures.

On the governmental side the Service d'Information et de Diffusion (SID), linked directly to the Prime Minister's office, spends some three million francs a year on surveys which are commissioned from the various institutes of public opinion. With the help of a monthly confidential barometer on public opinion and a series of *ad hoc* polls the SID reports to the government on the electorate's opinion of what the government is doing, globally and sector by sector. It also measures the attitudes of the electorate on any given issue to help the government make its decisions and follows the fluctuation of opinion day by day when there are serious social conflicts (e.g. strikes) and international conflicts (e.g. Gulf War). The major parties and potential presidential candidates commission surveys which are usually not published. Their rhythm accelerates as an election approaches, becoming first weekly, then, as the campaign advances, daily. Images of the candidates, election issues, electoral alliances are thus regularly tested and the results commented on by public opinion specialists.

The influence of opinion polls on electors was considered so great in France in the 1970s that a law was passed on 19 July 1977 to prevent 'the publication, circulation and commentary' of any opinion poll 'having a direct or indirect link' with the election during the week preceding each ballot and on election day itself. The same law also created an Opinion Poll Watchdog Committee whose task was to verify 'the objectivity and the quality of the polls published or circulated' at all times outside the forbidden period.

The hegemony of television communication and the rise in popularity of the polls came at a time when politicians and parties in France were realizing how necessary it was given the presidentialization of the regime to rationalize their election campaigns and, more widely, their political communication.[14] The first election campaign to be directed by a political campaign consultant was that of a candidate at the presidential election of 1965—Jean Lecanuet. The consultant was Michel Bongrand. Since then all the major election campaigns—presidential campaigns, general election campaigns, European election campaigns, even local campaigns—have been orchestrated by consultants: Jacques Séguéla for François Mitterrand in 1981 and 1988; Thierry Saussez and Gérard Demuth for Valéry Giscard d'Estaing; Elie Crespi for Jacques Chirac, etc.

Two main models of political persuasion dominate French election campaigns.[15] The first is a socio-political approach, the second more influenced by psychology, even psychiatry. The first model is founded essentially on the belief that there is a strong link between social class and political behaviour. This classical sociological analysis is, however, enriched by quantitative and qualitative analyses which enable the political scientist to define subgroups within the electorate and target them. Once the electorate/market has been defined and analysed the candidate/product should in theory be adapted to it. But both practitioners and politicians are convinced that candidates cannot be marketed as easily as commercial products. They must have credibility and that is founded on past action and on conviction and is not easily fabricated. The second model is socio-cultural and is based on analyses of styles of life and ways of thinking and not on social class, income, or education. The strength of the model is said to lie in the fact that it is not based on any pre-constructed hypothesis. It does not depend on any global explanation of society as the class model does. Analyses of this sort have been widely used by the COFREMCA who were used as consultants by Valéry Giscard d'Estaing. Jacques Séguéla also used the results of such studies when he built the portrait of François Mitterrand based on 'tranquil strength' (*la force tranquille*), stressing F. Mitterrand's common sense and realism and claiming he was in touch with the daily lives of the French.

The style and content of election campaigns have been modified by the new political technologies. The changes in style have not however, *pace* some journalistic analyses,[16] emptied the message of its content and concentrated exclusively on the packaging. The rationalization of campaigning has, however, simplified and streamlined the electoral message. Campaigns are now dominated by a central theme, popularized by posters and their slogans ('United France' (*La France unie*) in 1988, 'tranquil strength' in 1981 for François Mitterrand).

Spectacular effects are sought to dramatize the situation. In 1988 for instance at the beginning of his television campaign broadcast François Mitterrand projected a 90-second multiple-image clip—

similar to those pop singers use to illustrate their songs. Here the images constituted a history of France in the world since the Revolution of 1789, recalling the historical tradition of the left and situating the candidate within the history of France.

Politicians choose the issues they would like to dominate the campaign with the help of opinion polls. They are never sure, however, that they will in fact be able to set the agenda. The confrontation of candidates and interviews in the press, on radio, and on television play a considerable part. Quotations such as Giscard's remark to Mitterrand in 1974, 'You don't have the monopoly of caring' (*Vous n'avez pas le monopole du cœur*) make the headlines and set off new debates, sometimes very far from those the candidate would like to engage in.[17] The number of issues discussed is limited but there is a debate and it remains politically significant. In 1988 the IFRES exit poll showed the differential rating of issues by the voters for the different presidential candidates. Unemployment, low salaries, education, pensions, and law and order for those who voted for François Mitterrand at the second ballot; law and order, unemployment, private enterprise, education, and immigration for those who preferred Jacques Chirac. The negative vote (voting against one candidate by voting for his rival) was low. Only 21 per cent of voters at the second ballot claimed this was their strategy (IFRES exit poll, 8 May 1988).

There is a school of thought that holds that a 'new voter' has come into being who is less faithful to a particular party because he votes less according to his social class or the political socialization he received in his youth and because a higher level of education and information has freed him from ready-made ideologies.

The scant electoral data available on such questions leads us to cast doubt on this view of things. In 1958 a panel survey by IFOP calculated that some 59 per cent of voters had supported the same party in January 1956 (the last general election of the Fourth Republic) and in November 1958 (the first general election of the Fifth Republic). This meant that 41 per cent could be considered floating voters during this period of crucial change. 31 per cent voted to the right, 10 per cent to the left.[18] In 1981 in the presidential election which brought the left to power for the first time since 1958, Louis Harris France found that out of a panel of 250, 63 per cent remained stable and only 27 per cent were floating voters. The proportion is clearly below that of 1958.[19] In 1986 IFRES found 29 per cent of floating voters in a panel of 1,480.

Conclusion

The behaviour of electors has become more sophisticated and less easily predictable but the floating voter remains the exception not the rule. Opinion polls now seek to discover which candidates or parties voters are hesitating between; opinion polls also endeavour to analyse the transfers of support between the first and second ballots. The various means of communicating with the voter have not changed fundamentally but they are now used within the context of a campaign strategy. The outline of the message is conveyed by slogans and posters; the mass rallies in the major French towns are timed to coincide with the main news programme on television at 8 p.m.; the time allocated free of charge on radio and television—the election address, which is delivered free of charge to each elector—is used both to present and promote the candidate and to insist on the major issues seen to be favourable to the candidate; the tours of markets, of shops, the innumerable handshakes have come more and more to be seen as photo-opportunities. Door-to-door canvassing is unknown in France. Indeed there is much less involvement of the party faithful in the campaign than there is in Britain. The election addresses are sent out from the town halls so there is little addressing of envelopes. The hustings are now much less important than they were. Presidential candidates tend not to have groupies following them around. So there is really not all that much that activists can do save sell the party newspaper on the markets or stick posters on unauthorized sites. Perhaps that is why no pollster in France has sought to quantify the extent to which the electorate actually helps the parties' campaign. The press plays its role but never descends to the depths of personal vilification that it does in Britain. There is no truly national press in France, whether quality or popular, and this of course limits the role of the press during election campaigns. The big regional newspapers, such as *Ouest France* which is the daily with the biggest circulation in France, are largely apolitical.

The real problem that the new methods of electioneering raise in

France is less a rather mythical depolitization than the ever-increasing financial cost of election campaigns at all levels. This explains in part the political corruption charges (like those of Urba-Gracco in 1990–1 on the financing of the presidential campaign of François Mitterrand in 1988) individuals and organizations face today. Parties and candidates hide both the enormous size of their election expenses and the illegal means they use to finance them (forged bills, fake societies, bribes to the party or individuals given by firms obtaining public contracts at local or national level, etc.). Two laws, in 1988 and 1989, have endeavoured to introduce some morality into campaigning. The first law put a ceiling on election expenses for the first time: 120 million francs (£12 million) at the first ballot, plus 40 million (£4 million) at the second ballot for presidential campaigns; 400,000–500,000 francs (£40,000–50,000) depending on the types of constituencies at general elections.

It also introduced public financing of the political parties represented in the National Assembly or in the Senate. The sum allocated in the first instance was 14 million francs (£1.4 million)—3 francs per elector. The amount varies each year and is proposed and adopted within the framework of the national budget. The funds are allocated on the basis of the number of seats held. The Communist Party is against the public financing of political parties and has therefore consistently refused the money offered. The law also authorized within certain limits and under certain conditions donations to the parties from private donors and enterprises. This had hitherto been forbidden by law and to some extent explains why more devious means of financing parties had in some cases been resorted to.

The second law in 1989 put a ceiling on local election expenses in towns with over 9,000 electors and on European election expenses (80 million francs per list—£8 million).

Election expenses were considered to be those spent in the twelve months preceding the first day of the month in which the election was to be held. The second law also forbade some forms of campaigning with the intention, no doubt, of limiting temptations to spend. For three months before polling day no posters can be put up on commercial hoardings and no telephone campaigns can be waged. Parties and candidates are still forbidden to buy television time; only the free allocations of time may be used.

The effect of these new laws remains to be seen. The accounts of the recent past, however, have not yet been balanced and the suspicion of political corruption still hangs over France's political parties.

Notes

1. See P. Braud, 'Élire un Président . . . ou honorer les dieux?', *Pouvoirs*, 14 (1980), 15–28
2. See J.-L. Quermonne, *Le Gouvernment de la France sous la Ve République*, 3rd edn. (Paris: Dalloz, 1987); and H. Portelli, 'Les Partis et les institutions,' *Pouvoirs*, 49 (1989), 57–68
3. C. de Gaulle, '15 décembre 1965: Troisième entretien radiodiffusé et télévisé avec M. Michel Droit', *Discours et messages*, iv: *Pour l'effort, août 1962–décembre 1965* (Paris: Plon, 1970), 432–40.
4. See J. Charlot, 'Le Parti gaulliste', report to the Journées internationales sur de Gaulle en son siècle, Paris, UNESCO, 19–24 Nov. 1990 (to be published, Institut Charles de Gaulle).
5. See J. Charlot, 'Les Mutations du système des partis français', *Pouvoirs*, 49 (1989), 27–35. See also J. E. M. Schlesinger, 'The Reaffirmation of a Multi-party System in France', *American Political Science Review*. (Dec. 1990).
6. See H. Portelli, *Le Socialisme français tel qu'il est* (Paris: PUF, (1980), 147.
7. See A. Philippe and D. Hubscher, *Enquêtes à l'intérieur du Parti socialiste* (Paris: Albin Michel, 1991), 234.
8. See P. Perrineau (ed), *Régions: le baptême des urnes* (Bordeaux: Pedone, 1987), 19.
9. See SOFRES, *L'État de l'opinion 1989* (Paris: Seuil, 1989), 115.
10. See R. Cayrol, J. Blumler, and G. Thoveron, *La Télévision fait-elle l'élection?* (Paris: Presses de la FNSP, 1978); see also R. Cayrol, *Les Médias* (Paris: PUF, 1991).
11. See Cayrol, Blumler, and Thoveron, *La Télévision fait-elle l'élection?*
12. See A. Malraux, *Antimémoires* (Paris: Gallimard, 1967), i. 122.
13. See A. Max, *La République des sondages* (Paris: Gallimard, 1981), 29.
14. See M. Charlot, *La Persuasion politique* (Paris: A. Colin, 1970); M. Noir, *Réussir une campagne électorale: suivre l'exemple américain?* (Paris: Les éditions d'organisation, 1977); and D. Lindon, *Le Marketing politique* (Paris: Dalloz, 1986).

15. See D. Boy, E. Dupoirier, and H. Meynaud, 'Le Marketing politique: de la conviction à la séduction', *Pouvoirs*, 33 (1985), 121–30
16. See R.-G. Schwartzenberg, *L'État-spectacle* (Paris: Flammarion, 1977).
17. See D. Wolton, 'Leaders d'opinion dans une campagne présidentielle: un collège invisible', in *L'Élection présidentielle, 24 avril–8 mai 1988, Le Monde dossiers et documents* (May 1988), 50–5; see also J.-L. Missika and D. Bregman, 'Les Priorités comparées des candidats et des médias', ibid. 26–7.
18. See *Sondages*, 4 (1960), 25.
19. See Cayrol, *Les Médias*, 462–4.

References

Boy, Daniel, Dupoirier, Elizabeth, and Meynaud, Hélène, 'Le Marketing politique: de la conviction à la séduction', *Pouvoirs*, 33 (1985), 121–30.

Braud, Philippe, 'Élire un Président . . . ou honorer les dieux?', *Pouvoirs*, 14 (1980), 15–28.

Cayrol, Roland, in D. Gaxie (ed.), *L'explication du vote: bilan des études électorales en France* (Paris: Fondation Nationale des Sciences Politiques, 1985).

—— *Les Médias* (Paris: PUF, 1991).

—— Blumler, Jay G., and Thoveron, Gabriel, *La Télévision fait-elle l'élection?* (Paris: Presses de la FNSP, 1978).

Charlot, Jean, 'Les Mutations du système des partis français', *Pouvoirs*, 49 (1989), 27–35.

—— 'Le Parti gaulliste', report to the Journées internationales sur de Gaulle en son siècle, Paris, UNESCO, 19–24 Nov. 1990 (to be published, Institut Charles de Gaulle).

Charlot, Monica, *La Persuasion politique* (Paris: A. Colin, 1970).

De Gaulle, Charles, '15 décembre 1965: Troisième entretien radiodiffusé et télévisé avec M. Michel Droit', *Discours et messages*, iv: *Pour l'effort, août 1962–décembre 1965* (Paris: Plon, 1970), 432–40.

Lindon, Denis, *Le Marketing politique* (Paris: Dalloz, 1986).

Malraux, André, *Antimémoires* (Paris: Gallimard, 1967).

Max, Alfred, *La République des sondages* (Paris: Gallimard, 1981).

Missika, Jean-Louis, and Bregman, Dorine, 'Les Priorités comparées des candidats et des médias', in *L'Élection présidentielle, 24 avril–8 mai 1988, Le Monde dossiers et documents* (May 1988), 26–7.

Noir, Michel *Réussir une campagne électorale: suivre l'exemple américain?* (Paris: Les Éditions d'organisation, 1977).

Perrineau, Pascal (ed.), *Régions: le baptême des urnes* (Bordeaux: Pedone, 1987).

Portelli, Hugues *Le Socialisme français tel qu'il est* (Paris: PUF, 1980).

—— 'Les Partis et les institutions', *Pouvoirs*, 49 (1989) 57–68

Quermonne, Jean-Louis, *Le Gouvernement de la France sous la Ve République*, 3rd edn. (Paris: Dalloz, 1987).

Schwartzenberg, Roger-Gérard, *L'État-spectacle* (Paris: Flammarion, 1977).

SOFRES, *L'État de l'opinion 1989* (Paris: Seuil, 1989).

Wolton, Dominique, 'Leaders d'opinion dans une campagne présidentielle: un collège invisible', in *L'Élection présidentielle, 24 avril–8 mai 1988, Le Monde dossiers et documents* (May 1988), 50–5.

8

Germany

MAX KAASE

At the end of the 1980s, events in Germany took a turn which made all other developments in electioneering seem trivial. They culminated in the election of 2 December 1990, in which the five states of East Germany (GDR) joined with the eleven states of West Germany (FRG) The constitutional logic of the unification process meant that East Germany had to be completely absorbed into the institutional and legal order of West Germany. The transfer set the stage for a fast and unprecedented process of socio-political transition in the old GDR together with a feedback to the old FRG which provides a major topic for study in its own right. The need to establish a democratic political culture in the part of the country which had lived for forty-five years under Communist rule and indoctrination raises fascinating questions about political socialization. But for this chapter we have to recognize that the general election of 1987 was the last to take place in the old FRG; new theoretical paradigms will now be needed, and longitudinal analyses of German elections and voting behaviour will become much more complicated.

The Constitutional and Legal Context of Elections and Campaigns

Federal elections are conducted under the regulation of a federal election law (*Bundeswahlgesetz*). The most important features of this law are that *de facto* the German electoral system is one of proportional representation, although it is modified in substance by adding a clause denying parties obtaining less than 5 per cent of the valid votes (or less than three direct constituency seats) parliamentary representation. Every voter has two ballots, one (the first ballot–*Erststimme*) for a constituency candidate elected by relative majority vote, and one for a party list (the second ballot–*Zweitstimme*—a rather misleading term, since it is this ballot which determines the final distribution of seats in the federal parliament, the Bundestag).[1]

Up to 1987 in the FRG, there were 248 constituency seats plus 248 seats distributed according to state party lists (plus 22 seats from West Berlin not directly decided by the people of Berlin, but by the West Berlin parliament because of the Four-Power status of Berlin). In 1990, after the unification, the respective numbers were 328 and 656 (the 1990 Bundestag has 662 members because of six surplus mandates—*Überhangmandate*). Article 39 of the Basic Law requires that general elections take place every four years within a narrowly defined time frame; there is no constitutional right for the head of government (Chancellor–*Bundeskanzler*) to dissolve parliament. Only under extreme, constitutionally defined circumstances has the Federal President(*Bundespräsident*) the right to dissolve parliament prematurely.[2]

Article 21 of the Basic Law places special emphasis on the role of political parties in the political process. Thus, it cannot come as a surprise that this regulation has from the beginning encouraged the parties to demand that this special role must be accompanied by the provision of public subsidies. The debate on the financing of parties and of political campaigns in West Germany has had a varied history. There was no public financial support for political parties until 1954. After 1954, parliaments and governments found various, constitutionally highly ambiguous ways of finding access to public subsidies.[3] The situation became so controversial that the Constitutional Court (*Bundesverfassungsgericht*) was asked for a ruling. On 19 July 1966, it issued its first major statement in the matter, declaring unconstitutional the public financing of parties except for campaign purposes. Reasonable subsidies for electoral campaigns were regarded as acceptable because of the important role of elections and political parties in the political process. The public controversy ended, at least for a while, when parliament in July 1967 decided on a Party Law (*Parteiengesetz*) which was much modified in 1983 and 1988, and again in 1990 because of the German reunification. There seems to exist general agreement among observers that the main function of the Party Law has been to provide sufficient public financing for the parties.[4] Overall public financing of political parties by 1989 for a legislative period of four years amounted to about 3,500 million marks. Of this, roughly 700 million (£200m) was for campaigning in state and European general elections.[5]

Under the Party Law, each political party that obtains at least 0.5 per cent of the valid votes (second ballot) at federal elections, receives in relation to its share of the popular vote, 5 DM *per eligible voter*. Through a complicated procedure, all political parties with at least 2 per cent of the popular vote receive additional subsidies. These, together with the 5 DM, amount to a total of about 6.50 DM per eligible voter, or 194 million marks for the general election of 1987.[6] The overall public campaign reimbursement to all political parties for the 1990 general election with its increased electorate was 361 million marks.[7]

There is one additional important feature which reflects the constitutionally elevated role of political parties in Germany. Various legal provisions have guaranteed political parties, within limits, the right to broadcast political commercials on television and on radio before elections free of charge (except for production costs). The spots are limited in time (2½ minutes) and number and are allocated to the individual parties more or less in accordance with the strength of parliamentary representation.[8] These regulations, however, reflect the specific nature of the German electronic media system. Up to the middle 1980s, this system was exclusively public in nature; the two major networks responsible for three channels were ARD (two channels—ARD1 and ARD3) and ZDF (one channel). Both networks are mostly funded by viewer fees; the remaining revenues (ARD *c.*20 per cent; ZDF, *c.*40 per cent) come from advertising strictly limited to the time period between 6 p.m. and 8 p.m.

In the mid-1970s, a heated debate began on the introduction of privately owned television and radio stations.[9] As a consequence, various networks were established of which two have turned out to be particularly important: RTLplus started broadcasting on 2 January 1984, and SAT1 started its programmes on 1 January 1985. Since these channels could initially only be received by households connected to a cable system, the spread of the networks was a slow process, and they played almost no role in the campaign for the 25 January 1987 general election. By mid-1991, however, the situation had completely changed: in the 'old' FRG more than two-thirds of all households had access to these (and additional) private stations, and, even more importantly, in those households the four major TV networks (ARD, ZDF, RTLplus, SAT1) are almost on equal footing. Since the private channels must be exclusively financed by advertising, one effect of the 'dualization' of the German electronic media system was that the campaign for the 1990 general election for the first time introduced a substantial amount of paid television and radio advertising by political parties.

For the sake of completeness, it should be added that in the 'new' *Länder* the system of mass communication is in a process of transition for the print media as well as for the electronic media. Since even before unification at least 80 per cent of the GDR population could receive ARD1 and ZDF, for the December 1990 election both stations were available to almost everybody there, in addition to the—reformed—former GDR channels. However, since the private channels could only be obtained via satellite antennas, it can safely be assumed that former GDR citizens had almost no exposure to them.

Political Interest, Campaigns and Political Participation

For many Western democracies, the 1950s and early 1960s are regarded in retrospect as a time of quiet, consensus-orientated politics. In West Germany, this thrust was reflected in the emphasis on the 'economic miracle', the need for political and social reconstruction, the integration into the Western alliance and the establishment of a stable three-party system (Christian Democrats—CDU/CSU; Social Democrats–SPD; and Liberals–FDP). 1966 marks a major political change in that for the first time the SDP entered a federal government (the so-called 'Big Coalition' of CDU/CSU and SPD) and, with Chancellor Willy Brandt, in 1969 became the senior partner in an SPD–FDP government which lasted until 1982 and produced, as well as the new *Ostpolitik*, a broad range of socio-political reforms. This period not only marks the final acceptance of liberal democracy in West Germany, but also a process of politicization culminating in what observers have called a 'participatory revolution'.[10] Between 1972 and 1983, this politicization has also been reflected by turnout rates of about 90 per cent for general elections. Interestingly enough, turnout in 1987 fell to 84.4 per cent and in 1990 reached only 78.5 per cent in the old FRG and 77.6 per cent in the New Germany; 78.5 per cent in 1949 (only 'old' FRG) was the former all-time low mark.

These turnout data do not necessarily indicate a negative trend, but it is possible that elections are becoming less popular as modes of political involvement, in contrast to forms of direct participation such as, for example, citizen initiatives. The decline in turnout has occurred despite the fact that the amount of money in the federal budget for campaign subsidies has risen from 147 million marks in the period 1973–6 to 266 million marks for 1984–7.[11] According to the official reports legally required from the political parties, for the 1984–7 electoral period campaign expenditure for general elections amounted to 400 million marks, for European elections to 230 million marks, for *Länder* elections to 420 million marks, and for local elections to 270 million marks. Informed observers argue that these amounts are misleading because a substantial share is 'illegally' used by the parties to cover the basic costs of the party organization (in 1966 the Constitutional Court ruled that public subsidies to political parties must be for campaign purposes only). Probably, instead of the 1,300 million marks, only 1,000 million marks were actually spent on election campaigning.[12] Although precise longitudinal data are not available, Landfried argues that between 1961 and 1987 parties seem to have doubled their campaign expenditures for general elections; for 1987, the direct campaign expenditures for CDU/CSU, SPD and FDP were almost 200 million marks.[13]

The politicization of the West German electorate has also resulted in a weakening of established voter ties to political parties (dealignment). There has been a continuous increase in the number of floating voters, of split ticket voters and of voters who reach their final voting decision only very close to election day.[14] Clearly, the emergence of television as the most relevant and, in the eyes of the voter, most trustworthy source of political information, together with these changes in voter orientations should lead to a substantial change of emphasis in campaign strategies. Information gathered by Landfried for the 1980 general election campaign at least hints at how central campaign headquarters used their resources.[15]

Schleth's analysis of CDU/CSU expenditures in the 1961 election campaign, though not fully comparable, indicates that the cam-

TABLE 8.1 *Campaign expenditures of parties, 31 March–5 October 1980 (%)*

Money was spent on	CDU/CSU 1980	CDU/CSU 1961	SPD	FDP
Newspaper advertisements	20	20	26	35
Billboards	20	22	29	46
Publications (brochures, newspapers)	35	19	34	
Radio, TV, film	3	16	4	5
Meetings	17	14	7	5
Other	5	10	0	9
Sum (million marks = 100%)	42.5	17.0	39.1	7.8

Source: Figures from Schleth *Parteifinanzen*, 88 and for CDU/CSU in 1961 Landfried, *Parteifinanzen und politische Macht*, 256–8.

paign strategies may not have changed drastically over time.[16] In addition, Landfried's data, especially for the two large parties, look surprisingly similar. Thus one cannot help reaching the conclusion that, even for the parties themselves, campaigning contains a lot of ritual, repetitive elements, and justifies the popular view of election campaigns as basically boring or even superfluous. But this is only one side of the coin. The rise of television and in particular the diffusion of modern campaign techniques from the United States to Europe has created new perspectives on campaigning.

Television and Political Campaigning

Social scientists in the early 1960s were impressed by findings from voting and mass communications research that information from the mass media was at best able to stabilize political orientations, but could not change them. These findings were of course from a period in which television was just beginning to take its now dominant place. Nevertheless, one consequence of these findings was that voting behaviour research was slow to pay attention to the role of the mass media. This situation prevailed longer in Europe than in the USA because of the different organizational structure of the electronic mass media—public in Europe, and largely private in the USA. In addition, in the USA the weakness of the political parties and the emphasis on individual candidates, be it for president or for other political offices, accentuated the role of television in the conduct of campaigns.[17]

In West Germany, it was not so much in electoral research as in mass communications research that the impact of the mass media and especially of television on society was slowly reconsidered. This change in perspective is particularly prominent in the work of Elisabeth Noelle-Neumann, professor of mass-communications studies and at the same time director of the well-known private market research institute, Institut für Demoskopie (IfD) in Allensbach. This redefined emphasis became politically relevant when in the context of the general election of 1976, Noelle-Neumann, based on a preliminary version of her theory of the spiral of silence (*Schweigespirale*) and on empirical data, claimed that the CDU/CSU, with 48.6 per cent of the second ballot vote only just failed to secure an absolute majority of seats because of the hostility of television journalists.[18] The argument cannot be developed in detail here. It must suffice to say that Noelle-Neumann presented empirical findings seemingly showing that during the 1976 campaign one element of the overall climate of political opinion— personal communication—clearly favoured the CDU/CSU opposition in the sense that those people who relied mostly on personal information expected the CDU/CSU to win the election. But people who regularly watched political television programmes became much more inclined than those who hardly watched to believe that the incumbent SPD–FDP government would win the election. This 'dual climate of opinion' could emerge because for this election the opinions of journalists and the citizens were especially wide apart, and those of the journalists who saw SDP and FDP ahead were also particularly homogeneous.[19] Noelle-Neumann's insinuation was, of course, that the dual climate of opinion was consequential also for the outcome of the election, although this was never explicitly stated.

In the scholarly realm, these findings triggered a fierce debate, and their validity has remained ambiguous. In political terms, however, the Noelle-Neumann study can be regarded as the decisive factor which convinced the CDU and CSU that the West German ARD television system, in particular, was so biased against the two parties that the road to private TV networks had to be paved.[20]

This dualization of the TV market was put into effect in the mid-1980s. However, since the early 1970s the CDU–CSU had started to reconsider the role of the mass media on the outcome of elections. It is not by accident that Peter Radunski, who had earned a degree in political science and then worked in various capacities for the CDU, became the federal manager (*Bundesgeschäftsführer*) of the CDU throughout the 1980s. His knowledge of findings from electoral research (e.g. dealignment processes) and his command of the relevant American mass communications literature enabled him to convince his party that campaigns in the age of television had to be completely different from earlier days.[21]

Since political parties up to 1990 were restrained by the public ownership of the electronic mass media system, which prevented the buying of advertising time for political communications, more indirect ways of gaining influence on the electronic media had to be considered. One such way was to reinforce the long established tendency to recruit people into leading network positions on the basis of their party affiliation. In the 1970s, after the 1976 general election failure, the CDU/CSU was especially successful in launching affiliated journalists into positions of influence in the electronic media.[22] Another way is to catch the mass media in their own 'logic' by creating political events just for the purpose of being reported by the media (so-called pseudo-events). A third example is the increasing emphasis on promoting politicians rather than political issues, a phenomenon which has become known as 'personalization' of politics.

All this reflects a changing perspective about the role of mass media as a political intermediary. Elections and campaigns are now regarded as just one symbolically and institutionally dramatized, but time-bound, event in an ongoing political process. Parties see their role as placing 'their' actors, events, and themes on the public agenda; in this effort knowledge of the 'media logic'[23] helps them to instrumentalize the media. It is thus not surprising that some of the most revealing books on campaigning have been written by people working in political parties.[24]

The continuing struggle between political parties and the media has deflected the attention of political scientists from the far-reaching consequences of these developments for the nature of the democratic political process.[25] But even in the age of direct politics, for a large part of the people politics continues to be a distant affair. This is why the mobilization of voters has remained such an important part of campaigning.

The parties believe that campaigning through advertising has little impact in convincing new voters, but that it has an impact by making the parties visible, and supporting a favourable climate of opinion. Therefore, the broadcasting of party commercials, free of charge, on public television has become an important element in recent campaigns. However, the number of such spots was limited (in 1990, CDU and SPD were permitted eight spots on each of the two major networks), and their placement right behind the evening news gave viewers every opportunity to escape them before the 'real' programme started.

With private channels, however, the situation has at least changed. Within limits, parties can now purchase time for their commercials to be placed anywhere they like in the programmes. Although prices were only discounted by 10 per cent from those of spots for 'normal' products and fees reached DM 25,000 for 30 seconds, the SPD and CDU each bought twenty-six such spots on RTLplus and 27 on SAT1: the smaller parties decided not to incur this sort of expense. This, in the long run, may turn out to be a structural problem because it opens the way to grave inequalities. Another interesting feature of the 1990 campaign was that the CDU bought fifty additional spots in two small channels (PRO7 and Tele 5) in order to reach specific types of viewers (in particular, young people). These are the first hints that the 'dualization' of the electronic media system in Germany may also have far-reaching consequences for campaign strategies in the future.

There is one further aspect of the introduction of private TV in Germany which needs mentioning. Content analyses of political information in public TV and private TV have shown that there are substantial differences, not only in the sheer amount of political coverage (particularly in public TV), but also in the way politics is presented (private channels do it less politically).[26] These developments may contribute to known changes in public perceptions of what is political and may thus also have an impact on the political process.[27]

One aspect of election campaigns which, since the famous 1960 Nixon-Kennedy confrontation, has become important has been debates between the leading competitors. In Germany such debates took place between 1969 and 1987 on the Thursday before the Sunday election day and were always broadcast by both ARD 1 and ZDF. Analyses of these debates show that, while over time they have become less appreciated by the public, they still have a substantial impact on voter information and probably also some impact on voting behaviour.[28] This seems to provide the reason why Chancellor Helmut Kohl in 1990, feeling that this time he could only lose from participation, decided not to join in the debate, despite strong challenges by the SDP leader Oskar Lafontaine. As a consequence, the debate did not take place.

The Role of Public Opinion Polls in West German Politics

Public opinion polls have always been and are still regarded as a mixed blessing. Political polling has been regarded either as a threat to responsible élite politics or as a desirable addition to plebiscitary elements in the democratic decision-making process. However, this debate has long since lost its teeth. Opinion polling by now has become a way of life to most citizens and political actors; this is especially true before elections (and one has to keep in mind that in Germany now there are eighteen—one federal, one European, and sixteen at the state level, without including the various local elections).

As in most liberal democracies, opinion surveys became institutionalized after World War II. In West Germany, the Americans have contributed a lot to that institutionalization, and by the mid-1950s the polling techniques were used competently by a broad spectrum of private market research firms.[29] Of those, the Allensbach Institut für Demoskopie was the first one regularly to 'predict' election outcomes based on representative sample surveys of the voting age population; it has continued to do so up to the present day, and has been very accurate in its predictions.

In the mid-1960s, there existed a substantial amount of public controversy over whether poll results should be made publicly available at all, or only at certain times (e.g. up to two weeks before an election), or without any limitation. But electronic and printed media discovered that publishing poll results plainly attracted a great deal of public interest. As a consequence, starting six to eight weeks before the election, weekly polls are now published by newspapers, magazines, and television and are paid for by the media and therefore not subject to political pressure. This development has neutralized any idea political parties might have had of using polling data as a direct instrument in campaigning.

The acceptance of public opinion polls by the media has gone far beyond obtaining voting intentions. Starting in 1977, the Mannheim-based Forschungsgruppe Wahlen e.V (initially founded by Max Kaase, Uwe Schleth, and Rudolf Wildenmann at the University of Mannheim in 1965) does monthly surveys of the voting-age population for the ZDF ('Politbarometer'), including the distribution of party preferences, and the data are presented once a month on ZDF in its evening news programme. These reports are by now so much a part of the regular information programme that there is no controversy about them; they are accepted as a normal part of the network's obligation to inform the public about politics. In addition, almost every week some newspaper publishes a poll on the present distribution of party preferences.

Of course, political parties also regularly commission public opinion polls. Some of these are funded from public subsidies for campaign expenditures, some are funded through public money regularly given to the party foundations. Changes between the 1960s and 1980s in this respect certainly have taken place in that initially the wealth of polling information now present was not available. Generally, it is out of the question for a party to plan its campaign without having regular and systematic information about the state of public opinion. Whereas we have not yet seen, as in the USA, the large-scale rise of political consultants as a profession, each party at least has access to university-based advisers who may bring academic expertise to the preparation of campaign strategies.

From 1966 TV (ARD and ZDF) has also routinely used social science techniques to forecast elections on election day once the polls have closed at 6 p.m. Both public stations rely on three bases of information: exit polls, actual precinct results, and, for background information, findings from surveys conducted in the week before the election. In all three instances, the rise of modern electronic communication (especially telephone surveys which permit researchers to contact respondents up to the Saturday before the election) has resulted in a situation where about 30 minutes after the polls have closed the highly competitive TV stations present election forecasts which are so precise that by 7 p.m. at the latest politicians are already being interviewed live on the outcome of the election. This is a far cry from the 1965 situation where it was 9 p.m. before the first and not very reliable forecasts were presented on TV.

At times, there were voices claiming that all this speed and precision in predicting elections on TV was bound to frustrate voters and make them feel that it was not worth taking the trouble to go to the polls. Such voices are hardly heard today, but the question remains whether all this scholarly expertise together with electronic gadgets and computer-driven graphics do not deflate the meaning of the vote and contribute to political alienation.

Instead of a Conclusion

Panta rei—everything changes. This certainly applies to politics and electioneering in Germany. Over the last three decades, processes of social change have eroded established milieux and, as a consequence, have severed traditional ties between social groups and political parties (such as those between Catholics and the CDU/CSU). The impact had been heightened by the fact that social groups once at the centre of political action (like the labour movement) have lost in absolute size and in political influence. All this has, in Germany as elsewhere, resulted in more electoral volatility, in more changes of government directly through elections rather than through changes in coalition composition, and in increasing difficulties for the parties as they try to mobilize their voters. The causal nexus between these changes and especially changes in the system of mass media is unclear; most likely, both processes are contingent on each other.

Obviously, such transitions cannot happen without also influencing electoral campaigns. We have seen these influences emerge in every aspect of electioneering. Nevertheless, at least for the Federal Republic, the institutional and constitutional context has so far set limits on the impact of these massive social and technological forces. In this sense, one could also argue that *plus ça change plus c'est la même chose.* This argument may, however, be just a reflection of our inability to perceive gradual changes, however deep-reaching in consequence, as changes at all.

Notes

1. For details of the German electoral system, see Max Kaase, 'Personalized Proportional Representation: The "Model" of the West German Electoral System', in Arend Lijphart and Bernard Grofman (eds.), *Choosing an Electoral System: Issues and Alternatives* (New York: Praeger, 1984), 155–64.
2. For an example, see Max Kaase, 'The West German Election of 6 March 1983', *Electoral Studies*, 2 (1983), 158–66.
3. Hans Herbert von Arnim, *Die Partei, der Abgeordnete und das Geld* (Mainz: v. Hase & Köhler, 1991), 54–9.
4. For general concerns and considerations, see von Armin, *Die Partei*; and *Die neue Parteienfinanzierung* (Wiesbaden: Karl-Bräuer-Institut des Bundes der Steuerzahler e. V., 1989); Karl-Heinz Nassmacher, 'Parteienfinanzierung als verfassungspolitisches Problem Aus Politik und Zeitgeschichte', Suppl. to the weekly *Das Parlament*, B 11/89 (10 Mar. 1989), 27–38; and Nassmacher, 'Structure and Impact of Public Subsidies to Political Parties in Europe: The Examples of Austria, Italy, Sweden and West Germany', in Herbert E. Alexander (ed.), *Comparative Political Finance in the 1980s* (Cambridge: Cambridge University Press, 1989), 236–67.
5. Von Arnim, *Die neue Parteienfinanzierung*, 156.
6. Ibid. 58–61.
7. Von Arnim, *Die Partei*, 305.
8. For details, see Klaus Schoenbach, 'The Role of Mass Media in West German Election Campaigns', *Legislative Studies Quarterly*, 12 (1987), 373–94.
9. Max Kaase, 'Fernsehen, gesellschaftlicher Wandel und politischer Prozess', in Max Kaase and Winfried Schulz (eds.), *Massenkommunikation: Theorien—Methoden—Befunde*, 30, special issue of the *Kölner Zeitschrift für Soziologie und Sozialpsychologie* (Opladen: Westdeutscher Verlag, 1989), 97–117.
10. Samuel H. Barnes, Max Kaase, *et al.*, *Political Action: Mass Participation in Five Western Democracies* (Beverly Hills, Calif: Sage, 1979); M. Kent Jennings, Jan van Deth, *et al.*, *Continuities in Political Action: A Longitudinal Study of Political Orientations in Three Western Democracies* (Berlin: Walter de Gruyter, 1990).

11. Karl-Heinz Nassmacher, 'Parteienfinanzierung im Wandel', *Der Bürger im Staat*, 39, No. 4 (Stuttgart: Landeszentrale für Politische Bildung, 1989), 271–8.

12. Ibid. 175–6.

13. Christine Landfried, *Parteifinanzen und politische Macht: Eine vergleichende Studie zur Bundesrepublik Deutschland, zu Italien und den USA* (Baden-Baden: Nomos, 1990), 257.

14. Russell J. Dalton and Robert Rohrschneider, 'Wählerwandel und die Abschwächung der Parteineigung von 1972 bis 1987', in Max Kaase and Hans-Dieter Klingemann (eds.), *Wahlen und Wähler: Analysen aus Anlass der Bundestagswahl 1987* (Opladen: Westdeutscher Verlag, 1990), 297–324.

15. Landfried, *Parteifinanzen und politische Macht*, 256–8.

16. Uwe Schleth, *Parteifinanzen: Eine Studie über Kosten und Finanzierung der Parteitätigkeit, zu deren politischer Problematik and zu den Möglichkeiten einer Reform* (Meisenheim am Glan: Anton Hain, 1973).

17. Richard L. Rubin, *Press, Party, and Presidency* (New York: Norton, 1981).

18. Elisabeth Noelle-Neumann, 'Das doppelte Meinungsklima: Der Einfluss des Fernsehens im Wahlkampf 1976', in Max Kaase (ed.), *Wahlsoziologie heute: Analysen aus Anlass der Bundestagswahl 1976*, *Politische Vierteljahresschrift*, 18, Nos. 2/3 (Opladen: Westdeutscher Verlag, 1977) 408–51; and *Öffentliche Meinung: Die Entdeckung der Schweigespirale* (Frankfurt-am-Main: Ullstein, 1989).

19. Noelle-Neumann, 'Das doppelte Meinungsklima', 436.

20. Kaase, 'Fernsehen, gesellschaftlicher Wandel, und politischer Prozess'.

21. Peter Radunski, *Wahlkämpfe: Moderne Wahlkampfführung als politische Kommunikation* (Munich: Olzog, 1980); and 'Strategische Überlegungen zum Fernsehwahlkampf', in Winfried Schulz and Klaus Schönbach (eds.), *Massenmedien und Wahlen* (Munich: Öchläger, 1983), 131–45.

22. Albrecht Kutteroff, 'Politische Macht und Massenmedien: Veränderung der politischen Macht und des politischen Seltverständnisses', in Jürgen W. Falter, Christian Fenner, and Michael Greven (eds.), *Politische Willensbildung und Interessenvermittlung* (Opladen: Westdeutscher Verlag, 1984), 372–80.

23. David L. Altheide and Robert P. Snow, *Media Logic* (Beverly Hills, Calif: Sage, 1979).

24. For example, Peter Radunski, *Wahlkämpfe*.

25. Examples indicating an increasing awareness of this problem are Austin Ranney, *Channels of Power* (New York: Basic Books, 1983); and Kaase, 'Massenkommunikation und politischer Prozess', in Max

Kaase (ed.) *Politische Wissenschaft und politische Ordnung* (Opladen: Westdeutscher Verlag, 1986), 357–74.

26. See Erwin Faul *et al.*, *Die Fernsehprogramme in dualen Rundfunksystem* (Berlin: VDE-Verlag, 1988); Heribert Schatz *et al.*, *Strukturen und Inhalte des Rundfunkprogramms der vier Kabelpilotprojekte*, vol. 23 of the Begleitforschung des Landes Nordrhein-Westfalen zum Kabelpilotprojekt Dortmund (Düsseldorf: Presse—und Informationsamt der Landesregierung Nordhein-Westfalen, 1989; and Barbara Pfetsch, *Politische Folgen der Dualisierung des Rundfunksystems in der Bundesrepublik Deutschland: Konzepte, Analysen zum Fernsehangebot und zum Publikumsverhalten* (Baden-Baden: Nomos, 1991).

27. Kaase, 'Massenkommunikation and politischer Prozess'.

28. Helmut Norpoth and Kendall L. Baker, 'Politiker unter sich am Bildschirm: Die Konfrontation von Personen und Sachthemen in den Fernsehdiskussionen 1972–1980', in Max Kaase and Hans-Dieter Klingemann (eds.), *Wahlen und politisches System: Analysen aus Anlass der Bundestagswahl 1980* (Opladen: Westdeutscher Verlag, 1983), 600–21; and Peter R. Schrott, 'Electoral Consequences of "Winning" Televised Campaign Debates', *Public Opinion Quarterly*, 54 (1990), 567–85.

29. Max Kaase, 'Public Opinion Polling in the Federal Republic of Germany', in Karl Cerny (ed.), *West Germany at the Polls* (Washington, DC: American Enterprise Institute, 1978), 195–225.

References

Altheide, David L. and Snow, Robert P., *Media Logic* (Beverly Hills, Calif.: Sage, 1979).

Arnim, Hans Herbert von, *Die neue Parteienfinanzierung* (Wiesbaden: Karl-Bräuer-Institut des Bundes der Steuerzahler e. V., 1989).

—— *Die Partei, der Abgeordnete und das Geld* (Mainz: v. Hase & Koehler, 1991).

Barnes, Samuel H., Kaase, Max, *et al.*, *Political Action: Mass Participation in Five Western Democracies* (Beverly Hills, Calif.: Sage, 1979).

Dalton, Russel J., and Rohrschneider, Robert, 'Wählerwandel und die Abschwächung der Parteineigung von 1972 bis 1987', in Max Kaase and Hans-Dieter Klingemann (eds.), *Wahlen und Wähler: Analysen aus Anlass der Bundestagwahl 1987* (Opladen: Westdeutscher Verlag, 1990), 297–324.

Faul, Erwin, with Behrens, Peter, Grundheber, Horst, and Willems,

Brigitte, *Die Fernsehprogramme im dualen Rundfunksystem* (Berlin: VDE-Verlag, 1988).

Jennings, M. Kent, van Deth, Jan, *et al.*, *Continuities in Political Action: A Longitudinal Study of Political Orientations in Three Western Democracies* (Berlin: Walter de Gruyter, 1990).

Kaase, Max, 'Public Opinion Polling in the Federal Republic of Germany', in Karl H. Cerny (ed.), *West Germany at the Polls* (Washington, DC: American Enterprise Institute, 1978), 195–225.

—— 'The West German Election of 6 March 1983', *Electoral Studies*, 2 (1983), 158–66.

—— 'Personalized Proportional Representation: The "Model" of the West German Electoral System', in Arend Lijphart and Bernard Grofman (eds.), *Choosing an Electoral System: Issues and Alternatives* (New York: Praeger 1984), 155–64.

—— 'Massenkommunikation und politischer Prozess', in Max Kaase (ed.), *Politische Wissenschaft und politische Ordnung: Analysen zu Theorie und Empirie demokratischer Regierungsweise* (Opladen: Westdeutscher Verlag, 1986), 357–74.

—— 'Fernsehen, gesellschaftlicher Wandel und politischer Prozess', in Max Kaase and Winfried Schulz (eds.), *Masssenkommunikation: Theorien—Methoden—Befunde*, 30, special issue of the *Kölner Zeitschrift für Soziologie und Sozialpsychologie* (Opladen: Westdeutscher Verlag, 1989), 372–80.

Kutteroff, Albrecht, 'Politische Macht und Massenmedien: Veränderung der politischen Macht und des politischen Selbstverständnisses', in Jürgen W. Falter, Christian Fenner, and Michael T. Greven (eds.), *Politische Willensbildung und Interessenvermittlung* (Opladen: Westdeutscher Verlag, 1984), 372–80.

Landfried, Christine, *Parteifinanzen und politische Macht: Eine vergleichende Studie zur Bundesrepublik Deutschland, zu Italien und den USA* (Baden-Baden: Nomos, 1990).

Nassmacher, Karl-Heinz, 'Parteienfinanzierung als verfassungspolitisches Problem Aus Politik und Zeitgeschichte', supplement to the weekly newspaper *Das Parlament*, B 11/89 (10 Mar. 1989), 27–38

—— 'Structure and Impact of Public Subsidies to Political Parties in Europe: The Examples of Austria, Italy, Sweden and West Germany', in Herbert E. Alexander (ed.), *Comparative Political Finance in the 1980s* (Cambridge: Cambridge University Press, 1989), 236–67.

—— 'Parteienfinanzierung im Wandel', *Der Bürger im Staat*, 39, No. 4 (Stuttgart: Landeszentrale für politische Bildung, (1989), 271–8.

Noelle-Neumann, Elisabeth 'Das doppelte Meinungsklima: Der Einfluss des Fernsehens im Wahlkampf 1976', in Max Kaase (ed.), *Wahlsoziologie heute: Analysen aus Anlass der Bundestagswahl 1976, Politische*

Vierteljahresschrift, 18/2–3 (Opladen: Westdeutscher Verlag, 1977), 408–51.

—— *Öffentliche Meinung: Die Entdeckung der Schweigespirale* (Frankfurt-am-Main: Ullstein, 1989).

Norpoth, Helmut, and Baker, Kendall L., 'Politiker unter sich am Bildschirm: Die Konfrontation von Personen und Sachthemen in den Fernsehdiskussionen 1972–1980', in Max Kaase and Hans-Dieter Klingemann (eds.), *Wahlen und politisches System: Analysen aus Anlass der Bundestagswahl 1980* (Opladen: Westdeutscher Verlag 1983), 600–21.

Pfetsch, Barbara, *Politische Folgen der Dualisierung des Rundfunksystems in der Bundesrepublik Deutschland: Konzepte, Analysen zum Fernsehangebot und zum Publikumsverhalten* (Baden-Baden: Nomos, 1991).

Radunski, Peter, *Wahlkämpfe: Moderne Wahlkampfführung als politische Kommunikation* (Munich: Olzog, 1980).

—— 'Strategische Überlegungen zum Fernsehwahlkampf', in Winfried Schulz and Klaus Schönbach (eds.), *Massenmedien und Wahlen* (Munich: Ölschläger, 1983), 131–45.

Ranney, Austin, *Channels of Power: The Impact of Television on American Politics* (New York: Basic Books, 1983).

Rubin, Richard L., *Press, Party, and Presidency* (New York: Norton, 1981).

Schatz, Heribert, *et al.*, *Strukturen und Inhalte des Rundfunkprogramms der vier Kabelpilotprojekte*, vol. 23 of the Begleitforschung des Landes Nordrhein-Westfalen zum Kabelpilotprojekt Dortmund (Düsseldorf: Presse- und Informationsamt der Landesregierung Nordrhein-Westfalen, 1989).

Schleth, Uwe, *Parteifinanzen: Eine Studie über Kosten und Finanzierung der Parteitätigkeit, zu deren politischer Problematik und zu den Möglichkeiten einer Reform* (Meisenheim am Glan: Anton Hain, 1973).

Schoenbach, Klaus. 'The Role of Mass Media in West German Election Campaigns', *Legislative Studies Quarterly*, 12 (1987), 373–94.

Schrott, Peter R. 'Electoral Consequences of "Winning" Televised Campaign Debates', *Public Opinion Quarterly*, 54 (1990), 567–85.

9

Italy

STEPHEN GUNDLE

The Italian political system has been long renowned for its static qualities, for its resistance to change of all types. Yet in the course of the 1980s the pattern of electioneering evolved radically as new techniques and codes of campaigning were widely adopted. Not only did television become more important than ever before but party-centred rallies, posters, and word-of-mouth strategies were displaced by media-orientated forms of political communication in which the emphasis shifted from parties towards leaders and candidates. As part of the trend towards political marketing, even telephone canvassing and direct mail shots were introduced. By a variety of observers this process of change was hailed, from its very earliest manifestations in the late 1970s, as part of a deplorable trend towards Americanization that would result in Italian political life losing its distinctive cultural and ideological traits with political communication becoming virtually indistinguishable from entertainment. This view was given little credence by the experts. While one or two also spoke of Americanization, and even of Italy being 'the most "Americanized" European country' in its acceptance of media-related techniques,[1] most political scientists and sociologists of the mass media dismissed the idea as absurd. To put Italy on a par with the United States was to confuse a recent and largely cosmetic use of modern technologies of communication with a consolidated, and continually evolving, tradition of campaigning in which the media played a central, and even dominant, role in all phases of the electoral process. This was unlikely to occur in Italy, it was argued, because of the structural constraints of a political system marked by parliamentarianism, proportional representation, entrenched loyalties, and political control of the mass media.[2]

Although the term was widely used, sometimes in inverted

commas, sometimes not, no attempt was made in the debate on new trends in political communication to define or query the concept of Americanization. This theoretical paucity contrasted sharply with the careful discussion of its various possible meanings and implications which occurred in the course of the 1980s among students of Italy's post-war social and cultural development. To sum up briefly it may be said that Italy, like every other country in Western Europe, underwent a process of modernization after 1945 in which American images, products, ideas, customs, and values acted as a powerful model. However, even where such ideas and products were attractive to large numbers of people or were promoted with vigour by American political, cultural, or economic élites their impact was a complex process, often partial and usually unpredictable in its consequences. It was profoundly conditioned both by the cultural and political context and the filtering mechanisms of traditional élites, religious authorities, and left-wing ideologies. American notions and techniques found their readiest application when established procedures were in crisis or had lost relevance either because of inherent weaknesses or as a result of social and economic change.[3]

It is in this context that developments in electoral campaigning need to be considered. New procedures pioneered in the United States have not been adopted purely because technological change has rendered them possible, or even because certain politicians and political parties have been ready to exploit them. Of crucial importance has been the erosion of old forms of political communication and consensus aggregation, and the more general crisis of the party system as a whole. The principal aim of the present chapter is to examine the interrelationship of these factors and to assess the real extent of innovation.

Campaigning in the 1950s and 1960s

The 1948 election was one of the most bitterly fought in post-war Europe and without doubt the most divisive in the history of the Italian Republic. It institutionalized within the domestic political system the international divisions of the Cold War years and it sanctioned the hegemony of the Christian Democrats over the government and of the Communists over the opposition: roles which each would still conserve over forty years later. During the campaign the dominant codes and trademarks of the political parties were fixed in the public mind; images were established that, no matter how much they evolved in practice over time, remained an essential part of Italian political life.

One of the key characteristics of the 1948 campaign was the active intervention of powerful international and national interests, mostly on the side of the pro-Western parties and in particular the DC. The United States made it plain that not only would Marshall aid cease but military intervention might follow if Italians failed to recognize the merits of co-operation with the West. Over one million letters were sent by Italian-Americans to relatives and random citizens urging a non-Communist vote while Frank Sinatra, Jimmy Durante, baseball hero Joe Di Maggio, and other stars of Italian origin launched a radio appeal. The Church also presented the election as a choice between civilization and barbarism, the Pope himself intervening to invite Italians to take a stance 'either for Christ or against Christ'. Catholic Action set up a vast network of 18,000 civic committees at parish level with the aim of reducing abstentionism among the faithful. The DC's expensively-produced and varied propaganda included newsreels distributed in cinemas and posters and leaflets which sought to identify it as hostile to communism, favourable to social justice, and stern in its defence of the family. In one celebrated poster only a muscular arm wielding a sword bearing the legend 'Vote Christian' stood between a happy family and writhing snakes representing 'divorce' and 'free love'.

Against this barrage the Socialist and Communist parties, fighting jointly as the Democratic Popular Front, were unable to hold the support they won separately in 1946. The great strength of the left was its activist support: its rallies drew enormous crowds and its partisans were enthusiastic. But despite its adoption of Garibaldi as its symbol and its determined endeavours to present itself as the true defender of the national interest and even of Christian principles against De Gasperi and Pius XII, who were depicted as puppets of Truman and reactionary capitalist forces, its international sympathies undermined its credibility in two crucial areas. The Soviet Union was admired by some sectors of the population for its role in the defeat of Nazism and for its socialist system but it could offer next to nothing by way of material aid to a devastated country. Moreover, its credentials as a supporter of democracy and national self-determination were gravely damaged by the Communist seizure of power in Czechoslovakia and the more general extension of Soviet control in Eastern Europe. The left-wing parties were also a disadvantage on the propaganda plane. They were completely excluded from the government-controlled radio network and the short films that were made met with the refusal of distributors to show them in cinemas. Only in the field of posters and leaflets was an effort launched that was comparable to that of the DC.

In subsequent elections international involvement declined but the level of ideological confrontation remained high. Every party, from the neo-fascist Italian Social Movement (MSI) to the Communists, cultivated a distinctive political culture and impersonal identity which it expressed in the stern and uncompromising stances it set out, above all at election time. This applied even to the small centre parties (the Social Democrats, the Republicans, and the Liberals) who relied largely on what Parisi and Pasquino, in their typology of Italian voting behaviour, called a *voto d'opinione* (opinion vote). But it was particularly true of the DC and the PCI, whose robust and extensive subcultures produced a massive and regular *voto di appartenenza* (belonging or loyalty vote).[4] It was the dominance of the latter type of voting that ensured a very high degree of electoral stability.[5] Shifts of more than two or three percentage points were rare and even one extra point was enough for any party to proclaim a victory.

The presence of an electorate marked by a high level of ideological segmentation and of mass parties which covered the whole of society with a network of institutions, recreational activities, newspapers and festivals, inevitably had a profound effect on political campaigning. Although both major parties endeavoured to reach out beyond the confines of their subcultures to intercept different segments of the floating opinion vote, political leaders primarily addressed themselves to the converted, often in terms that, while highly significant for activists, were not necessarily meaningful for the uninitiated. An army of grass-roots activists then relayed simple decodified versions of these messages to ordinary voters, most of whom would be known to be actual or potential supporters. Newspapers were an important source of information for activists as they provided a blow-by-blow account of the development of the campaign. But their low readership, predictable centre-right orientation, or explicit party political affiliation and use of a technically sophisticated 'insider' language, meant they had little or no independent influence on the general public. In communicating political messages to a population that contained a by no means negligible proportion of poor and illiterate people, a greater role was probably played by the colourful and often witty posters that were displayed on billboards and specially erected temporary hoardings.

In many respects the two mass parties conducted their campaigns in a similar way. However, despite the many common characteristics they shared, there were important organizational differences between them. The strength of the PCI's support derived from the flexible mass-orientated style of activity Togliatti imposed on it after the war, but it also conserved the compactness and discipline of a highly integrated party. Consequently at election time the party machine could ensure that votes were directed with a high degree of precision to given candidates. The DC was more variegated. Its loyalty vote was essentially a Catholic vote that was mediated by the church and religious organizations. As a party, moreover, it was highly factionalized. Each faction mobilized electoral support by drawing on the interest groups or affiliated associations most closely associated with it (as well as regional strongholds). Because of its high degree of interpenetration with the state apparatus (a practice the PCI vividly denounced in 1953 by erecting giant-size knives and forks designed to portray the DC in the public mind as a party of greedy scoundrels incapable of distinguishing private interests from the public good) the DC also mobilized significant support amoung poor electors, particularly in the more backward southern regions, on the basis of collective or individual favours and promises of assistance. This third type of vote, identified by Parisi and Pasquino as a *voto di scambio* (exchange vote), produced often virulent local rivalries between candidates belonging to different factions. Eager to amass the three or four preference votes each elector could express among the candidates of his or her chosen party, candidates endeavoured both to act as the privileged voice of given clienteles and to secure by a variety of means the backing of identifiable groups and individuals. Readily corruptible, the exchange vote was a resource which gave the DC a distinct advantage over other government parties as well as the Communists, who could endeavour to capture it only in the 'red' regions of central Italy where they gradually acquired a reputation for honest and efficient local administration.

In contrast to countries with bi-polar or presidential systems, the pattern of political communication in Italy was little altered by the advent of television. A limited number of national politicians were certianly rendered more visible by *Tribuna politica*, which was broadcast regularly during election periods from 1960, but the country's high level of politicization and complex party system meant that neither their image nor their standing was substantially modified.[6] Although the Communist daily *L'Unità* was quick to highlight the fact that Togliatti's 'calm words' and 'convincing mode of arguing' had been heard by an audience of fifteen million people when he first appeared on screen during the 1963 election campaign,[7] generally speaking the language of politics remained erudite and dense. Even if politicians had wanted to break out of their habitual insider mode of communication or known how to, they faced a structural obstacle in the form of a panel of journalists drawn from the parliamentary press corps whose main concern was often less to elicit reponses to their questions than to score political points of their own. Togliatti, for example, regularly tangled with Romolo Mangione, a journalist of Social Democratic persuasions who was not above confronting the Communist leader with embarrassing quotations from the PCI press that he had in fact invented himself. But most party spokesmen were happy to strike the sort of aggressive, antagonistic posture that confirmed the prejudices of adversaries and won the applause of supporters who, prior to the later 1960s, were more likely to gather in bars, party sections and recreational centres to cheer on their favourites and comment on their performances than to be watching at home.

The Innovations of the 1980s

An observer transported from the 1960s to the present would find a number of features of Italian election campaigns unchanged. The same parties with more or less the same symbols dominate the political system. The Communists remain the largest opposition party while the Christian Democrats are still the largest force in governmental coalitions that to all intents and purposes reproduce the centre-left alignment first established following the co-optation of the Socialists in 1963. Despite their local government experience and near accession to government office in the late 1970s, the Communists remained a force in the 1980s that both powerful domestic interests and the United States preferred to see in opposition. Despite at least a quarter of a century of on-off collaboration Socialists, Republicans, Liberals, Social Democrats, and Christian Democrats nevertheless all still sought to highlight their separate and distinctive qualities before the electorate. There is continuity also in the forms of campaigning. Although reduced in size and fewer in number, election rallies retain a certain importance in large cities. The last two days of campaigning in Milan in 1983 saw the Republicans and Socialists competing to see which party could draw more people into Piazza Duomo for its closing rally, while the Communists, as always, brought their campaign to a close with a mass rally in Rome's Piazza San Giovanni. The television tribunes are little changed too. Although, since the 1975 reform of RAI, they have been regulated and monitored directly by a Parliamentary Commission of Vigilance in which all parties are represented according to their proportionate strength, RAI-TV's main contribution to the campaign still consists of party secretaries and spokesmen responding to the questions of a panel of newspaper journalists.

Yet the 1980s also saw substantial novelties which an observer from the 1960s would not readily recognize. The activist dimension of political campaigns for example is now much reduced. Although rank-and-file party members still play an important role in distributing leaflets and mobilizing the faithful, they no longer constitute the central vehicle of political communication, the channel through which most citizens would hear about an election and receive encouragement to vote. Instead radio and above all television have come to play the dominant part in distributing information about an election and determining the rhythms of the campaign.

Until the 1970s broadcasting mattered little. The state monopoly radio and television company RAI gave the campaign scarcely any coverage, even in news broadcasts, in accordance with a tradition of maximum depoliticization that marked all official media from the late 1940s. The *Tribune* were eagerly followed in part because they were exceptional moments, a rare chance to hear politicians speak directly on screen. Since the mid-1970s this has changed and RAIs three channels now offer a variety of opportunities for politicians to speak to the public and to debate with each other. During campaigns the parliamentary commission fixes down to the last second the time every party or list is to be allotted on each channel for its tribune appearances, brief self-managed slots and appeals to vote. However, in addition, current affairs programmes hold debates on specific issues and interview the protagonists of the campaign. It should not be deduced from this that all broadcasting is scrupulously fair. Whereas at one time news broadcasts used to be pro-government but not party-specific, now each of the RAI channels is a party fief. At the best of times news coverage is biased; during election campaigns it becomes blatantly so. Viewers of RAI-1 can expect to see and hear far more about the Christian Democrats than those of RAI-2 and RAI-3, who in any case are accustomed to hearing more about the Socialists and Communists respectively. A viewer of the news on any channel could be forgiven for thinking that no smaller parties existed. Although all appearances by candidates on non-political programmes are formally forbidden during campaigning, the level of party control is such that few are surprised when a prominent Christian Democrat pops up on RAI-1's popular Sunday afternoon show *Domenica in* or a RAI-2 reportage on Eastern Europe includes on-camera comments from a number of well-known Socialists.

A range of less party-dominated, more informal programmes on Italy's private broadcasting networks provide further opportunities for the electorate to compare the merits of the positions of the parties. The most significant innovation of all, however, has been the bombardment of paid spot announcements which all but the smallest parties now inflict on television viewers. Bought in packages at specially reduced rates from the private television entrepreneur Berlusconi, the spots are a form of communication that had no precedent in Italy (or Europe) before the late 1970s.[8] Brash, highly visual, and sometimes rich in production values, they are the most striking sign of the 'Americanization' of Italian politics that traditionalists and some left-wingers were swift to denounce as a regrettable degeneration. However, although they represented a significant innovation in political communication, their adoption did not really strike voters as something exceptional. Commercial television advertising in Italy increased dramatically in the 1980s, altering the people's relationships with images and products, and political parties merely adapted to this, making use of skills and opportunities that were on offer to businesses. However, this development has obviously entailed changes in the way campaigns are planned and conducted. In the 1960s some parties consulted advertisers and media professionals on an *ad hoc* basis. Most memorable, largely for its involuntary humour and the salacious remarks it gave rise to, was the poster campaign devised for the DC in 1963 by the Madison Avenue wizard Dichter which featured a nubile young woman and the slogan 'The DC is twenty years old'. Yet now advertising agencies make a decisive contribution to the formulation of strategies that have not only supplemented existing forms of campaigning but which have tended to displace them altogether. Not only have open-air rallies declined in import-ance and vitality (heckling, for example, has as good as disap-peared) but all activities involving the capillary action of rank-and-file activists have been undermined by the progressive adoption of many of the techniques of political marketing pioneered in the United States.[9] Once the parties had allowed their images to emerge spontaneously from the social processes of which they were a part, but in the 1980s this was much less the case. Private pollsters, image consultants, and agencies all gained a foothold in the political process.

Although each party still prides itself on its own peculiar tradition, the ideological content of election campaigns declined notably in the 1980s. Instead of stressing their traditional identities the parties sought to present themselves in positive terms as the bearers of policies that usually had more specific connotations to them than in the past. One contributory factor here was television, particularly private television, which invited parties and candidates to discuss given issues. But the press was also a factor. In the 1970s Italian newspapers broke out of their conventional political strait-jacket and for the first time began to treat the PCI as a normal component of the political system. Since that time a conscious effort seems to have been made to render the activities of parties and institutions more comprehensible to readerships that, while still low by comparison with other industrialized countries, are no longer as small as they once were. All major newspapers endeavour to play a mediatory role between the public and the political system by identifying themes such as corruption, pollution, and the public sector deficit which require specific responses and which tend to be overlooked in political debate. This agenda-fixing role, quite normal in advanced societies with high levels of social integration and literacy, has only succeeded in part, however, and tends to be performed consistently only by two new newspapers, the liberal left *La Repubblica* and the conservative *Il Giornale*, which both adopt an antagonistic attitude towards the political élite as a whole.

By publishing set-piece interviews with leading politicians and employing snappy headlines and cartoons which conveyed political disputes in terms of contests between individuals, the press undoubtedly contributed to the personalization of politics that was another feature of electioneering in the 1980s. Although the party secretaries still spoke as institutionalized persons in the party-orientated RAI, in other forums (the press, more informal programmes, and the parties' own election strategies) they emerged more forcefully. In a political system that had long seemed immune to personalization leader-figures grew in importance as parties became inextricably bound up in the public mind with their secretaries. Given that the first two politicians to undergo this familiarization, Enrico Berlinguer and Aldo Moro, the protagonists of the 1970s, were both rather remote, aloof figures given to expressing themselves in a dense and at times almost impenetrable political jargon, the hypothesis may be advanced that it was occasioned more by objective factors (the transfer of television-viewing from public places to the private homes, for instance) than subjective ones. But both the Republican Giovanni Spadolini and the Socialist Bettino Craxi, Italy's first two non-Christian Democrat Prime Ministers since 1945, who held office respectively in 1981–2 and 1983–7, achieved an unusually high degree of personal popularity by speaking plainly and seeking to establish a rapport directly with the electorate.[10] Naturally their parties took full account of this in devising their advertising strategies for the 1983 and 1987 election campaigns.

The process of personalization manifested itself at other levels too. The maverick Radical Party was the first to exploit the possibilities of private radio in the 1976 election but dozens of single candidates revised their campaign strategies to take account of it in 1979. The party machines, which conveniently frowned on any sort of individualism that might risk undermining ideological and political cohesion, were compelled to adapt in the light of new communicative possibilities and what were perceived to be the expectations of a growing opinion electorate. In drawing up their lists all parties offered slots in the 1980s to well-known figures from all sectors of civil society: intellectuals, businessmen, trade unionists, journalists, theatre and film directors, local mayors, etc. Although it was in fact a relatively marginal phenomenon, much controversy was caused by the way the parties seemed to compete to field show business personalities. In 1987 for example the veteran pop singers Gino Paoli and Domenico Modugno stood for the PCI and the Radicals respectively, while the PSI fielded the Milanese disc jockey Gerry Scotti and the DC the newscaster Alberto Michelini. The Radicals, who largely pioneered the media event as a political phenomenon during their campaigns on abortion and drugs in the 1970s, caused a sensation by sponsoring the candidature of the Hungarian-born blue-movie star Ilona Staller (Cicciolina). These candidatures were, to be sure, cherries on the cake but their presence obliged less well-known individuals to take vigorous steps to bring themselves to the attention of voters or risk oblivion. Well-connected and well-funded candidates were able to adopt high-profile strategies using local radio, press, and television, which added a new dimension to the growing phenomenon of intra-party competition. For candidates placed low down on their party list who had neither the resources to pay for publicity nor connections in the 'right' places, there often remained little choice but to resort to the sort of stunts William Porter observed in 1983. 'In Arpi, Cicero's homeland, the head of the ticket of the Italian Social Movement made speeches in Latin', he noted, while 'in Trieste, a female independent Communist candidate removed her clothes and harangued citizens on the beach in the nude'. In Verona, one candidate resorted to making speeches from a hot-air balloon.[11]

To sum up so far, the novelties in the practice of electioneering may be said to have involved an altered mass media system, a reduction in the input of conventional activism, a more assertive press, recourse to outside professional assistance by the parties and a greater emphasis on leadership.

The Causes of Change

Underlying these changes are the general processes of development in Italian society. In the period from the mid-1970s, the country underwent a social and economic transformation that made it urbanized and prosperous. This was by no means an even or harmonious process. But by the 1980s the fruits of prosperity had in some measure reached all quarters of society and Italians broadly shared a common pattern of culture and values. Overwhelmingly they received information and entertainment principally through the broadcast media. Consequently old divisions and identities which survived the earlier phases of development, albeit not without modification, began to wane while new ones formed beneath or alongside them. Established parties as a result had to learn to operate in a changed environment and come to terms with new pressures and demands. These processes cannot be examined here but three specific factors must be mentioned if the sources of new patterns of political competition are to be grasped.

In the first place the Italian mass media evolved considerably in the 1970s under the stimulus of social protest and political change. Instead of the instrumental domination of press and broadcasting by the economic élite and the DC that was the norm in the 1950s and 1960s, a more complex relationship emerged in which a wider range of viewpoints was represented and all parties took a share in the management of RAI, including even the Communists after 1976.[12] The most dramatic development, however, was the deregulation of broadcasting following a ruling by the Constitutional Court in 1976. The steady emergence between 1976 and 1984 of a mixed public–private system in which the three RAI channels were matched by three private networks controlled by the construction and advertising based enterpreneur Silvio Berlusconi altered the nature of electoral conflict because it furnished well-funded parties with an unprecedented chance to purchase space for national spot advertising.

Ideological change, social mobility, urbanization, higher standards of education, and the central position won by television in the transmission of information and entertainment all affected the country's complex cleavage structure and weakened the Catholic and Marxist subcultures. This meant that the loyalty vote, once so deeply entrenched as to determine the whole character of the electioneering process, was no longer as solid as it once was. Instead it was the opinion vote, estimated variously to include 20–30 per cent of the electorate, to which parties had to learn to address themselves even if they were mainly concerned to preserve their market share.

The decreasing capacity of the parties to structure and hegemonize public opinion coincided in the late 1970s with a series of reforms which extended party power over the public sphere and witnessed the partial incorporation of the PCI into the mechanisms of the spoils system. This severely compromised the standing of the parties as a whole and contributed to an unprecedented phenomenon of political disaffection which manifested itself in the rise of new anti-establishment parties (the Radicals, the Greens, the northern regional leagues), declining voter participation, and waning audiences for political broadcasts.[13]

It is against this background that the new departures in the communicative strategies of the parties need to be seen. For, as Marcello Fedele has noted, 'the spectacularization of politics appeared for the first time in the 1970s and coincided with a crisis in the representativeness of the whole party system'.[14] Far from being a simple consequence of technological change and new methods of marketing, the new electioneering was the symptom of a crisis in the prestige of the parties. Saddled with reputations that were either tarnished or outdated, and no longer able to mobilize voters on conventional bases, the parties accepted a media logic, abandoning even those reservations over personalization, which had been a strict taboo in an earlier phase of post-fascist democracy. In addition to highlighting leader-figures the parties sought through the media to convey political messages in simpler, more accessible terms. It remains to be assessed whether the conversion was a genuine one, motivated by a desire to establish a new relationship with a profoundly changed civil society, or whether it was more a cosmetic change motivated by a desire to preserve existing arrangements by means of the introduction of new tricks.

The Parties, the Political System, Political Communication

In the late 1980s new forms of campaign technology were widely adopted. While several parties consulted individual advertisers in 1983, commercial advertising agencies entered the fray only in 1987. Not only the Socialists and Christian Democrats drew on their services but also the small centre parties and even the Greens, despite very limited resources. Of the major parties, only the Communists went against the trend by making minimum use of television (ostensibly to avoid giving money to Berlusconi). Instead, by means of traditional activist forms of campaigning, supplemented by posters and newspaper advertisements, they tried to portray themselves as a party that was 'far removed from the intrigues, close to the citizens'. However, after dropping three percentage points in 1987, even the PCI began to show itself to be receptive to new tools of communication. It ran a successful media campaign in the 1989 European elections in which spot announcements were used sometimes featuring a new-born baby (to convey the 'new PCI' unveiled at the March 1989 party congress) and on other occasions the party leader Achille Occhetto. To the consternation of some, it actually organized its campaign around the personal qualities of its leading candidates (especially where these were popular mayors) in the local elections of 1990.[15]

The party which did most to pioneer the techniques of modern political communication in Italy was the PSI. It skilfully used new techniques in the early 1980s to gain media attention, constructing an image of modernity, dynamism, efficiency, and vitality, and breaking a pattern of political debate focused largely on the DC and PCI. Thus it was well placed to conduct a high-profile campaign in 1987. Devised by the Armando Testa agency, it focused heavily on the party's forceful leader Bettino Craxi as it had done in 1983. Although the party's slogan was 'Il PSI cresce l'Italia' ('Italy has grown with the PSI'), it was Craxi whose portrait appeared above it on billboards throughout the country and who featured in the simulated interviews that constituted the bulk of the party's spot announcements. These were incessant and repetitive in their identification of the PSI with the period of stability and economic growth over which Craxi had presided as Prime Minister. From the sheer quantity of Socialist spot announcements the party might be thought to have simply adopted a strategy of indiscriminate image bombardment. In fact it was more sophisticated. It aimed to appeal to television viewers as a whole (one of its secondary slogans 'perhaps a carnation would suit *you*' explicitly invited voters to consider switching to the PSI) but in a differentiated fashion: in the morning messages specific to pensioners were broadcast, at midday to housewives, in the afternoon and early evening to young people, and only in the evening to the electorate as a whole.

The one party to compete with the PSI in terms of the visibility and professionalism of its campaign was the DC. Still smarting from its loss of six percentage points in 1983 and aware that it would face stiff competition from a PSI aiming to siphon off votes from both the conventionally dominant parties, the DC called on the services of the Italian affiliate of Jacques Séguéla's French-based multinational advertising agency RSCG, which had devised Mitterrand's highly successful 'La force tranquille' campaign in 1981. The result was a campaign based on extensive market research, in which no Christian Democratic politician appeared (least of all Craxi's chief antagonist Ciriaco De Mita); it aimed to activate the most primary secularized motivations for identification with the party. With slogans such as 'Forza Italia' ('Come on, Italy') and 'Fai vincere le cose che contano' ('make the things that matter count') it presented itself as a modern party firmly rooted in the texture of everyday values shared by most ordinary Italians. Its posters and spot announcements, richly coloured like the commercials for Barilla pasta and Il Mulino biscuits, featured peasants leaving for the fields at dawn, school-children singing, happy young people, family birthdays, and country weddings. All this was accompanied by a mixed male and female Coca Cola style chorus, emotively orchestrated by Ennio Morricone, singing the following refrain 'For a smile, for freedom, for a great dream of love, for a life full of calm, for your home and job and the future of your children—Come on Italy! Come on Italy! Come on Italy!' Rigorously pre-political in its imagery, the campaign aimed to remind voters of the DC's basic character as a solid, down-to-earth, moderate party in contrast with the cynical yuppie-type values of the PSI.

These two campaigns were both judged to have been successful by media professionals and the politicians (Craxi attributed 1 per cent of the PSI's 2.5 per cent increase to the Testa agency's posters and spot announcements).[16] However, generally speaking, the parties have not adapted well to the exigences of the new media-style campaigning. The smaller parties were awkward and hesitant in 1987, lurching from inappropriate negative advertising in the case of the PLI ('Free yourself of them'—i.e., the other parties—

'Vote Liberal') and the PRI ('When two argue'—i.e. DC and PSI—'the PRI takes over the driving position') to the brash personalization of the Social Democrats' uninspiring leader Franco Nicolazzi. The notoriously clientelistic PSDI perhaps strained the credence of the electorate more than any other party by calling in one announcement for a higher standard of ethics in public office (like his predecessor Nicolazzi was forced to resign a year later, after becoming embroiled in a bribery scandal). The same awkwardness and naïvety could be seen in the performances on local television of single candidates for parliament or council posts in the late 1980s. In the Autumn of 1989 *La Repubblica's* television critic wrote as follows after viewing a compilation of spot announcements broadcast during the campaign for the Rome city council elections:

We have seen personal advertisements, sometimes very amateurish, of the most varied candidates. The candidate Portoghesi who promised (or threatened) to sort out the problems of the periphery by building lots of beautiful squares. The populist candidate who, after having cracked out the slogan 'a man among the people, a man for the people' turned to his small son to ask him 'Isn't it true, Matteo?', and the child gravely assented. The culturist candidate who asked loudly 'Culture?', and provided his own reply. 'Yes please', as though he was discussing an aperitif. The efficiency candidate who showed himself playing tennis during a pause in the electoral battle: young modern, dynamic, probably a manager. The obliging television journalist who met the candidate Carraro and asked him obsequiously: 'Minister Carraro? Manager? Rome needs a manager, doesn't it?'[17]

In another incident a candidate hit on the idea of using a polystyrene copy of Rome's Mouth of Truth monument as a backdrop for his live broadcast. The effect was spoiled when it fell to the ground, striking him on the head.

It is not surprising that there should have been difficulties, resistances, and inconsistencies in the conversion to modern media-orientated demands and modes of communication. Even in the behaviour of the two parties whose campaigns were best co-ordinated and directed there were contradictions and anomalies. The reasons are bound up with the nature of the political system and the ingrained habits of the parties. Indeed it may be argued that there were profound structural obstacles in the political system to the sort of procedures and expectations that were generated by the broadcast and print media. In their attention both to the personality of leaders and candidates, and in their efforts to focus discussion on themes deemed to be of interest to voters, they appeared to present political contests as though they were being fought along bipolar lines. Given that the United States is widely viewed as the home of norms of media behaviour as well as modern techniques of political marketing this is perhaps inevitable, but a 'media logic' conceived in these terms clashed with a political culture and institutional framework organized on the basis of quite different premises. Let us look at these points in a little more detail.

The stress on personality, on image, and on the individual qualities of candidates was favoured by the press and by television. In particular the informal, chat-show style election programmes of Canale 5 and Rete 4 (*Elettorando, Volti e voti, Onorevoli signore* etc.) drew attention to the interviewee rather than the party. This obviously met certain entertainment or 'human interest' criteria. Yet it had little to do with the dynamics of a parliamentary system based on proportional representation in which the key actors were parties whose ideological attachments and support bases were still strong. On the whole the parties disapproved of the practice of presenting single candidates on television as autonomous individuals but there was little they could do to prevent it. Why then did some parties themselves accept the role of personality at the top level and play on the way they became associated with their secretaries in the public mind? It can be said that the personalization of the leader was embraced as a campaign device where decline was impending or expansion deemed to be possible and where the secretary was proved to enjoy a higher personal standing in the polls than his party. Yet even where it occurred it did so within strict limits. Craxi, for example, was the first Italian politician to employ an image consultant. Not only did he change the symbol of his party in 1978 from the hammer and sickle to a red carnation but he himself deliberately dressed unconventionally (for a politician) in jeans and open-necked shirts. When he became Prime Minister in 1983 he wore managerial dark suits. By his assertive manner and plain speaking he won a regular place in newspaper headlines and satirical cartoons. Craxi's wife, Anna, also broke with the conventional veil drawn over the private and family lives of politicians and performed a 'first lady' role even to the point of being dressed free of charge by the designers Trussardi and Versace.

Yet Craxi did not present himself as a free-floating individual; rather he identified himself closely with the PSI. He was careful to be seen regularly wearing or holding a carnation and he also made a point of referring regularly to the democratic reformist tradition of his party and quoting figures from its pantheon like Filippo Turati and Bruno Buozzi.

A further area of tension between the media and the political system concerns issues. Both the visual and print media endeavour to raise practical themes deemed to be of interest to voters and in so doing they create an expectation that political conflict will take place over programmes. Yet because Italian politics is coalitional, and there are no institutional or electoral incentives such as those operative in France or Germany to encourage parties to form coalitions before elections, the decisive matter in any contest tends not to concern policy issues but political issues: who will lead the coalition and for how long? Should there be an explicit pact? Must it involve the same parties as before? Are any alternatives possible? These matters used to be secondary to the ideological conflict between the DC and PCI but since the Socialists adopted a more assertive line the sharpest conflicts have been between the DC and the PSI. These dominated the election of 1983 and even more so that of 1987. Because the press and television have only a very limited measure of autonomy from the political system and, indeed, are still largely subordinate to it, they have little choice but to register this primacy, albeit sometimes with ill grace. As Paolo Mancini has written, the function of the press, and sometimes television, is for Italian politicians primarily 'negotiational', i.e. they use the media to communicate with each other more than the electorate.[18] To simplify this form of communication and render it comprehensible, television and the press tend to personalize it, writing up the 1987 campaign for example as a struggle between Craxi and the DC secretary De Mita. Yet there are limits to how far the reality of a contest can be made to conform to this 'fictional' form. Despite the media's insistence on the De Mita-Craxi duel, the pair resisted all offers from Berlusconi's Fininvest company to stage a face-to-face debate before the television cameras. To this day the only such debate to have occurred in Italy was between Berlinguer and De Mita during the 1983 campaign. Broadcast on Rete 4, the transmission was notable for two things: first the two party leaders opted to address each other using the formal *Lei* mode instead of the familiar *tu* form by which politicians usually address each other; second the outcome of the cautious and civilized discussion was generally held to have been a draw.[19]

The importance of modern techniques of communication long went unrecognized by the Italian political élite and even today the scepticism towards advertising, market research, polling, and image-building is well-rooted. The parties had long held the masses in thrall; they had filled the country's squares over decades and mobilized huge rallies whenever the occasion demanded. Political leaders considered themselves to be the great communicators. They were therefore highly sceptical of the need for recourse to marketing techniques. Moreover, because politics had always been considered a voluntary activity, the input of professionals was seen as poisonous and unnecessary, part of a conspiracy to turn the political party into a soap bar (*partito-saponetta*).[20]

These views were perhaps held most strongly in the PCI. As the mass party *par excellence*, it was more deeply attached than others to the pedagogical style of propaganda that had been the norm in the 1950s and 1960s. Its whole apparatus was geared not towards communication with a volatile opinion electorate but rather towards the needs of a relatively stable network of militants, supporters, and sympathizers. As a result not only was there internal opposition to anything which smacked of 'Americanization' but there were structural difficulties in adapting to new forms of electoral competition. In the first place the size of the party did not help it to compete in the costly field of television advertising because all its resources were taken up by the running of an enormous machine staffed by 2,500 full-time officials (in addition to loss-making newspapers, magazines, and publishing enterprises). Secondly, the PCI in any case had a particularly 'heavy' identity well-established in the public mind, that had certainly undergone modifications since 1948, but which could scarcely be altered by a few eye-catching spot announcements. Thirdly, as a force with a global ideological perspective it was not well-attuned to the issue-based politics favoured in the media.[21] Yet in the 1980s some changes did occur. The PCI sought to turn itself outwards, using mass culture and its celebrated political festivals to communicate with broader strands of the population. It broke with the practice of publicizing only the party label in elections and used telephone canvassing, direct mail shots, and advertisements in the mainstream press to reach potential voters and supporters who would be unlikely to come into contact with the party apparatus or the Marxist subculture.

Even in the case of a party like the PSI, which appeared to have absorbed the lessons of political marketing, experts remained substantially external to the decision-making process. The Socialists had a clear communicative strategy based on Craxi and two or three other spokesmen and they turned party conferences into US-style conventions whose main purpose was to launch the party image. With their razzmatazz, futuristic scenographies designed by the architect Panseca, uniformed hostesses, and orchestrated adoration of the leader, these occasions made a notable impact. Despite all this the PSI leadership kept control of the planning and execution of election campaigns; although the Testa agency had a major input in 1987 it was called in at short notice and given a narrow brief. What this suggests is that the figure of the political consultant and a fully-fledged conception of political marketing are likely to remain unknown in Italy. In a system with highly structured parties in which the mass media are subordinate to the political élite, the most that can occur is for parties to draw on the expertise of specialists deemed to belong to their 'area'.[22] But even this is limited, first by the concern of the apparatus to perform as many strategic functions itself, even to the point of training its own technical personnel,[23] and second by the reluctance to admit publicly or even express generic approval for the use of image advisers and the like even though such people in reality are consulted not infrequently.[24] The only professional category independent of party that the parties are happy to draw on interchangeably is that of commercial advertising agencies such as Testa, RSCG, Young and Rubicam, etc., which indicates that electoral aesthetics is the area in which most change has occurred.

One feature not examined hitherto is opinion polls. In bipolar and presidential systems these provide a key tool whereby the press and television create news, interpret the mood of the electorate, and force the parties or candidates to adjust their strategies. The virtual impossibility of indicating accurately and regularly the level of support for the parties in a highly complex multi-party system such a Italy where voting patterns are relatively stable and shifts on the whole small, confirms the pre-eminence of the political system over the mass-media system. In fact polling has been carried out since the war by the Gallup affiliate DOXA and, in the last twenty-five years or so, by a range of other organizations (Demoskopea, SWG, etc.). But only in the last fifteen years have newspapers been willing to commission them from time to time, not least because of their very mixed record. In 1976 the polls forecast the advance of the PCI but not that of the DC. In 1979 they were broadly accurate in their predictions of the outcome. On the strength of this a range of publications (*Il Giornale*, *La Repubblica*, *Panorama*) used polls in 1983. Yet they proved to be wildly inaccurate, failing to foresee the big drop in DC support, the very modest rise in PSI strength, and the substantial continuity in PCI votes. Inevitably therefore they were used very warily in 1987. Of national newspapers, only *La Repubblica* presented the specially commissioned polls as news items. Once again the predictions were wrong. Whereas the PRI and PCI were seen to be on the increase and the DC destined to drop points, both the former two parties fell back while the DC held its position and the PSI advanced a couple of points. There are only two areas in which polling organizations have made a contribution to the electoral process. By indicating the popularity ratings of politicians and public attitudes on specific questions, they have keyed in with the broader trend towards personalization and issue-orientated politics. In this sense they are also used by some parties which employ organizations close to them (Eurisko for the DC, Macno for the PSI) to keep a check on the situation. In addition DOXA performs an important role on the post-election Monday afternoon when, after one and a half days of voting, its projections of overall results based on a small sample of precincts furnish the basis for discussion on the continuous broadcasts staged by each of RAI's three channels. Furnished in advance of the first meaningful results supplied by the Interior Ministry, and often contemporaneously with the assessments of the PCI's experts, DOXA's projections constitute part of a show involving entertainers, politicians, and commentators.

It is open to doubt whether even the high profile media strategies of the PSI and the DC have contributed much to the electoral fortunes of the two parties. Despite the positive comments of some Socialists there is no evidence that the party's recent successes owe anything to its electoral communications. Indeed there are grounds for supposing that these have had at best a very limited impact. One reason for this is that the opinion electorate, which is mainly

northern, urbanized, and educated, would seem to be least susceptible to the charm of commercials of the type that have been
adopted. This category of voters is not devoid of ideological and
cultural characteristics, as sometimes seems to be assumed, and it
is concerned with social and moral questions in addition to
economics. Not surprisingly the Greens and the Radicals have
emerged due to its support.

The image of a party can be supervised and 'constructed' only to
a certain extent. It is the sum not just of actions, statements, events,
and personalities which the leadership seeks to bring to public
attention, but of the totality of events and reactions that it is
implicated in. Thus the image of modernity cultivated by the
Socialists has been compromised by the party's eagerness to join
with the DC in dividing up the public sector into spheres of
influence and its involvement in a variety of corruption scandals at
local level.

Although the press and the broadcast media have served to
render visible aspects of the electoral process in Italy that were
once hidden from view, it would be wrong to imagine that they
have heralded 'modernization' in any unambiguous sense. On the
contrary, in two ways media techniques have reinforced traditional
practices. First, because commercial advertising is often crudely
associated with modernity in Italy, parties have been able to seize
on new opportunities for political communication to build images
(based on personality, dynamism, etc.) that serve to recycle the old
in a new, more attractive form without usually undertaking any
substantive change. Second, creation of the expectation that, in
addition to parties, candidates will conduct multi-media publicity
campaigns has raised the costs of electioneering enormously.[25] The
competition for preference votes necessitates independent financing
which in some zones may be acquired by mobilizing the support of
an interest group or base association or in others by the clandestine
'purchase' of packets of votes by means of favours, promises or, in
parts of Sicily, Calabria, and Campania, alliances with organized
crime.

The exchange vote has long been corrupted by the simplest and
most basic of bribes. In the fifties the shipping magnate and
Monarchist Party mayor of Naples Achille Lauro used to distribute
one half of a pair of shoes to the subproletarian inhabitants of the
city's Spanish quarter on the eve of elections, promising that the

other half would be made available in the aftermath of a positive result. In other cities, packets of pasta were quite regularly distributed at political rallies. This sort of practice has for the most part been eliminated or rendered more sophisticated, but not always. In the Rome city council election in 1989 one shop in the San Lorenzo quarter offered two packets of pasta, one litre of olive oil, two cans of tomatoes, and half a kilo of coffee free of charge to every registered inhabitant. Those accepting this unusual offer found in their bags a ticket urging electors to vote for the Socialist Sandro Tinto and also (much to the party's annoyance when the episode finished up in the press) the PSI number one Franco Carraro.[26]

It is common for ministers and influential deputies to build up a block of supporters by supplying and promising favours, supplemented by the support of those who have benefited from a legislative measure or well-directed public spending initiative (or hope to do so) and accords with the heads of hospitals, sports associations, and business groups able to deliver the votes of those under them. In the bitter comedy film *Il Portaborse* (The Lackey), released in 1991, the protagonist, an unscrupulous young minister, adds two further dimensions to his campaign: a deliberate image of dynamism and modernity presented on television and electoral fraud. The film may be a caricature, but it was accurate enough in its portrayal of cynicism and malpractice to draw howls of protest from outraged politicians.[27]

For the larger government parties electoral volatility can be countered to some extent by clientelism, which is a crucial pillar of the DC's system of power. In the south of the country, and to a lesser extent in the north, it is a mass structure capable of delivering huge blocks of votes. The existence of this structure also helps the party preserve its control over representatives who might otherwise be carried away in their individual coalition-building. Given that the DC has lost support in the north and grown in the south, and that the PSI's increase has been mainly concentrated in the south, it can be legitimately argued that this response to the waning of the loyalty vote was ultimately more significant than the adoption of campaign methods geared to the opinon vote in terms of the results it delivered. For these two parties, spot advertising, homely slogans, avuncular images, and showbusiness sparkle served to conceal old practices rather than move beyond them. In less sophisticated campaigns such as that of the Social Democrats in 1987 the link between clientelism and modernity was almost explicit. In one advertisement Nicolazzi stepped out of a black limousine to be asked by a journalist, 'What will become of the young people?' 'The young?', replied Nicolazzi, waving his arm and heading off towards a large official-looking building, 'Tell them to come with me.'

Conclusion

At the root of new forms of electoral campaigning in Italy stand social and political changes. Gradually, and in recent years more rapidly, old identities have been eroded under the impact of social and economic development and the resulting élite changes and responses. Political militancy has declined and social life has become less ideologically determined. Italy has also become a television and media-saturated society. All this hit old campaign methods geared to a loyalty vote that, while still strong, has been eroded at the margins and is less central to the electoral process. Although they were frequently reluctant to do so, the parties have added new electioneering techniques to old ones in order to present themselves attractively to a changed electorate. In provoking specific innovations the earthquake in broadcasting was crucial. But more important still was the sharp drop in the prestige and representativeness of the established parties from the late 1970s. Indeed the demise of the state's monopoly over broadcasting was arguably one of the first tangible products of this crisis.

Unquestionably the parties have been affected by the new terms of campaigning. A younger generation of media-literate men and women, at ease in a television studio and at home with modern visual communication, now run the media campaigns of the major parties. Sometimes they are shunted to one side by the real power-brokers once a contest is over but by no means always, as their skills are increasingly seen to be of use even outside electoral moments. Yet new techniques have not just signalled change. Their adoption has also been a way of renewing politics without respond-ing to demands for more fundamental reform in institutional practices, public policy, and the forms of political competition. To describe the 'spectacularization' of politics as a whole in these terms would be an exaggeration. For changes in political communication can never simply be a mask. If only to a small extent, they affect the substance of political conflict. But the cosmetic factor was certainly part of the process. Most of the parties, in different ways, were locked into patterns of conduct that they were unwilling to revise. None truly accepted a logic of communication as the central and exclusive factor in its electoral strategy. Instead convenient elements were absorbed and put to use to shore up or supplement old practices or, more frequently, to supply a necessary and otherwise improbable image of modernity. For the government parties, experiments in political marketing have been just one response to their declining appeal and to the difficulties experienced by the PCI since the late 1970s on the planes of culture, ideology, organization, and politics. They have been mixed with a more serious and far-reaching expansion in clientelism, which in some cities of the south has been used as a deliberate strategy to undermine the loyalty vote of the PCI. In such zones, where the stakes involved in the mixture of business and politics are high, electoral malpractices and ballot-rigging are not unknown.

Does this mean that it is impossible to discuss the Americanization of electioneering in Italy? The impression cultivated both by exponents of political marketing and its detractors is that the adoption of the techniques associated with it leads inevitably to a political system assuming in the long run the characteristics of American-style moderate bipolarism. In relation to Italy this view has been dismissed on the grounds that not only are the history, cultures, and ideological composition of the political system very different from America but the institutional structure and electoral system are too. But this does not mean that Americanization is therefore meaningless as a concept. On the contrary, precisely the point about it is that it is ambiguous, often incomplete, and unpredictable in its consequences. In the political field, the filtering role of the receiving country's procedures, customs, and institutions is invariably so pronounced that techniques and even strategies pioneered in the United States can be emptied of any ideological content and adopted by any type of political force. The meaning of Americanization therefore can only be determined by carefully examining the impact of these in specific contexts. Whereas in some instances external inputs may contribute to dynamic innovations occurring at a variety of levels, in others, such as Italy, they may have a very different connotation, reinforcing and perpetuating old practices in a revised form.

Notes

1. C. Marletti, 'Ascesa e ridimensionamento delle politiche di immagine nei partiti (1974–1984)', in G. Pasquino (ed.), *Mass media e sistema politico* (Milan: Franco Angeli, 1986), 104.

2. It is not possible here to list all the contributions to the debate on changing patterns of political communication in Italy. Of particular interest are the following: C. Marletti, 'Il "Potere dei media": sulla crescente interazione fra communicazione e politica', *Il Mulino*, 32/288 (1983), 580–98; G. Bechelloni, 'Una campagna elettorale "nuova" produce risultati "vecchi"?', *Problemi dell'informazione*, 8/4 (1983), 533–51; P. Mancini, 'La propaganda elettorale negli stati Uniti', *Il Mulino*, 33/291 (1984), 56–76; G. Pasquino, 'I mass media e la communicazione politica' in id., *La complessità della politica* (Bari: Laterza, 1985); G. Statera, 'Vecchi e nuovi modelli di communicazione politica: dalla politica degli apparati alla politica spettacolo', in Pasquino, *Mass media e sistema politico*; 'Introduzione' to P. Mancini (ed.), *Come vincere le elezioni: le campagne elettorali negli Stati Uniti* (Bologna: Il Mulino, 1988); G. Pasquino, 'Alto sgradimento: la communicazione politica dei partiti', *Problemi dell'informazione*, 3/4 (1988), 477–97; P. Mancini, 'Tra di noi: sulla funzione negoziale della communicazione politica', *Il Mulino*, 39/328 (1990), 267–87.

3. Compare S. Gundle, 'L'americanizzazione del quotidiano: televisione e consumismo nell'Italia degli anni Cinquanta', *Quaderni storici*, 21/62 (1986), 561–94 (pp. 564–9). Of particular relevance to the debate on Americanization are 'L'America arriva in Italia', a monographic issue of *Quaderni storici*, 20/58 (1985); P. D'Attore (ed.), *Nemici per la pelle: sogno americano e mito sovietico nell'Italia contemporanea* (Milan: Franco Angeli, 1991) (see esp. the chapters by D'Attorre, Wanrooij, Ventrone, Gundle) and D. W. Ellwood (ed.), *Hollywood in Europa 1945–60* (Florence: Ponte alle grazie, 1991).

4. A. Parisi and G. Pasquino, 'Relazioni partiti-elettori e tipi di voto' in G. Pasquino (ed.), *Il sistema politico italiano* (Bari: Laterza, 1985).

5. In fact recent research suggests that electoral behaviour in Italy was much less static than has usually been supposed, but because much of the vote-switching was self-cancelling an overall stability was maintained. See P. Corbetta, A. Parisi, and H. Schadee, *Elezioni in Italia*

(Bologna: Il Mulino, 1988) and M. Caciagli and A. Spreafico (eds.), *Vent'anni di elezioni in Italia 1968–1987* (Padua: Liviana, 1990).

6. The *tribune politiche* were organized rather like press conferences. Only one politician was usually present at each broadcast and he responded to the questions of the journalists, who had a chance usually to ask no more than two questions and two supplementary questions. The moderator took no active part.

7. A. Gismondi, *L'Unità*, 22 Aug. 1963; see the page of articles re-evoking the event published in *L'Unità*, 15 Oct. 1990.

8. See P. Martini, 'Molti affari, molta politica: nei rapporti con i partiti il lato forte di Berlusconi', *Problemi dell'informazione*, 15/4 (1990), 513–28, p. 525.

9. See D. Masi, *Come 'vendere' un partito* (Milan: Lupetti & Co., 1989).

10. Prior to Spadalini and Craxi no Prime Minister received an approval rating that was lower than 26% or higher than 40%. P. Luzzatto-Fegiz, 'Political Opinion Polling in Italy', in R. Worcester (ed.), *Political Opinion Polling: An International Review* (London: Macmillan, 1983), 143.

11. W. Porter, 'The Mass Media in the Italian Elections of 1983', in H. Penniman (ed.), *Italy at the Polls, 1983* (Durham N. Carolina: AEI/Duke University Press, 1987). 146.

12. As far as the treatment of social and political questions was concerned the post-reform arrangements had two effects. First, news reporting became more competitive and coverage was widened. Second, political reporting generally became less orientated towards the government and more orientated towards the parties but without losing any of its starchiness and linguistic indigestibility. Indeed, in some areas including electoral broadcasting, the situation was actually worsened. In the wake of the reform the timid experimentation of the early 1970s (in two programmes, *Dibattito aperto* and *Tribuna popolare* members of the public and trade unionists were invited to ask questions instead of members of the parliamentary press corps) was terminated and the original formula rendered rigid and artificial by parties keen to avoid the slightest possible chance of embarrassment ('We do not want to win in the tribunes, but above all we do not want to lose' one politician told their organizer, Jader Jacobelli). See J. Jacobelli, 'Le elezioni sui teleschermi', *Problemi dell'informazione*, 7/4 (1983), 497–509.

13. Given that voting is semi-compulsory and turn-out has stayed consistently high in the post-war years, the parties have not had to worry unduly about physically getting voters to the polling stations. However, turn-out declined from a peak of 90.9 per cent to 84.5 per cent between 1976 and 1987 while the numbers of blank and spoiled

ballots increased from approximately one million between 1958 and 1976 to over two million in 1983 and 1987.

14. M. Fedele, 'Il problema delle "reti effettive" nei processi di communicazione politica', in Pasquino, *Mass media e sistema politico*, 85.

15. See the article by Alfredo Sandri of the regional secretariat of the PCI in *L'Unità* (Emilia-Romagna suppl.), 27 Mar. 1990. Significantly it is entitled 'E "americana" la campagna elettorale del PCI?'.

16. Masi, *Come 'vendere' un partito*, 88. Masi, and G. Calvi and G. Minoia, *Gli scomunicanti: la pubblicità politica com' è e come potrebbe essere* (Milan: Lupetti & Co., 1990) offer professional assessments of the various parties' campaigns.

17. *La Repubblica*, 4 Nov. 1989.

18. Mancini, 'Tra di noi'.

19. Organized by Rete 4 when it was still owned by Mondadori, the debate was published the day after it was broadcast in *La Repubblica*, also owned by the group.

20. Calvi and Minoia, *Gli scomunicanti*, 11–21.

21. On the problem of the mass party and especially the PCI, see Pasquino, 'I mass media e la comunicazione politica' and G. Grossi, *Rappresentanza e reppresentazione: percorsi di analisi dell'interazoine fra mass media e sistema politico in Italia* (Milan: Franco Angeli, 1985), ch. 3.

22. Calvi and Minoia, *Gli scomunicanti*, 103–4.

23. For example the PCI held a *stage* on modern political communications for its local and regional cadres at the 1990 National *L'Unità* festival in Modena. Its title was 'Propaganda addio'.

24. See the interviews on this topic with leading politicians published in July 1991 in *L'Unità*.

25. In 1985 the journalist Giorgio Bocca estaimated that 500 million lire were needed to secure election as a deputy and 300 million as a local councillor. Many candidates spend far more than this. In 1987 Mino Martinazzoli was calculated to have spent 1,000 million lire and his DC colleagues Goria and Formigoni 5,000 million lire each (although the latter admitted only to costs of 250 million). F. Cazzola, *Della corruzione* (Bologna: Il Mulino 1988), 153–4.

26. *La Repubblica*, 22 Oct. 1989.

27. The film, a great success at the box office, was seen to have been influential in the result of the May 1991 referendum in which a majority voted to abolish the system of multiple preference voting (widely regarded as a source of corruption). Instead voters will only be able to express one preference.

References

In addition to the materials cited in the text, the following works contain much useful information on electioneering in Italy. Two journals which regularly publish analyses of political campaigning and communication are *Il Mulino* and (with special reference to the mass media) *Problemi dell' informazione*.

Alberoni, F. *et al.*, *L'attivista di partito: un' indagine sui militanti di base nel PCI e nella DC* (Bologna: Il Mulino, 1967).

Baranski, Z. and Lumley R., *Culture and Conflict in Postwar Italy* (London: Macmillan, 1990).

Cheli, E. *et al.*, *Elezioni in TV: dalle tribune alla pubblicità—la campagna elettorale del 1987* (Milan: Franco Angeli, 1989).

Facchi, P. (ed.), *La propaganda politica in Italia* (Bologna: Il Mulino, 1960).

Galli, G., *Il bipartitismo imperfetto: communisti e democristiani in Italia* (Bologna: Il Mulino, 1966).

Ginsborg, P., *A History of Contemporary Italy: Society and Politics 1943–1988* (Harmondsworth: Penguin, 1990).

Jacobelli, J. (ed.), *La comunicazione politica in Italia* (Bari: Laterza, 1989).

Manoukian, A. (ed.), *La presenza sociale del PCI e della DC* (Bologna: Il Mulino, 1968).

Penniman, H. (ed.), *Italy at the Polls 1976* (Washington, DC: AEI 1977).

—— (ed.), *Italy at the Polls 1979* (Durham: Duke University Press/AEI, 1979).

—— (ed.), *Italy at the Polls 1983* (Durham: Duke University Press/AEI, 1987).

Statera, G., *La politica spettacolo* (Milan: Mondadori, 1986).

Tinacci Mannelli, G. and Cheli E., *L'immagine del potere: comportamenti, atteggiamenti e strategie d' immagine dei leader politici italiani* (Milan: Franco Angeli, 1986).

10

Scandinavia

PETER ESAIASSON

Whatever horrors World War II brought to the Scandinavian countries it did civilize electioneering. As things returned to normal after the war the democratic parties agreed upon certain practical rules of the game. In Sweden the common belief in democracy was manifested in unanimous decisions to cut down on the distribution of printed pamphlets, to begin the putting up of posters at a fixed day five weeks before the election, and to grant every party equal rations of petrol. Similar agreements were made in Denmark and Norway. Only in Finland was the situation different. The country's dramatic history, its special relations with the Soviet Union and its strong Communist Party, made a climate of basic trust between the main political actors a virtual impossibility.[1]

A characteristic of the early post-war election campaigns in Scandinavia was the strong position of the political parties. The daily papers were closely tied to a specific party and could be relied upon to render supportive service in editorials as well as in news coverage, whereas the state-regulated radio provided every party with a new and far-reaching channel for campaigning. Through political meetings the parties could address a large percentage of the electorate directly. Organized interest groups of workers, farmers, and employers contributed money and personnel. Having long-term commitments to a party, many voters had decided how to vote long before the election. The main object of the campaigns was to motivate the party's supporters to turn basic commitments into actual votes.

Half a century later the Scandinavian parties have lost their firm

The author would like to thank Lars Bille, Tor Bjørklund, Mikael Gilljam, Tom Moring, Bo Reimer, Henry Valen, and Anders Widfeldt for valuable suggestions and comments.

control over the formation of political opinion. The media no longer function as passive megaphones. Public meetings have ceased to draw major crowds. Organized interests have started to act independently during the campaigns. Increasingly volatile voters can no longer be counted on as guaranteed supporters. This general development has occurred throughout the world, but the rate of change seems to have been unusually high in Scandinavia.

Important Election Campaigns

During the past two decades the importance of Scandinavian election campaigns has increased significantly. One indicator illustrating the development is the size of the floating vote. In the 1950s only 7–10 per cent of Norwegian or Swedish voters changed party between elections. Today, the number of party switchers has passed the 20 per cent level in Norway and Sweden as well as in Denmark. The most dramatic increase in the floating vote took place in the early 1970s, although Norway reached an all-time high in the election of 1989 (30 per cent).

A parallel development can be found regarding the voters' timing of party choice. Since the 1950s the number of voters reporting that they made their voting decision during the election campaign has more than doubled (in the latest elections 20–40 per cent in all Scandinavian countries). Furthermore, in Denmark and Sweden the voters' attachment to the parties has declined since the late 1960s. Thus, there is more at stake in today's Scandinavian election campaigns than in the battles of the 1950s and early 1960s.[2]

Another factor underlining the growing importance of the campaigns is the decreasing correlation between class and partisanship. Scandinavia, traditionally one of the strongholds of class-based electoral behaviour, has seen a trend towards increased issue voting. As the voters become more sensitive to specific issues it is more crucial for the parties to influence the agenda of the election debate.[3]

The Legal Framework

There are few legal restrictions on electioneering in Scandinavia. For instance, the parties, as well as the individual candidates, are free to spend any sum of money they can raise during the campaigns. However, there have been some changes of the parliamentary electoral systems and the administration of voting procedures with consequences for the election campaigns. (The regulation of election broadcasts will be discussed later.)

In the early 1950s, Sweden, Denmark, and Norway replaced the d'Hondt proportional method for allocation of seats to parties in multi-member constituencies with a modified version of the Sainte-Laguë method (using 1.4 as the first divisor). The logic behind this change was to make it less profitable for the parties to join in electoral alliances (and to guarantee the continuous under-representation of the small Communist parties).[4]

Denmark in 1953 and Sweden in 1970 abolished their Upper Chamber, thereby making the formation of government directly dependent upon the election outcome. Since the government can no longer get along by leaning on support in the upper chamber— a strategy that for a long time secured the power position for the Swedish Social Democrats—every single election has become more important.

A third change with consequences for election campaigns lies in the introduction of legal threshold rules for the gaining of parliamentary representation (2 per cent of the national vote in Denmark, 4 per cent in Norway and in Sweden). Having small parties oscillating about the magic threshold has increased the incentives for tactical voting.

Taken together, the changes in the electoral systems have added to the increasing importance of the election campaigns. Since they have to choose between a number of parties with different chances of gaining parliamentary seats, the voters are offered an increasing amount of political stimuli. The parties, in their turn, are more motivated to involve themselves in attractive issues.

As far as electoral systems go, Finland is a deviant case. First, only the Finnish people elect a President (with a six-year term). The presidential candidates, who are sponsored by the parties, do campaign on their own, but they are in no way as active as their counterparts in France and the United States.

Secondly, the Finnish parliamentary electoral system offers the voters a decisive influence on the ordering of party candidates. Indeed, the voter casts his vote exclusively for a candidate, the party's total vote being the sum of the votes for its candidates. This provides for a decentralized campaign with a fair amount of within-party competition, a political element practically unknown in Norway and Sweden.[5] Since the introduction in 1978 of compulsory primary elections for the selection of candidates, the tendency towards individually orientated campaigns has been increased. It is only in Finland that well-known sport stars and media personalities can rocket into parliament.[6]

The most important Scandinavian experiment in the administration of voting procedures concerns advance voting. In 1969 the Swedish Riksdag decided to allow advance voting in postal offices for any voter in the preceding twenty-four days, this being the world's most liberal rule. The reform got a positive reception; during the 1980s almost four out of ten votes were cast at a post office. In fact, the liberal rule for advance voting is likely to have contributed to an upsurge in Swedish turnout (for the period 1970–1988 the average turnout was 89.8 per cent as compared to 82.6 per cent for the preceding two decades).[7] However, a fall in turnout lately shows that allowing advance voting is no panacea (the turnout dropped to 86.0 per cent in the 1988 election). Likewise, Finland, after adopting the Swedish model in the 1991 election, witnessed a decline in the turnout figures (by 4.3 per cent).

Duration of Campaign

The normal Scandinavian routine is to let every parliament run its full course. The Norwegian constitution does not allow early dissolutions; parliamentary elections have been held on the second Monday of September every fourth year since 1945. In Sweden only one out of fifteen post-war elections has followed on an early dissolution and in Finland only two out of thirteen. Hence, the parties have had plenty of opportunity to plan and prepare for the campaign.

In Denmark, however, only two parliaments have been close to running a full four-year term since 1964. Because of unclear majority situations the Danes have been asked to cast their votes on the average every second year, with forty-two months as the maximum period between elections, and eight months as the minimum (in all there have been twenty post-war parliamentary elections). The elections have often been called with short notice, thereby minimizing the time for preparation.

Considering the frequency of elections it is no wonder that Denmark has the shortest campaigns in Scandinavia, lasting only about three weeks. Sweden represents the other extreme. The 'hot' phase of the Swedish campaigns begins some five to six weeks before election day, the third Sunday in September. The party leaders start to tour the country even earlier, in late July. With campaigns lasting four to five weeks, Finland and Norway fall in between the two extremes.

As the potential importance of campaigns increases one might expect the parties to be tempted to extend the period of intense campaigning. In fact, this is what has happened in Sweden. Until the mid-1960s the parties used to hold back their public efforts until the final four weeks. In Norway, however, the duration of campaigns has remained more or less the same since 1945. Danish campaigns have, if anything, shortened compared with the 1950s. Finland moved the fixed day of election from July to March in 1966, which complicates any comparisons.

One reason for starting late lies in the fear that long periods of campaigning could be counter-productive; extensive campaigns may, quite simply, tire the electorate. Tradition, of course, is another factor explaining the late start of campaign in Norway. Also, it should be noticed that there is no official starting point for campaigns in Scandinavia.[8]

There are, indeed, indicators showing that the elections cast longer shadows in advance. In the late 1960s, the Swedish parties started to hold their party congresses a full year before the election to come, using the occasion as a starting-point for the unofficial campaign. In earlier years, the parties used to meet as late as June, three to four months prior to the election. A similar development can be seen in Norway. In Denmark, the parties claim to be always on the alert for the possibility of an election. Certainly, the international trend towards permanent campaigns is also visible in Scandinavia.[9]

Campaign Meetings

In the first campaigns after the war, the Swedish parties could make direct contact with a considerable portion of the electorate simply by holding thousands of public meetings at which candidates and leaders spoke. According to various opinion polls nearly one-third of the people interviewed reported having attended a campaign meeting. Corresponding data are not available for the other Scandinavian countries, but an estimation is that attendances at meetings were only slightly lower than in Sweden. It was not only the party's speakers that held attraction for the Swedish voters. The Swedish parties utilized propaganda movies with probably greater consistency and efficiency than anywhere else in the world, offering those who attended meetings a combination of amusement and ideological edification.[10]

Over time, however, fewer voters bothered to attend traditional campaign meetings. By 1956, the number of self-reported meeting attenders in Sweden was down to 16 per cent and after the breakthrough of television in the 1960s the number of attenders was halved once again (to 7 per cent in 1960 and 1964). The corresponding figure in Finland and Norway was about 10 per cent for the late 1950s.[11]

Beginning in the late 1960s, the parties tried to revitalize this traditional form of direct voter contact. The new formula was to arrange series of short meetings in crowded places—if the voters didn't come to the parties, the parties had to come to the voters! These so called 'town-square meetings' have increased the share of voters attending campaign meetings, but only moderately (to about 10–13 per cent in Sweden, 10 per cent in Norway, and 8 per cent in Denmark).[12]

Canvassing and Workplace Activities

In contrast to their Anglo-Saxon counterparts Scandinavian party workers have regarded door-to-door canvassing as a somewhat improper campaign technique. Conservative and liberal campaigners especially are afraid that the voters will dislike it as an invasion of their privacy. Only during the first post-war period did the doorbell ringers, mainly agrarians and social democrats, manage to canvass a substantial part of the electorate (according to a Swedish Gallup poll from the local election of 1946, 12 per cent of the voters were canvassed).[13]

Since then, with an electorate better educated in the art of voting, and with slightly less devoted activists, the number of canvassed voters has gone down. Today, the parties visit the homes of only a marginal proportion of the electorate (4 per cent in Norway in 1973, 2–4 per cent in Sweden 1982–8).

A special case of direct personal campaigning, seldom treated in the international literature, but often discussed in the Scandinavian context, lies in organized workplace activities, i.e. personal contacts made by party activists at factories, offices, and other places of work.

Although difficult to depict in detail, the general pattern of these contacts is clear. The Social Democrats, and, to a lesser extent, the Communists, have been helped by their connection with a trade union. At the opposite end of the ideological spectrum, the Conservatives enjoyed support from authoritative employers, who could urge their employees to vote the 'right way'. Likewise, the Agrarians were supported by the Agrarian Unions.[14]

Survey research evidence is scarce but in Sweden it suggests that the parties have increased their workplace activities during the last decades, but that the activist–voter contacts are of a limited range (from 1946 to 1988 the number who reported having been urged to vote for a party at their workplace rose from 3 per cent to 7 per cent). More impressive figures can be found in a report from a state commission, where the parties are said to have personal representatives at one-third of all major workplaces.[15]

That workplace activities could be of crucial importance is evident taking into consideration the more informal and unorganized political discussions that occur in everyday life. Survey research from all Scandinavian countries shows that about three-quarters of the voters are engaged in political discussions at their workplace during election campaigns. In this respect the workplaces are centres of agitation for the political parties.[16]

Paid Media Channels: Pamphlets and Advertising

Since the late 1800s centrally produced, mass-distributed pamphlets have played a central role in party campaigning. The circulation figures have been surprisingly stable over time and have always outnumbered the electorate many times over. With fixed days of election, Finnish, Norwegian, and Swedish parties can plan the production and distribution of pamphlets in advance. The Danish parties are working under more unpredictable conditions, which explains why the distribution seems to be somewhat less extensive when compared with the other Scandinavian countries. Finnish candidates only, having to display themselves individually before the electorate, produce pamphlets of their own.[17]

The pamphlets seem to be relatively widely read. Judging from the results from the National Election Studies about half the electorate in Norway and Sweden read at least one of the party's brochures. The figure in Denmark is 10 per cent lower. Compared to the 1950s, the readership of brochures seems to have increased, especially in Finland and Norway. An explanation for the increase, of course, could lie in the rising level of education. However, since the competition from television and the press has sharpened, this does not necessarily mean that the relative importance of pamphlets has increased. Printed pamphlets probably peaked as a powerful campaign in the first decades of this century.[18]

Direct mail was introduced in Finland in the late 1950s, and has been used in the other countries as well, although on a smaller scale. A major difference as compared to the USA is that the parties normally use direct letters for propaganda purposes. Fund-raising through direct mail has never been big business in Scandinavia.[19]

As in most Western democracies party advertising has been restricted to newspapers and magazines. Although little is known in detail, it seems that the Danish, Finnish, and Norwegian parties have recently started to put more money into newspaper advertising. The Swedish parties launched major advertising campaigns in the 1940s. Since the 1960s, the parties have preferred to put their money into fewer but bigger full-page advertisements. The total amount of advertising, though, remains more or less constant.[20]

Campaign advertising has probably never had any major impact on the outcome of elections. This may change in the future. Although small in scale, broadcast political advertising has made its début on local cable television (Finland), on local radio (Finland and Denmark) and on national cable television (Sweden).[21] Given the current expansion of commercial television in Scandinavia, the potential impact of TV advertising is likely to grow in the next decade. However, one should remember that advertising on television may be less effective in a multi-party system than in the American two-party context. Since the Scandinavian parties have to fight multi-front wars, it is probably less useful to follow the strategy of negative campaigning, so dominant in the USA today.

The Free Media

Since the Scandinavians are the world's most persistent newspaper readers, the press continues to be an important campaign channel for the parties. During the post-war period, the media market has undergone a process of concentration typical of the press in the West. While the combined circulation figures have risen (considerably in Sweden and Finland, moderately in Denmark and Norway), the number of daily newspapers has been sinking continuously. The so called 'death of the newspapers' has been most noticeable in Denmark, while the smaller newspapers have managed relatively best in Norway (from the 1940s to the 1980s the number of newspapers sank from about 120 to 40 in Denmark, from about 190 to 150 in Norway, and from about 200 to 120 in Sweden). Hence, parties of today have fewer daily newspapers to use as campaign channels but in terms of circulation they are stronger. Most importantly, over 90 per cent of the Scandinavian electorate still read a daily newspaper at least once a week.[22]

Living in the era of television it is easy to forget that the radio had already had a major impact on electioneering. Introduced in the 1930s, radio election programmes made their definite breakthrough in the late 1940s. By then, most Scandinavian voters had regular access to the radio, spending on average two to three hours a day listening to the new medium. In Sweden, about 80–90 per cent of the electorate followed at least one of the election broadcasts. In Finland and Norway, the corresponding numbers were lower, but still impressive (audience figures of 50–60 per cent). When questioned, politicians as well as voters rated radio as the most important campaign channel during the 1950s. Lasting until 1960 in Denmark and Sweden, and until the mid-1960s in Finland and Norway, the radio's period of primacy was short but uncontested.[23]

Since the state regulation did not allow any news coverage of the campaign, the radio contribution to the campaigns consisted of special election programmes. In Denmark and Finland, the parties presented their manifestos in 15-minute talks. In Sweden and

Norway, the election broadcasting took new forms. The party leaders were questioned by representatives of the other parties. However, the most important programme was a debate between the party leaders a few days before the election. The parties confronted each other directly and the broadcast debate formed the natural climax of the campaign in all Scandinavian countries.[24]

Following a rapid increase in the number of licence holders, television took over as the most important campaign channel. In both Denmark and Sweden, the first TV election was in 1960, when about two-thirds of the electorate watched the televised election broadcasts. Due to complicating geographical conditions, the shift was delayed until 1965 in Norway and 1966 in Finland. At the end of the 1960s television reached the vast majority of the Scandinavian voters (in Denmark and Sweden over 90 per cent, in Finland 80 per cent, and in Norway 75 per cent). By then, the new medium had long confirmed its primacy in electioneering.[25]

However, one should note that the first TV elections in Scandinavia were staged more or less completely by the parties; while television gained control over the voters, the parties kept control over television.[26] The radio's tradition of functioning as a passive election platform for the parties, restricting its election broadcasts to presentational programmes and debates, was taken over by television. Thus, the concluding debate between the Swedish party leaders in September 1960, was broadcast some weeks *before* the 'great' American duel between John F. Kennedy and Richard Nixon, which is known as the first televised debate with, potentially, a decisive influence on the election outcome.

Today, the format of special election programmes is similar all over Scandinavia. Following the Swedish pattern there are three major types of programmes: first, hour-long interviews with the party leaders (since the late 1960s the 'cross-examinations' are conducted by independent journalists, not by party representatives); second, one or two issue-orientated debates; and, finally, a few days prior to the election, a debate between the party leaders. In Norway and Sweden, a separate debate between the two major contenders for the premiership may be added. In Denmark only, each party is allocated fifteen minutes of free air time, the basic cost of production being covered by the Danish Broadcasting Company.

In the special election programmes, the parties represented in parliament are ensured equal time.[27] Denmark, however, has still more egalitarian regulation. Following a ruling by the Danish Supreme Court in 1959, the right to equal time is ensured to *every* party fighting the parliamentary election. Undoubtedly, the regulation has helped new and small parties to make their voices heard during the campaigns. A practical consequence is that the concluding debates between the party leaders are considered to be less decisive in Denmark. Having up to fifteen participants, and mixing the established parties with more or less obscure newcomers, the debates tend to be rather chaotic.

Controlling the Free Media

In learning how to cope with the TV medium, the parties faced a new challenge—the advent of more professional, resourceful, and assertive political journalism in the mid and late 1960s. Starting in radio and television, the journalists refused to settle for passive roles as mediating campaign channels for the parties. Referring to their position as the third (fourth) estate, and helped by general ideological radicalization of the political climate, journalists wanted to take an active part in setting the agenda for debate and scrutinizing politicians' standpoints. It is in this area that the major changes in campaigning have occurred during the past decades.

A first sign of the new situation for the political parties was that TV journalists took over the questioning of party leaders from the party representatives. Even more importantly, both television and the radio started to cover the election campaigns in their news programmes. From now on the party representatives had to give increasing attention to news journalism, having to be prepared to answer aggressive questions from journalists. The press also began a process of emancipation from the parties, although at a slower speed.[28]

Underlining the free media's key position in the campaigns is the substantial increase in election coverage since the 1950s. Most evident, of course, is the emergence of everyday news coverage by radio and television. The newspapers have followed suit. Between 1956 and 1976 the Swedish press doubled its news coverage of the elections. If available, it is likely that corresponding data from the other Scandinavian countries would show the same tendency.

Moreover, since the late 1970s in Sweden and the 1980s in Finland and Denmark, local radio and regional television have covered the elections from their own geographical horizon. The latest addition to the supply of electorally relevant media is national cable television penetrating to steadily increasing proportions of the electorate. As compared to the 1950s, the Scandinavian voters are offered many times the number of political stimuli through an increasing number of non-partisan media.

The change in the relationship between politicians and the media first became visible in Sweden and Denmark during the years 1966–8. A few years later, in the early 1970s, the Norwegian and Finnish parties started to experience the same difficulties in controlling the political agenda of debate.[29]

In analytical terms, television and radio have moved from passivity to activity, while the press has moved from partisanship towards neutrality. Thereby the free media have changed from an effective campaign channel to an independent actor in election campaigns, having a strong influence on what issues actually are to be discussed.[30]

Centralized Party Campaigns

To deal with the new situation in political opinion formation the parties have taken to centralizing. Compared to the 1950s, the central party offices have strengthened their control over campaigning. Most parties nominate a central leadership, which is in everyday contact with the regional party organizations during campaigns. Thereby the parties try to communicate a united strategy of reaction to events during the campaigns, be it to a verbal stumble by the party leader when questioned on television, or to a sudden initiative from another party.[31]

The parties carefully avoid giving up any power over decisions. The role of professional public relations men is restricted to practical matters and the suggestions of ideas. Small and poor parties handle the public relations aspects of campaigning themselves. However, in planning the campaigns the richer parties may have contacts with internationally known political consultants. Although no systematic evidence is at hand, such consultations seem to have become more frequent during the 1980s.[32]

In local campaigning MPs play a crucial role. As well-known personalities, they have good chances of getting publicity in the newspapers; over 90 per cent of the Swedish MPs reported themselves to have been interviewed by some local media during the 1985 campaign. The candidates are normally loyal party workers, emphasizing the issues put forward by the central party leadership (in a Swedish study, 85 per cent of the MPs were classified as 'party campaigners', thus leaving the number of 'individual campaigners' at 15 per cent). The disciplined candidates are of great help to the central party leadership in the efforts to create a unified issue-image during the campaign.[33]

Again, the Finnish electoral system provides a deviant case. Having to obtain personal votes, Finnish candidates for parliament have incentives to compete internally with candidates of the same party. Also, it is only in Finland that the candidates are beginning to create campaign organizations of their own.[34]

The heaviest burden in the centralized campaigns, however, is shouldered by the party leaders. Having been leading spokesmen and the most important actors in election campaigns since the turn of the century, the party leaders have come even more to the forefront during the past decades. It is the party leader's responsibility to handle the demands of the new media situation during campaigns.[35]

Until the late 1960s public speeches were the dominant feature in the party leaders' campaigning. Although perceived as highly important, performances in election broadcasts and a few debate confrontations with other party leaders were small in number. With the emergence of active and more assertive political journalism all this began to change. In order to profit from the mass media's growing hunger for news, the party leaders have increased the number of campaign performances, arranging daily press conferences and various media events ('photo-opportunities').

The development is very distinct in Sweden. In the 1968 election, the first with regular news coverage on television, the average number of campaign performances made by the party leaders increased from 27 to 49, while the percentage of press conferences doubled (from 9 to 20 per cent). Since then, the number of campaign performances has increased more or less constantly, reaching an all-time high of 104 in the 1988 campaign. In this campaign, also, for the first time more campaign performances were devoted to press conferences and media events than to campaign speeches.[36]

In Norway the development seems to have run parallel to Sweden, albeit with a few years' time-lag. In Finland, also, the party leaders tour the country regularly. In Denmark, however, the party leaders seem to be less active in this respect. During the short campaigns the dominant strategy is to give daily press conferences at Christiansborg in Copenhagen (the seat of the Folketing), and to make relatively few performances in other parts of the country.[37]

To summarise the development from the parties' point of view: the party leaders' campaigning remained stable until the late 1960s and early 1970s. The leaders addressed the voters directly at public meetings and were reported more or less extensively in the press. Election broadcasting provided larger audiences, but the party leaders still had the opportunity to develop their standpoints relatively undisturbed. Not until the breakthrough of active and aggressive political journalism did the basis of campaigning change. Since then, the party leaders'—and hence, the parties'—messages to the voters have been filtered through questioning journalists.

Political Money

The cost of campaigns has increased during the post-war period. Compared to states allowing paid TV-advertising, however, Scandinavian campaign expenditures are limited. The richest party, the Swedish Social Democrats, spent an equivalent of £3.5 million on advertising during the 1988 campaign. Small and poor parties like the Swedish Communists and the Danish Christian People's Party spend less than £0.1 million.[38]

The greatest change in Scandinavian political expenditure concerns the costs for personnel. With the introduction of public subsidies—in Sweden and Finland during the 1960s, in Norway in 1970, and in Denmark during the 1980s—the parties got resources to professionalize their organizations. In accordance with the size of the public subsidies, the Swedish and Norwegian parties have the strongest organizations, while the Danish parties have the lowest number of employed personnel. Obviously, the professional organizations have played an important part in the efforts to centralize campaigning.[39]

Furthermore, the new form of political financing has had some side-effects. With the introduction of public subsidies, the parties have become more reluctant to accept direct contributions from interest group organizations. The alternative strategy chosen by many interest groups is to take active part in political opinion formation by urging support for their demands during campaigns. Thereby, competition over setting the agenda for debate has been even more sharpened. Indeed, in comparison to the rather concordant party choir of yesterday the modern Scandinavian election campaign is a cacophony of voices.

Conclusion

During the past decades, much has changed in Scandinavian election campaigning. The core theme is that the parties have lost ground; voters as well as the media have become increasingly independent. The basic trends can be found in all Scandinavian countries.

However, there are differences between the individual countries. The changing situation first became visible in Sweden and Denmark in the late 1960s. In Norway and Finland the parties kept their grip over political opinion formation to the early 1970s. Denmark went through a rapid development culminating in the 'earthquake-election' of 1973, but since then the parties have recovered somewhat. Finland, with a constitution giving incentives for individualized campaigning, is the most deviant case in Scandinavian electioneering. The Swedish and Norwegian parties, who used to have the most faithful voters and the most loyal media, have been the most weakened.

Moreover, the Scandinavian example shows that we are too often subject to simplified generalizations regarding the impact of television on today's politics. From post-war history we learn that the development should be described in accordance with a long-range model: (1) the breakthrough of radio, (2) television takes over, (3) the journalists move in. It was not until the journalists started their process of emancipation that the parties began to lose their grip over political opinion formation. It is not to be taken for granted that the voters have won from the development.

Notes

1. Admittedly, not even the older history of Nordic election campaigns is as shady as in many countries. Cornelius O'Leary's book *The Elimination of Corrupt Practices in British Elections 1868–1911* would not have been as voluminous had he written on Scandinavia. On the agreements between the political parties in Sweden, see Esaiasson (1990: 183, 194). On the relationship among the Finnish political élite, see Moring (1989: 40–99).

2. See Borre (1984), Tonsgaard (1989), Valen *et al.* (1990: 28), Listhaug (1989: 115–17), Gilljam and Holmberg (1990: 105–7). For comparative analysis, see Asp *et al.* (1987), Granberg and Holmberg (1988), Berglund and Lindström (1978: 81–91).

3. For analyses of issue voting in Scandinavia, see Holmberg and Gilljam (1987: 285–95), Borre (1984), Valen and Aardal (1983), Listhaug (1989: 37–67).

4. For a comparative analysis of the Scandinavian election systems, see Särlvik (1983).

5. It should be noted that the Danish electoral system offers an opportunity to cast votes for either a party or an individual candidate. During the past decade, the number of personal votes has started to increase.

6. See Törnudd (1968), Thomas (1985), and Sundberg (1991).

7. Holmberg and Gilljam (1987: 77–80).

8. Cf. Pesonen (1968: 186–7), Esaiasson (1990: 52–3).

9. See Koblik (1980), Bille (1991).

10. See Esaiasson (1990: 354–5; 1991).

11. Esaiasson (1991), Pesonen (1968: 184, 197), Valen and Katz (1964: 100–6).

12. Esaiasson (1991), Asp *et al.* (1987).

13. See Valen and Katz (1964: 100–6), Esaiasson (1990: 355–9, 389–416; 1991).

14. The Finnish election of 1958 offers an example of concrete support. The members of the Agrarian Union in a rural commune donated to the party a part of their income from milk sent to the local dairy (Pesonen 1968: 197). Also, see Esaiasson (1990: 359–61).

15. Sigeman (1975).

16. Sigeman (1975).

17. Cf. Bille (1991), Elklit (1991).

18. Asp *et al.* (1987), Pesonen (1968: 180–2), Valen and Katz (1964: 128–31).

19. The Danish Conservatives have been most successful in raising

campaign money from direct mail (Bille *et al.* 1991). See also Wiberg (1991), Pesonen (1968: 180–2), Valen and Katz (1964: 113–15, 128–31).

20. Björklund (1991), Bille (1991), Elklit (1991), Esaiasson (1991).
21. Sundberg (1991), Elklit (1991).
22. Thomsen (1968; 1987), Höyer (1968), NOU (1982), Weibull (1983), Sauerberg and Thomsen (1977), Asp *et al.* (1987).
23. Sauerberg and Thomsen (1977), Esaiasson (1990: 370–2, 426–31), Pesonen (1968: 181–2), Valen and Katz (1964: 113–15, 133–4).
24. See Lund (1975) and Björklund (1991).
25. See Sauerberg and Thomsen (1977), Asp *et al.* (1987), Björklund (1991).
26. The distinction between power over the voters and power over the media is taken from Asp (1983, 1986); cf. Katz (1971).
27. A minor deflection from the rule of equal time is that the Social Democratic Party is allowed an extra representative in the concluding debate.
28. As late as the 1980s, the Swedish press showed tendencies to favour their 'own party' and 'own party bloc' in the news coverage (most of all the centre party press, thereafter the Social Democratic press and the Conservative press) (Asp 1990). See also Asp (1982), Sauerberg and Thomsen (1977), Björklund (1991).
29. Asp (1983, 1986), Esaiasson (1990), Sauerberg and Thomsen (1977), Siune (1982), Östby (1991), Moring (1989: 132–54).
30. Cf. Asp (1983), Östby (1991).
31. Bille (1991), Koblik (1980).
32. For instance, were the Swedish Social Democrats helped by the French 'political guru' Jacques Séguéla in planning the campaign of 1991.
33. See Holmberg and Esaiasson (1988: 168–204).
34. See Thomas (1985). In Denmark, however, the same tendency towards individualized campaigns is beginning to show (Bille *et al.* 1991).
35. Over the years 1956–68 the ability of the Swedish voters to identify photographs of the party leaders more than doubled (the number of persons interviewed making 4 out of 5 correct identifications increased from 34% to 87%): Esaiasson (1985: 61–7). In the daily papers, the number of news articles concentrating on a party leader increased from 11 to 37% (Asp 1990).
36. Esaiasson (1991).
37. Cf. Björklund (1991), Bille (1991).
38. Esaiasson (1990: 348–401, 443–4), Bille (1991). In 1948, the Swedish Social Democrats spent about £0.1m. At the time, however, both the Conservatives and the Liberals had higher campaign expenditures (£0.2m and £0.15m respectively).
39. e.g. Wiberg (1991).

References

Asp, K. (1982) 'Väljarna och massmediernas partiskhet', in *Väljare Partier Massmedia: Empiriska Studier I Svensk demokrati* (Stockholm: Liber).

—— (1983), 'The Struggle for the Agenda: Party Agenda, Media Agenda and Voter Agenda in the 1979 Swedish Election Campaign', *Communication Research*, 10: 333–55.

—— (1986), *Mäktiga massmedier: Studier I politisk opinionsbildning* (Stockholm: Akademilitteratur).

—— (1990), 'Medierna och valrörelsen', in M. Gilljam and S. Holmberg (eds.), *Rött Blått Grönt* (Stockholm: Bonniers).

—— Esaiasson, P., and Hedberg, P. (1987), 'Kommunikation och påverkan: Valkampanjernas betydelse i Norden', paper presented at the VII Nordiska Stadskunskabskongress, Copenhagen.

Berglund, S., and Lindström, U. (1978), *The Scandinavian Party System(s)* (Lund: Studentlitteratur).

Bille, L. (1991), 'The 1988 Election Campaign in Denmark', *Scandinavian Political Studies*, 14/3: 205–18.

—— Elklit, J., and Jakobsen, J. V. (1991), 'Denmark: The 1990 Campaign', in D. M. Farrell and S. Bowler (eds.), *Election Campaigning in a Comparative Perspective* (London: Macmillan).

Bjørklund, T. (1991), 'Election Campaigns in Postwar Norway (1945–1989): From Party-Controlled to Media-Driven Campaigns', *Scandinavian Political Studies*, 14/3: 279–301.

Borre, O. (1984), 'Traek af den danske vælgeradfærd', in J. Elklit and O. Tonsgaard (eds.), *Valg og Vælgeradfærd: Studier i dansk politik* (Aarhus: Politica).

Elklit, J. (1991), 'Sub-national Election Campaigns: The Danish Local Elections of November 21, 1989', *Scandinavian Political Studies*, 14: 219–40.

Esaiasson, P. (1985), *Partiledarna inför väljarna: Partiledarnas popularitet och betydelse för valresultatet* (Göteborg: University of Göteborg, Department of Political Science).

—— (1990), *Svenska valkampanjer 1866–1988* (Stockholm: Allmänna förlaget).

—— (1991), '120 Years of Swedish Election Campaigns: A Story of the Rise and Decline of Political Parties and the Emergence of the Mass Media as Power Brokers', *Scandinavian Political Studies*, 14/3: 261–78.

Gilljam, M., and Holmberg, S. (1990) (eds.), *Rött Blått Grönt En bok om 1988 fors riksdagsval* (Stockholm: Bonniers).

Granberg, D., and Holmberg, S. (1988), *The Political System Matters:*

Social Psychology and Voting Behavior in Sweden and the United States (Cambridge: Cambridge University Press).

Holmberg, S., and Esaiasson, P. (1988), De folkvalda: En bok om riksdagsledamöterna och den representativa demokratin i Sverige (Stockholm: Bonniers).

—— and Gilljam, M. (1987), Väljare och val i Sverige (Stockholm: Bonniers).

Høyer, S. (1968) 'The Political Economy of the Norwegian Press', Scandinavian Political Studies, 3: 85–143.

Katz, E. (1971), 'Platforms and Windows: Reflections on the Role of the Broadcasting in Election Campaigns', Journalism Quarterly, 48: 304–14.

Koblik, S. (1980), 'Towards an Analytical Model for Swedish Election Campaigns', Statsvetenskaplig Tidskrift, 83: 23–36.

Listhaug, O. (1989), Citizens, Parties and Norwegian Electoral Politics 1957–1985 (Trondheim: Tapir).

Lund, E. (1975), 'Valgudsendelser i radio og TV 1924–1974/75', Pressens Årbog (Copenhagen: Pressehistorisk sellskab).

Moring, T. (1989), Political Elite Action: Strategy and Outcomes (Helsinki: Commentationes Scientiarum Socialium).

NOU (1982), Maktutredningen: Rapporten om massmedier (Oslo: Universitetsforlaget).

O'Leary, C. (1962), The Elimination of Corrupt Practices in British Elections 1868–1911 (Oxford: Oxford University Press).

Østbye, H. (1991), 'Media in Politics: Channels, Arenas, Actors, Themes', in K. Strøm and L. Svåsand (eds.), Challenges to Political Parties (forthcoming).

Pesonen, P. (1968), An Election in Finland (New Haven, Conn.: Yale University Press).

Särlvik, B. (1983), 'Scandinavia', in V. Bogdanor and D. Butler (eds.), Democracy and Elections (Cambridge: Cambridge University Press).

Sauerberg, S., and Thomsen, N. (1977), 'The Political Role of Mass Communication in Scandinavia', in K. Cerny (ed.), Scandinavia at the Polls (Washington, DC: American Enterprise Institute).

Sigeman, T. (1975), Politisk propaganda på arbetsplatser: Rättsläge och förekomst (Stockholm: SOU).

Siune, K. (1982), Valgkampe i TV og radio (Aarhus: Forlaget Politica).

Sundberg, J. (1991), 'Campaign Strategies in National and Local Elections: Finland in a Comparative Perspective', paper, ECPR Workshop on Election Campaigning in Western Europe, Bochum.

Thomas, A. (1985), 'Members of Parliament and Access to Politics in Scandinavia', in V. Bogdanor (ed.), Representatives of the People?

Parliamentarians and Constituents in Western Democracies (London: Gower).

Thomsen, N . (1968), *Partipressen* (Aarhus: Politica).

—— (1987), 'Politisk kommunikation, massmedier og opinion', in *Dansk politik under forandring 1945–1985* (Copenhagen: Forskningssekretariatet).

Tonsgaard, O. (1989), 'Vælgervandringer og vælgerusikkerhed', in J. Elklit and O. Tonsgaard (eds.), *To folketingsvalg: vælgerholdninger og vælgeradfærd i 1987 og 1988* (Aarhus: Politica).

Törnudd, K. (1986), *The Electoral System of Finland* (London: Hugh Evelyn).

Valen, H., and Aardal, B. (1983), *Et valg i perspektiv: En studie av stortingsvalget 1981* (Oslo: Statistisk Sentralbyrå).

—— and Katz, E. (1964), *Political Parties in Norway: A Community Study* (Oslo: Universitetsforlaget).

Valen, H., Aardal, B., and Vougt, G. (1990), *Endring og kontinuitet Stortingsvalget 1989* (Oslo: Statistisk Centralbyrå).

Weibull, L. (1983), *Tidningsläsning i Sverige: Tidningsinnehav, tidningsval, läsvanor* (Stockholm: Liber).

Wiberg, M. (1991), *The Public Purse and Political Parties: Public Financing of Political Parties in Nordic Countries* (Helsinki: The Political Science Association).

11

Japan

GERALD L. CURTIS

Introduction

Japan's experience with political parties and elections goes back over a century. The first parliamentary election was held in 1890, for an electorate restricted to male property owners—just 1 per cent of a total population of forty million, or one in twenty-five adult men. The suffrage gradually expanded over the next three decades, and in 1925 Japan adopted universal manhood suffrage.

In the decade which followed, parties became increasingly important and electoral competition grew in intensity. Even though military involvement in politics brought about the demise of the party system in the late 1930s, Japan did not discard elections entirely even during World War II. An election was held in 1942 in which several politicians ran as independents against the government-sponsored Imperial Rule Assistance Association. A number of the successful independents in that wartime election went on to play important roles in post-war politics.

Highly competitive elections, well-organized political parties, large-scale election campaigning, a distinctive system of electoral districting, and a functioning parliament—or Diet, the Prussian term the Japanese adopted as the official Western language name for their parliament and the name by which it is still known today—thus existed in Japan well before General Douglas MacArthur arrived and the American Occupation embarked upon its political reform programme. Japanese political democracy and many important aspects of its electoral system and campaign practices have their roots in the political system of the pre-war period and have evolved out of a long and quite distinctive tradition.

Japan's electoral system is a good example of the continuity between the pre- and post-war eras. Under today's electoral system for the lower house of the Diet, the country is divided into 130 districts which elect a total of 512 members. Almost all the districts elect three, four, or five members.[1] Each voter has one non-transferable vote so the winners are the three, four or five candidates that poll the largest number of votes. The system stimulates intense competition between candidates of the same party in districts where a party is strong enough to run two or more candidates. Moreover, with many candidates in a single district, the electoral system makes it possible for candidates to win with 15 per cent or even less of the popular vote.

In Japanese this system is known as the 'medium-size election district system' (*chūsenkyokusei*). Interestingly, the label reflects its pre-war architects' conception of 'medium' as being midway between the prefecture-wide large election-district system that Japan used from 1900 to 1919 and the small single-member constituency system employed from 1919 until the shift to the medium-size district system in 1925. This new system, devised in anticipation of the introduction of universal manhood suffrage, was expected to help both major conservative parties existing at that time to win seats in districts where they faced strong opposition from candidates of working-class parties. The American Occupation authorities experimented with a different election system in the first post-war election, but shortly thereafter permitted a return to the more familiar medium-size district system of the pre-war era.

Another significant continuity with the pre-war period is the presence in Japan's election law of extensive restrictions on campaign practices. Many present-day regulations such as limits on the duration of the formal campaign period, restrictions on the types and quantity of written materials candidates may distribute to voters, the prohibition of house-to-house canvassing—and many other limitations on campaign activities that are legitimate and commonplace in the United States and elsewhere—were first introduced in the period between the two world wars.

These pre-war controls on campaign activity were eagerly sought by the conservative parties in large part because they were expected to disadvantage the fledgling working class parties. But it also was believed that the reforms would reduce campaign spending and thereby help weed out corruption from the system. Most of these pre-war restrictions and prohibitions were abolished initially by the American Occupation authorities, but they were reintroduced gradually in subsequent years. In contrast to the pre-war period, however, election campaign restrictions have enjoyed the support of almost all political parties. The parties on the left, in particular, fear that campaigning would cost even more than it consumes now if restrictions were relaxed. Strict regulations on campaign practices also draw broad support among Japan's Diet members regardless of party affiliation because they make it difficult for new and relatively unknown politicians to get their name and message out to voters, and thus strenghten the re-election prospects of incumbents.

During the past fifteen years Japan has given a new twist to its long history of extensive campaign restrictions. It has revised its laws regulating campaigning and political funding in ways that distinguish sharply between party and candidate campaigns. It has done so in an effort to weaken the role of individual politicians in obtaining votes and to strengthen the vote-mobilizing role of political parties. In its political reforms it has tried to counteract the trend toward increasingly personalized campaigning that has become characteristic of virtually all advanced democratic countries in recent years.

Candidate-centred campaigning, as it is now practised in the United States and other countries, is a peculiarly modern feature of democratic politics, a consequence of the impact of modern mass communications on party organization and campaign practices. Politician-based local organization and personalized campaigning are old traditions in Japan, however, and Japanese of all political persuasions tend to be convinced that they reflect the peculiar backwardness of Japan's political culture. In the popular Japanese view, only mass membership parties offering voters clearly defined programmes and election campaigns which are debates between parties over their respective platforms rather than constituency struggles between individual politicians are the mark of a truly modern polity.

Over nearly two decades, in an effort to force behaviour to accord more closely with this model of 'modern' party politics, the Election Law and Political Funds Regulation Law have tightened restrictions on candidate campaigns while loosening or even eliminating many limits on the campaign activities of political parties.

Understanding the dynamics of Japanese election campaigning means first of all comprehending this distinctive Japanese separation of candidate and party campaigning.

Parties and Candidates

A vast array of legal restrictions and prohibitions regulate candidate campaigns in Japan. In addition to a ban on all campaigning beyond a 15-day official campaign period, and the above-mentioned ban on house-to-house canvassing, both of which apply to candidate and party alike, there are restrictions on candidate speech-making activities and a prohibition of the distribution by candidates of written materials (handbills, newsletters, campaign buttons, and so on) except for those the election law expressly permits. These sanctioned materials include some 35,000 postcards and, depending on the size of the district, between 60,000 and 100,000 handbills. During the official campaign period, candidates can display their campaign posters only on government-provided poster boards; they may use a specified number of additional posters to publicize the time and place of a planned speech. To deter candidates from looking for loopholes in these provisions, the Home Ministry's official campaign handbook warns that restrictions on written materials include 'newspapers, name cards, greeting cards, posters, signs, paper lanterns, placards, postcards, telegrams, slides, movies, neon signs, advertising balloons, and characters written on walls or fences or in the sand [on the side] of the road'.[2]

Since the legal changes made in 1975, however, political parties are free to engage in a great variety of campaign activities prohibited to candidates. Parties may distribute unlimited numbers of handbills through the post or on the street for example, so long as the ban on house-to-house canvassing is respected by avoiding direct delivery to residences. But there is an important catch regarding the distribution of written campaign materials that reflects the law's attempt to separate parties from candidates: none of these handbills may mention the name of any candidate.

Before the reform in 1975 neither parties nor candidates could buy television time or newspaper space for political advertisements. Today, however, there are no limits on political party paid advertisements on television or radio or in newspapers or magazines. Parties may even run four newspaper advertisements during the official election campaign period at government expense. But there again is the crucial catch: it is against the law to mention the candidacy of any individuals in these party advertisements. Party leaders and other Diet members may appear in these advertisements only in the context of their party roles, since the purpose of the advertisements supposedly is to promote the party's policies, not to publicize its candidates. Mention of the fact that these party leaders will themselves be running in the election, much less a personal appeal for voter support, is a violation of the law.

Individual candidates are prohibited from purchasing any advertising time on television or radio or space in newspapers or magazines, as they were before 1975. Instead, the government provides each candidate with funds to publish five newspaper advertisements of specified length and make four television and two radio appearances of five and a half minutes each. These candidate speeches are broadcast one after another early in the morning and late in the evening during the short campaign period. They are literally 'appearances' in that candidates are prohibited from using film footage, props, or any other paraphernalia. Interestingly, the election law also attempts to discourage negative campaigning by imploring candidates to act 'responsibly' by avoiding statements in these media appearances that would damage the reputation of other candidates, parties, or political organizations.

There was a flurry of excitement when the reform liberalizing political party media advertising was first introduced. Parties hired Japan's best advertising agencies to create both short spot commercials and longer documentaries for television for use during the campaign. But this enthusiasm for media advertising waned once it became evident that party advertisements were of scant help to voters trying to decide which particular candidate to vote for. Consequently, though both electronic and print media saturate Japan, the regulations that prevent parties from advertising their candidates and candidates from advertising themselves severely constrain the use of the media as a campaign tool.

A related phenomenon is the limited importance of political consultants and market research specialists in Japanese election campaigns. A small political consulting industry does exist. All major advertising companies have political consulting departments.

There are also a number of companies that specialize in political consulting—one estimate is that there are around fifty firms doing about $15 million in business annually.[3]

Big advertising firms have been important in creating television commercials for the ruling Liberal Democratic Party (LDP) and to a lesser extent for the opposition parties. The small independent political consulting companies mostly have handled individual candidate campaigns. They design posters, computerize voter address lists, give advice about slogans, and in some cases use market research techniques to test voter response to different issues to prepare the candidate's standard campaign speech.

This is a far cry from the role of the high-powered American campaign consultant. An article that appeared in the *Nihon Keizai Shinbun*, Japan's top economic newspaper, about campaign consulting reveals how trivial is much of what passes for political consulting in Japan. Opening provocatively enough with the line 'Roger Ailes, watch out,' the account in fact relates how one political consulting firm designed a campaign poster for a candidate. The article in particular describes how the consultants discovered that candidates were not bound by the 42 cm by 40 cm size limit for campaign posters so long as the posters were displayed before the formal campaign period. The firm thereupon produced one nearly twice the size of a conventional poster. Not only that, slogans were printed vertically on both sides of the picture, which showed the candidate from his waist up (rather than just his face). *Nihon Keizai Shinbun* writer's conclusion? 'Unlike conventional campaign posters, which simply show the face and the name of the candidate, the poster is likely to make a strong impression.' Heady stuff for the political advertising industry. Political consulting is one American dominated industry that seems safe from Japanese competition for some time to come. Parenthetically, some American political consultants have attempted to break into the Japanese market, but apparently with very little success.

The Centrality of Candidate Campaigns

Despite a legal framework designed to discourage candidate-centred campaigning and to turn the spotlight on parties and their policies, the fundamental characteristic of Japanese election campaigning continues to be the centrality of the individual politician. Extremely weak, almost non-existent, party organization at the local level means that individual politicians must build their own electoral machines, raise their own money, and run their own campaigns. This is especially true for LDP candidates. Even in the case of the Socialist Party, which now rarely runs more than one candidate in a district, the absence of strong local-level party organization means that candidates must rely on their own resources and on those of particular labour unions with which they have close personal connections.

Thus the heart of the Japanese election campaign is the effort by individual politicians to develop their own local organizations, secure the backing of powerful interest groups in their districts, and maximize their share of the vote in a particular section of the constituency where their personal ties are the most extensive. In working toward these goals, the stress is on constituency service to convince voters that the candidate has the clout in Tokyo to bring the district new roads and bridges, industrial development, and higher living standards.

Because of the legal restrictions on campaigning, most of the effort to mobilize voter support takes place before the official campaign period begins. As long as candidates do not mention that they are planning to run in a particular election, they are able to do many things banned during the official campaign period. Most campaigning in Japan comes to a screeching halt as soon as the official campaign period begins.

The restrictive campaign provisions of the election law have the perverse consequence of discouraging politicians from openly seeking support on the basis of policy and party programme. Unable to send a newsletter or give a speech in which they explicitly ask for support in a particular election without violating the ban on pre-election campaigning, Japanese politicans concentrate instead on expanding personal contacts, meeting people in small group settings, and building their political machine. The legal framework of campaigning in fact provides few incentives to frame appeals in terms of broad party goals or to devote much attention to national or international issues. The regulations rather strengthen the personalistic base of political organization and the local orientation of politicians running for national-level office.

Japanese politicians expend enormous energy establishing direct contact with a large number of voters and enmeshing themselves in webs of personal relationships to snare still other voters' support. To that end, nearly all candidates develop elaborate mass membership supporter organizations (called *kōenkai*). The emphasis on personal and continuous campaigning is a major reason why candidates who are placed highest among the losers in a district—coming in fifth in a four-member district for example—often win in their subsequent election effort. They are simply able to spend more time campaigning between elections than those who won.

Given weak party organization and the importance of personal ties and webs of social relationships in organizing politician support organizations, it is not surprising that the great majority of Diet candidates hail from the districts in which they run. Candidates with backgrounds in local elective politics and former national government bureaucrats running from their home-town constituencies together account for about half the members of the Diet. But the most striking evidence of the impact of localism and personalism on candidate recruitment is the extraordinarily large number of offspring of retiring or deceased Diet members running for, and successful in, Diet elections.

Roughly 40 per cent of the LDP's Diet members are such second-generation politicians. There are fewer such politicians in the opposition camp, but the phenomenon itself is common to most of Japan's political parties. Second-generation candidates have certain obvious advantages, given the personalistic nature of Japanese political organization. They have high name recognition and they can tug at the strings of personal loyalty that tie the Diet member to his *Kōenkai*'s leaders and rank-and-file members.

For the local politicians who largely comprise the leadership of these personal organizations, the Diet member's key function is to provide what the Japanese like to call a 'pipe' to the central government's pork-barrel. When a Diet member retires or dies, the leaders of his organization want to keep their particular pipe in place in order to continue to control the distribution of resources that flow out of it. A second-generation candidate rarely has had any local political experience before contesting his father's Diet seat, and is thus dependent on the support of his father's organization. Accordingly, he is both less able and disinclined to replace the leaders of his father's organization with other people, as a powerful local politician with loyal supporters of his own might want to do.

The dynamics of the system, in other words, make it rational for a retiring Diet member to select a successor who can retain his followers' loyalty, and for his followers to back someone dependent on them for support. This has thrown the balance in favour of selecting the second-generation political aspirant.

The prevalence of political dynasties receives much unfavourable commentary in Japan and it has contributed to the cynicism many Japanese feel about their political leaders. There is scant evidence to suggest the practice will soon end, however. The matter is complicated by the fact that second-generation Diet members are among the country's most popular politicians. Many of them spent the years while they were waiting for their fathers to pass on the reins of power by working in large banks and corporations, often involving a period of residence in the United States or some other foreign country. Some of them tend to have a better feel for the life of the typical urban Japanese salaried worker and a more cosmopolitan outlook than is true for the local politician or the national government bureaucrat who has spent his career dealing with domestic issues. Thus their appeal is strong particularly among the most modern and affluent groups in Japanese society. Second-generation candidates are successful at the polls and they dominate the pool of political talent from which the next generation of political leaders will be drawn.

The combination of highly personalized campaign organizations and an election districting system that pits one LDP candidate against another has produced a turnover rate among LDP Diet members that is astonishingly high, given the fact that this party has dominated the Diet for more than thirty-five years. In the most recent lower-house election in February 1990, for example, only 83 per cent of incumbents seeking re-election were successful. While the LDP lost 14 seats overall in the race, 46 of its incumbents were defeated. Moreover, a number of elderly incumbents retired before the election, many out of concern that they might lose to a younger and more energetic new LDP candidate if they ran. In fact new candidates outnumbered incumbents in the 1990 election— the first time that has happened since the current party system came into being in 1955. There were also more new candidates elected (133) than ever before, producing a Diet contingent with one-quarter freshman members. Of LDP winners, 16 per cent were new; in the JSP a massive 41 per cent were candidates elected to the Diet for the first time.

This turnover pattern is an important advantage of the medium-sized electoral system, given the weakness of the oppostion parties. It has infused new blood into the LDP, kept its incumbents from becoming complacent about their re-election prospects, and helped the party avoid the atrophy one might expect in a party perenially in control. The turnover rate would be much lower if Japan adopted a first-past-the-post, single-member districting system, as the 98 per cent re-election rate in the US House of Representatives suggests.

The 'Money Politics' Dilemma

The personalism and localism of Japanese political organization and election campaigning impose an enormous financial burden on Diet candidates and produce problems of political corruption that are well known. Political life in Japan is extraordinarily expensive, especially for LDP politicians. Since campaigning is perennial despite legal stipulations to the contrary, and because a Diet member or aspirant must build his own political machine to cultivate voter support, a tremendous amount of time and energy has to be given to raising money.

No one knows precisely how much money the Japanese electoral process consumes. The Political Funds Regulation Law requires politicians, political parties, and other political organizations to submit annual income reports. But it is an open secret that income reported is only the tip of an enormous iceberg of political contributions.

For example, it was widely reported that LDP Secretary-General Ozawa amassed a $300 million party campaign war chest for the February 1990 lower-house election. In addition, if each LDP candidate raised and spent on average close to a million dollars, which is a reasonable estimate, then the LDP and its 338 candidates probably spent well over half a billion dollars on the election. Further, when expenditures of the other parties and the $235 million in public financing are added,[4] it is not unreasonable to estimate the total cost of the 1990 lower-house race at one billion dollars.

Even in years when there are no elections, the cost of doing the daily business of being in national politics is enormous. LDP Diet members spend on average between $50,000 and $100,000 a month to keep their enterprise going. And many spend far more than that. According to a recent report of a group of ten reform-minded first-term LDP Diet members who created a 'Utopia Club', each of the ten spends an average of $1 million a year, the most frugal half that amount, and the biggest spender nearly half as much again. Diet salaries and other financial support provided by the government total less than $150,000 a year. Therefore, each of these freshman Diet members has to come up on his own with close to a million dollars a year on average.[5] Needless to say, senior Diet members, not to mention faction leaders, have much higher expenses.

There is little mystery as to how these vast sums are spent. At least half goes for staff and office rental expenses. In contrast to the large government budget for congressional staff in the American system, the Japanese government pays for only two secretaries per Diet member, without regard to seniority or election district population. Diet members may hire as many additional staff assistants as they wish, but at their own expense.

The government also provides each member with a small two-room suite in one of the two lower house member buildings. Members are free to rent additional space in commercial buildings in the area, which happens to be at the centre of the world's most expensive real estate market. In earlier years it was common for senior politicians to maintain a private office in a building in the vicinity of the Diet. It was relatively rare for back-benchers to do so. Since the early 1980s, and despite the enormous expense, it has become rather common among even junior LDP Diet members to rent a private office in addition to the office space provided in the Diet member building.

The size of the staffs of junior LDP Diet members has increased substantially in the past decade. Political funding reforms adopted in 1975, as discussed below, threw much more fund-raising responsibilities on individual Diet members, which in turn required more support staff to handle fund-raising chores. Wider politician involvement in the policy process, and the need to service constituents also have increased the pressures on Diet members to increase their staff. Even Japan's emergence as a global actor and the popularity of 'internationalization' has had an impact: a substantial number of LDP politicians now have foreigners—mostly American with an occasional European or South-East Asian—working as staff assistants in Diet member offices.

A private office serves other purposes as well. It gives the Diet member a chance to avoid having to spend his time greeting constituents, well-wishers, hangers-on, and various others who stream through the Diet building office day after day. A secretary can be placed there to say that the *sensei*—the honorific title by which Diet members are called—is off at some important meeting. Not insignificantly, a private office also has become a status symbol, a visible demonstration of the Diet member's political clout and his ability to afford his own space. Maintaining a private office and a staff that may consist of twenty or more people alone can cost close to a million dollars a year.

Because campaigning is a year round, ceaseless activity, Japanese politicians spend a small fortune on transportation and communication. Again citing Utopia Club figures, an average first-termer spends over $12,000 a month on these expenses. The Japanese government provides each Diet member with a free pass to use on the national JR railway system. A member living far from Tokyo can trade in the pass for a monthly transportation allowance of about $500 which, given the exorbitant cost of domestic air travel in Japan, is barely enough to purchase one round-trip ticket to many destinations.

There is no doubt that a great deal of the pressure on Japanese politicians to raise money would be relieved if the government made more money available for staff and transportation and provided more adequate office space. But it is just as difficult for Japan's Diet members to give themselves these benefits as it is for American Congressmen to give themselves a rise. So politicians have little choice but to go out into the political market-place looking for money.

Beyond the costs of staff and office, the heaviest financial burden on Diet members involves *kankonsōsai*, literally the 'ceremonies of birth, marriage and death'. According to one representative newspaper survey, an LDP Diet member or his representative attends 9.6 weddings a month on average and leaves a cash gift of $75–150 each time. This same survey found Diet members attending funerals on average 26.5 times a month, leaving a condolence gift of $75 each time. One member who was polled reported attending over a hundred funerals in a single month. Some politicians have ongoing contracts with mortuaries to send automatically telegrams of condolence in the politician's name to the relative of anyone who dies in the district.

The localism and personalism of Japanese political organization make it virtually impossible for politicians to avoid extensive involvement in these kinds of activities even if they wanted to. Gift exchange is so integral a part of Japanese social life that politicians risk being accused of being indifferent to their constituents and of forgetting who elected them to office if they do not actively engage in these financially taxing *kankonsōsai* activities.

In an effort to get some control over escalating costs, the Diet amended the election law in 1989 to forbid Diet members and other politicians from making monetary gifts at weddings and funerals they do not themselves attend. Non-monetary offerings, including flowers and incense sticks, are banned even if the politician is present at the ceremony. The amended law also prohibits politicians from providing *sake* to senior citizen social clubs or giving them financial support for recreational trips.

But the ink on the new law was hardly dry before loopholes were discovered. Nothing in the law prevents a Diet member's secretary, for example, from making a monetary gift in his own rather than the Diet member's name. Of course, everyone would know that the politician was the actual source of the gift. All it takes is one politician in a district to resort to a loophole like this before everyone else feels compelled to follow suit. There is no evidence that the 1989 amendment has had any substantial impact in reducing the heavy burden that *kankonsōsai* impose on the financial resources of Japan's politicians.

The other major expense incurred by Diet members involves servicing the politician's *kōenkai*, the personal mass membership support organization that provides the local organizational machinery and access to the electorate that every politician needs to run a successful campaign. It may seem odd to describe a politician's support organization as a financial burden on the politician rather than on the organization's general membership but in Japan *kōenkai* is just that. Utopia Club members report spending between 15 and 20 per cent of their budgets on printing and mailing *kōenkai* newsletters to members, paying for meetings, and sponsoring such special events as bus excursions to visit the Diet.[6]

Kankonsōsai activities are directly related to *kōenkai* maintenance. Attendance at weddings and funerals is part of the process of keeping up the morale of existing members and recruiting new ones. Each new name card obtained at such occasions is entered into the *kōenkai* name list. Newsletters and invitations to special events follow, all in the hope that the recipient will be inspired to help the politician in the next election campaign.

There is also a related, though almost always unreported *kōenkai* expense that probably raises the budgets of Diet members higher then even the most candid and reform-minded of them reveal. To keep the *kōenkai* operating smoothly, the Diet member or candidate has to reward the local politicians and other notables who provide the organization's leadership, much as powerful political machines in Mayor Daley's Chicago or Tammany Hall would see to it that 'ward heelers' would be adequately reimbursed for their shoe leather. (The Japanese refer to some of these payments as *ashidai*, 'foot money'.) It is in these interactions with local élites who supposedly have the ability to deliver votes that the dangers and temptations of corrupt behaviour—of paying for delivery of a specified number of votes—is most rife. Direct vote-buying is rare in Japan, but paying people who supposedly have the ability to deliver their particular group of supporters is not.

In contrast to the election law's myriad restrictions on campaign activity, Japan's law regulating political financing sets few restrictions on how politicians either raise or spend money. The Political Funds Regulation Law calls for public disclosure of political funds and sets limits on the total amount candidates may use in their election campaigns. Both politicians and contributors have been able to find so many ways to circumvent the disclosure requirements, however, that no one regards the annual political funding report issued by the Home Ministry as a reliable indicator of the amount or of the sources of most political funding. Furthermore, Diet members will readily admit that their campaign expenditures far exceed what the law permits, which range roughly from $100,000 to $150,000 depending on the population of the district.

The revision of the Political Funds Regulation Law in 1975 set limits for the first time on corporate contributions, limiting even the largest firms to no more than approximately $750,000 in contributions to political parties. Donations to any one faction or individual politician were limited to about $10,000. The revised law also sought to encourage individual, as opposed to corporate, contributions. It permits individuals to donate up to $150,000 to parties and $75,000 to factions and individuals. Such donations are tax deductible up to an amount that, combined with other tax-deductible contributions, do not exceed 25 per cent of annual income.

This reform of the law was pushed through by the late Prime Minister Takeo Miki who was an avid student of British politics and a strong advocate of political reform. Miki's purpose in revising the law was to strengthen parties and weaken factions. But long established patterns of political behaviour have a way of frustrating the goals of the most ardent political reformers. Contrary to the hopes of the Prime Minister, and the fears of the party's faction bosses, a shift to a more party-centred pattern of political funding did not materialize. Corporate financing of political funding did not diminish and donations by individuals did not rise significantly.

Instead, the reform had a number of unanticipated and mostly deleterious effects on political funding patterns in Japan. Two are particularly noteworthy. A far heavier fund-raising burden was placed on the shoulders of individual politicians, resulting in the expansion of staff mentioned earlier. And by setting limits on corporate contributions and generally making fund-raising more complicated, the reform forced politicians to develop new fund-raising techniques and to spread a wider net and spend more time and energy than ever before in the search for funds.

Factions quickly adjusted their fund-raising techniques to accommodate the law's new restrictions. No longer able to rely on a single faction leader to collect huge sums from a few major business sources, senior faction members banded together to pool their efforts to raise money for the faction and to provide funding for new candidates unable to raise large amounts of money themselves.

Moreover, senior and junior politicians alike found themselves forced to rely on their own fund-raising efforts to a much greater extent than was true before the law was revised. No longer able to depend on the faction to provide the major share of their funding needs, candidates were pushed further into the arms of favour-seeking businessmen, both at the national and the local level. The

typical back-bencher relies heavily on constituency-based businesses for money and on Tokyo-based companies that his faction
leader helps him gain access to. There also appears to be a fairly
large number of politicians who go into personal debt to finance
their campaigns. As long as they are elected, they can keep on
borrowing to pay off earlier loans.

These kinds of fund-raising pressures create obvious temptations
to engage in corrupt activities that would provide some financial
breathing room. The dynamics of a system that requires the
surreptitious acquisition of an awesome amount of political money
have made political corruption a major problem in Japanese
politics, as was revealed most recently in a scandal involving a
company named Recruit.

This young diversified service company gave a large number of
politicians, and a few senior business leaders and newspaper
executives as well, the opportunity to make a killing on the stock
market by selling them shares in a subsidiary just prior to its listing
on the exchange. In some cases Recruit even lent the politicians the
money needed to buy the shares. These favoured insiders all made
windfall profits when the company went public.

Providing an opportunity to purchase shares in this manner is
not illegal under Japanese law except in situations where it can be
proved that the offer was a bribe made in expectation of a specific
favour. Government prosecutors were able to find enough incrimi-
nating evidence only to indict two politicians on suspicion of
bribery. Other recipients of Recruit largess, however, suffered such
severe public criticism that they were forced to resign their party
and government posts. None, however, resigned their seats in the
Diet as some people demanded.

The Recruit scandal sparked new calls for political reform
including not only the prohibition of specified activities—such as
insider trading—but a change in the medium-size election district
system as well. It has now become part of the conventional wisdom
in Japan that this system is the source of Japan's 'money politics'
and that it thwarts realization of the elusive goal of party-centred
election campaigns. A government advisory committee has recom-
mended adoption of a modified West German system, one in which
voters would choose some members of the lower-house in single-
member districts and others from a party list. Prime Minister Kaifu
made adoption of this new election system a major goal of his

administration. His efforts were frustrated, however, by opposition parties that feared that a single-member district system would strengthen the LDP, and by LDP politicians who feared what any change in the system they know so well might do to their re-election chances.

The local and personal bases of political organization in Japan have deep roots in Japanese history and social structure and are not likely to be eradicated by changing the electoral system, despite the widespread belief in Japan that single-member districts necessarily produce strong local party organization and party-centred campaigns. On this particular issue, the Japanese insist on pointing to the British example and steadfastly refuse to consider the implications of the experience of the United States where elections also are enormously expensive and campaigns are politician, rather than party, centred. In the Japanese context, adoption of a system of small single-member constituencies is all too likely to reinforce current patterns of highly personalized campaign strategies and a strong local orientation in candidate appeals. And it is certain to reduce the rate of turnover of new and incumbent candidates within the LDP that has been such an important feature of the medium-size election district system.

It is not at all clear what reforms would have an appreciable effect on the amount of money used in politics in Japan. Closing some of the loopholes in the present law might help. Currently, for example, there are limits on business contributions to any one factional organization or to a particular politician's organization, but politicians and factions may set up as many organizations as they wish, each of which is subject to the same $10,000 limit. And businessmen may treat the cost of purchasing tickets to fund-raising 'parties' as a business expense rather than as a political contribution.

There is a danger that more severe restrictions on corporate contributions and a thorough plugging of legal loopholes that permit politicians to circumvent virtually all existing restrictions on campaign funding might cure the disease, and kill the patient. The Japanese legal framework for campaigning is already extremely restrictive. Making it more so, and making those additional restrictions work, would raise serious questions about the openness of the campaign process.

There is no quick fix to the general problem of political money in modern democracies or to the specific form it takes in Japan. Reforms aimed at narrow, specific issues may have a more salutary effect than grand designs aimed at fundamental change. The building of adequate office space, for example, combined with a ban on the rental of commercial space, and increased government support of Diet member staff expenses, could significantly reduce fund-raising pressures on Japan's Diet members.

Beyond this, the only thing that may significantly ameliorate Japan's 'money politics' is politicians' self-restraint generated by fear that exposure of wrongdoing would undermine public support. In that sense, incidents such as the Recruit scandal have a positive impact on political behaviour even when they do not result in specific legal changes. But the process, needless to say, is an evolutionary one and will leave Japanese politicians and voters alike struggling with the issue of political money and corruption for a long time to come.

Candidates and Parties Revisited

Having raised money, built an organization, and concluded the pre-election campaign, the candidate for the lower-house enters into a two-week official campaign period. Because of the limitations on campaign practices, candidates run through a prescribed routine of sidewalk speeches and rallies. They also spend a good part of the day driving around in their campaign car asking voters for support over the car's loudspeaker.

Still, the official campaign is important in the electoral process in Japan. As Japan has become more urbanized and affluent, and as old values that tied people closely to their communities and community leaders have weakened, politician confidence that personal support organizations and the vote-mobilizing powers of local notables will produce enough votes for victory has declined. Thus the brief official campaign period offers candidates an opportunity to go after voters who have not been reached by their organization-based efforts and who have not yet decided whom to cast their vote for. The official campaign gives candidates the opportunity to secure the extra margin of support that can spell the difference between victory and defeat.

How important are campaigns—pre-election and the official

one—in getting elected in Japan? No one can hope to get elected without building a personal campaign organization and working energetically to get out the vote. But do most or even a large number of voters base their voting choice on the appeal of a particular politician, the charm of a campaign poster, or the request of a local leader of the candidate's support organization? Politicians seem to think so: after all, they spend an enormous amount of time and money to make these appeals. But are substantive issues and political party identification relatively inconsequential in Japanese elections?

The conventional view of Japanese voting behaviour is that issue salience is low and party identification weak. In rural areas in particular personal ties and social obligations are seen as the key to mobilizing electoral support. And regardless of the characteristics of the individual districts, the multi-member districting system itself ensures that voters will have to choose among individuals of the same party if they are inclined to vote for a party that runs more than one candidate.

This feature of the medium-size election district system makes it extremely difficult to discover what motivates voters when they make their voting choices. Japanese opinion surveys usually ask voters whether they vote for party or candidate, but in the Japanese system the question itself does not make much sense. Thus one has to analyse opinion data with caution and rely on other, less quantifiable indicators to gauge the degree to which issues and parties affect voter choice.

As far as issue salience is concerned, there has been a steady increase in the importance voters attach to national and international issues in voting over the past decade. Moreover, this seems to be almost as true now for rural as for urban voters. Mass communications, a mass higher education system, and the urbanization of rural areas have contributed to weakening the urban-rural cleavage that used to characterize Japan's political culture. The mass media saturates Japan. There is nearly 100 per cent literacy (and almost every Japanese graduates from high school). Virtually every household subscribes to at least one national newspaper and has at least one television set. The Japanese are not only bombarded with a constant flow of information; the news they receive is strikingly uniform because of the nation-wide coverage provided by major newspapers and television networks.

No doubt such information diffusion affects attitudes about politics and parties, as was demonstrated recently in public reaction to media exposure of the Recruit scandal and the coverage of the controversy revolving around the introduction of a consumption tax. In Japan, however, because of the strong personal and local ties that bind politicians and voters, a high threshold of discontent has to be breached before many voters will reject a candidate they formerly supported and shift to one identified with a different policy position. The combination of the Recruit scandal and the consumption tax did drive many people over this threshold, however, and resulted in the LDP's loss of its majority position in the 1989 upper-house election.

Issue salience can work to the LDP's benefit too. Opinion polls offer incontrovertible evidence that most voters are apprehensive about the kinds of policy changes that might be initiated if the LDP were to be replaced in government by one or more of the opposition parties. The LDP is no longer particularly popular in Japan, but the dominant view among the electorate is that it is the only party capable of governing. Needless to say, this view has had its impact on voting behaviour.

Voting behaviour in Japan, in other words, has become less predictable. Support for the LDP is soft and about 40 per cent of the electorate do not support any party. For the aspirant to high political office in Japan this has complicated the formulation of campaign strategies. Relying on the support of local élites and on personal support organizations alone to mobilize voter support is not sufficient. Elections are won on the margin and, with an electorate whose voting behaviour is less predictable than in earlier times, other factors—from the attractiveness of a candidate's poster to the popularity of a party leader or the emergence of a controversial policy issue—take on added importance.

Consequently, everything about Japanese campaigning has become more important: personal campaigning, party image, issue salience. There has been significant change over the past two decades which has made campaigning more sophisticated, intense, continuous, and expensive. But change has occurred within a context of extraordinary continuity. Some of the most important elements of continuity, as we have seen, go back not only two or three decades, but much further into Japan's modern history. Japan has followed its own particular path to reach the common ground of modern democratic campaign practices. It now also confronts a common problem of finding solutions to the serious problems these practices have created.

Notes

1. There are one single-member, four two-member, and one six-member districts.
2. Cited in Gerald L. Curtis, *The Japanese Way of Politics* (New York: Columbia University Press, 1988), 170.
3. See *Nihon Keizai Shinbun* 13 Jan. 1990.
4. The national budget for the 1990 lower-house election was approximately $235 million. Included in this budget are the allotments to candidates for television and press advertising, mailing of permitted written campaign materials, and the like. Also included are direct government expenses for the campaign brochure, a sheet containing the biographies and statements of each candidate that is produced for each district and mailed to every household.
5. On the Utopia Club, see Iwai Tomoaki, *Seiji Shikin No Kenkyú, Rieki Yúdó no Nihonteki Seiji Fúdó* (Tokyo: Nihon Keizai Shinbunsha, 1990); and Hirose Michisada, *Seiji To Kane* (Tokyo: Iwanami Shinsho, 1990).
6. The general practice is for people participating in such events to pay the basic cost involved. But the politician subsidizes the event by hosting lunches, providing souvenirs, staffing the occasion, and so on.

References

Blaker, Michael F. (ed.), *Japan at the Polls: The House of Councillors Election of 1964* (Washington, DC: American Enterprise Institute for Public Policy Research, 1976).

Campbell, John C. (ed.), *Parties, Candidates and Votes in Japan: Six Quantitative Studies* (Ann Arbor, Mich.: Center for Japan Studies, University of Michigan, 1981).

Curtis, Gerald L., *The Japanese Way of Politics* (New York: Columbia University Press, 1988).

—— *Election Campaigning Japanese Style* (New York: Columbia University Press, 1971).

Flanagan, Scott C., Kohei, Shinsaku, Miyake, Ichiro, Richardson, Bradley M., and Watanuki, Joji, *The Japanese Voter* (New Haven, Conn.: Yale University Press, 1991).

—— and Richardson, Bradley, *Japanese Electoral Behavior: Social Cleavages, Social Networks and Partisanship*, Sage Contemporary Political Sociology Series No. 06–024 (London: Sage Publications, 1977).

Passin, Herbert (ed.), *A Season of Voting: The Japanese Elections of 1976 and 1977* (Washington, DC: American Enterprise Institute for Public Policy Research, 1979).

Stockwin, J. A. A., *Dynamic and Immobilist Politics in Japan* (Basingstoke: Macmillan, 1988).

Walanuki, Joji, Miyake, Ichiro, Inoguchi, Takashi, and Kabashima, Ikuo, *Electoral Behavior in the 1983 Japanese Election* (Tokyo: Institute of International Relations, Sophia University, 1986).

12

The Impact of Electioneering in the United States

If elections in the rest of the world are becoming 'Americanized', then what is happening in America? The last forty years have seen a variety of notable changes in campaign technology, the role of political parties, and other important features of the electoral process. I shall attempt to distinguish between temporary changes associated with a specific set of historical events—in particular, with what Burnham[1] has referred to somewhat melodramatically as 'the cosmic smash-ups of the late 1960s'—and more permanent structural changes in the American electoral system.

Uncritical observers have, I believe, been too facile in seizing upon and extrapolating from the most salient electoral changes of the last generation. As a result, they have produced a caricature of contemporary American electoral politics—a colourful but sometimes misleading portrait of its current state and likely future prospects. In this essay, I draw upon events of the last forty years in attempting to clarify what is temporary and what is permanent, what is important and what is superficial in recent American electoral politics. The resulting picture features relatively more emphasis on underlying elements of stability than is currently fashionable, and more modest agnosticism concerning the political implications of the real and important changes that define the new American prototype.

The author thanks Christopher Achen, Richard Fenno, Wendy Schiller, and the editors for helpful comments on earlier drafts and Douglas Rivers for suggesting a statistical analysis of presidential campaign effects.

Candidate Selection

Over and above the numerous elections prescribed by the law, which were quite enough to bewilder the citizen, there were elections for choosing the representatives of the party. Besides the acts of the constitutional representatives of the people, the electors had also to follow and weigh those of the several series of representatives of the parties. The citizens were not equal to this task, and proved once more, and still more decisively, that the efficacy of the elective principle is limited.[2]

The most obvious and important changes in American candidate selection processes in the last forty years have been at the presidential level, where the uniquely American mechanism of direct primaries has become the dominant means of selecting the parties' presidential nominees. To Harry Truman, as Nelson Polsby has recalled, primaries were 'eyewash'. Adlai Stevenson in 1952 and even Hubert Humphrey in 1968 managed to be nominated without entering any primaries at all. More typically, in the 'mixed system' that emerged from the progressive reforms at the turn of the century and survived until 1968, presidential candidates would selectively enter primaries in several states in order to demonstrate their electability to the party leaders who actually controlled the nomination. Only in the last twenty years has an active and far-flung primary campaign become the main, and unavoidable, element in any serious quest for the presidency.

To a large extent this sea change is simply a matter of numbers: the proportion of each party's convention delegates selected in state primaries has doubled, from about 40 per cent before 1964 to about 80 per cent since 1980. But it is also a matter of legitimacy. The current primary-dominated system is the latest step in a long process of democratizing American candidate selection procedures. Like the changes from informal nominations to congressional caucuses, from congressional caucuses to national conventions, and from conventions to conventions-with-primaries, the change from a mixed system to a primary-dominated system was largely justified as an effort to create a more 'democratic' nominating process.[3] Indeed, the transitional experience of Hubert Humphrey in 1968 suggests that any future candidate who could, somehow, manage to win a presidential nomination without competing in the primaries might find that nomination so tainted in the public's estimation as to be nearly worthless.

A curious and significant feature of the current presidential primary system is that the various states vote sequentially over a four-month period. Thus, results in early states—amplified and interpreted by the news media—provide strong cues about the candidates' popularity to voters in subsequent primaries. One implication of this fact is that relatively unknown candidates may be able to parlay small-scale successes in the earliest states into significant national attention and support.[4]

This possibility has attracted more and different candidates than used to compete in presidential elections. For example, in December 1974, a Gallup poll asked Democratic voters to pick their first choice for the 1976 presidential nomination from a list of thirty-one major party figures. Jimmy Carter did not make the list. But by pulling off a few noteworthy early upsets, Carter managed to leapfrog over a field of better-known opponents to win the nomination. It is difficult to imagine a major party anywhere else in the world choosing as its leader a politician so inconspicuous only eighteen months earlier.

Carter's success dramatizes another important feature of the contemporary sequential primary system: its efficiency in 'winnowing' enough candidates out of the race to ensure that there will be a clear primary-season winner. Carter won his first primary, in New Hampshire, with less than 30 per cent of the vote in a crowded field. But he was able to capitalize so successfully upon that victory that most of his opponents were forced out of the race well before the end of the primary season. A similar dynamic has operated in other recent multi-candidate races. As a result, the national party conventions, which used to play an important role in the choice of party nominees, now serve essentially to ratify the outcome of the primaries and to launch the autumn campaign.[5]

Only a few states retain versions of the convention system for nominating candidates for state and local offices. Primary elections are common at all levels, but do not usually generate significant competition, especially if there is an incumbent in the race. Whereas two recent incumbent presidents—Ford in 1976 and Carter in 1980—have faced serious primary challenges, more than 90 per cent of incumbent senators and governors (and probably even larger proportions at lower levels) are unopposed within their party or defeat their strongest opponent by more than 50 per cent of the primary vote. Primary competition is more common when there is no incumbent running, but still by no means universal: 23 of the 59 first-term senators and governors in office in 1990 were nominated by primary margins of 20 per cent or less, while 22 were nominated by margins exceeding 50 per cent of the primary vote.

Partisanship

The old parties are breaking up with daily increasing rapidity, they can no longer contain the incongruous elements brought together under the common flag; it is all very well for them to go on bearing the old names to wrap themselves in the ancient traditions; these names and these traditions do not succeed even in disguising the absence of common ideas and aspirations. Compact and stable majorities are only a historical reminiscence.[6]

The 'decline of parties' has been one of the major themes in academic commentary on contemporary American electoral politics. It is not uncommon for analysts to refer to a 'massive decay of partisan electoral linkages', or even to 'the ruins of the traditional partisan regime'.[7] In some respects this change has been real and permanent and profound. In other respects it has been temporary or illusory or both.

The view that state and local party organizations have withered into insignificance is widespread but, apparently exaggerated.[8] It does seem to be true that candidates play a larger role, and parties a relatively smaller role, than they once did in media coverage of campaigns and in voters' thinking about electoral politics. For example, the ratio of 'candidate mentions' to 'party mentions' in some major print media increased from about 2 to 1 in the 1950s to about 5 to 1 in 1980.[9]

But the evidence offered most regularly in support of the claim of partisan decline comes from trends in the electorate's 'identification' with one or the other of the major parties.[10] The relevant data, which appear in Figure 12.1, do indicate a noticeable decline from 1964 to 1974 in the proportion of the public who said they thought of themselves as Democrats or Republicans. Self-designated 'strong' and 'not strong' identifiers combined made up 77

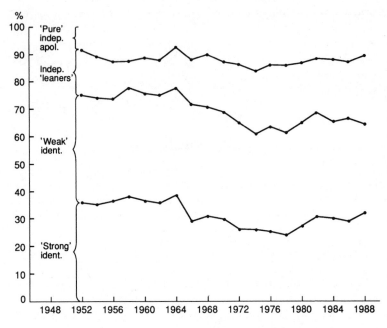

FIG. 12.1 *Trends in strength of party identification in electorate,*
1952–1988

per cent of the population in 1964 but only 60 per cent ten years
later.

It is worth noticing, however, that most of those who deny
thinking of themselves as partisans nevertheless allow that they
think of themselves as 'closer' to one party or the other. If we
include these 'leaners' among party identifiers, the much-vaunted
collapse of partisan loyalties looks rather meagre. Indeed, the
fraction of the public identifying with one party or the other by
this criterion has remained at a consistently high level for forty
years, varying between 82 and 92 per cent in every election since
1952, and rebounding by 1988 to a level closer to the top than to
the bottom of that range.

That the distinction between 'weak' identification and 'leaning'
is largely rhetorical should be evident from the vote choices of
people who place themselves in each category. 'Leaners' vote with

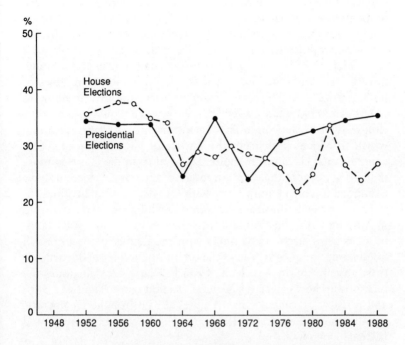

FIG. 12.2   *Total impact of party identification on voting behaviour in presidential and House elections, 1952–1988*

their party about 75 per cent of the time in House elections; the corresponding figure for weak identifiers is about 80 per cent. In presidential elections 'leaners' have actually been more loyal than weak identifiers, voting for their party's candidates about 80 per cent of the time.

The net result, illustrated in Figure 12.2, is that partisan loyalties had at least as much impact on voting behaviour at the presidential level in the 1980s as in the 1950s. In each period, by comparison with the vote choices of 'pure' independents, it appears that party loyalties of all sorts ('strong', 'weak', and 'leaning') shifted the votes of about one-third of the electorate, as compared to one-quarter or less in the troughs of 1964 and 1972. In this sense at least, the declining impact of partisanship in the 1960s and early 1970s was clearly a temporary phenomenon, attributable to specific candidates and events rather than to any permanent collapse of the 'traditional partisan regime'.

The corresponding trend for elections to the House of Representatives, also illustrated in Figure 12.2, tells a somewhat different story. Here there has been a more sustained decline in party voting, mostly attributable to the fact that incumbent representatives of both parties have been increasingly successful in appealing to voters across party lines. Even here, however, it would be a mistake to lose sight of the continuing significance of party identification, which is evident both from the impact of partisanship in recent congressional elections in Figure 12.2 and from the fact that more than 70 per cent of the voters in recent congressional elections have continued to vote in accordance with broader partisan loyalties.

Another way to illustrate the continuing influence of partisanship in American elections is to contrast the continuity and predictability of general election coalitions with the fluidity of coalitions in nominating campaigns, where the organizing influence of parties is truly absent. Following a lead of Key,[11] Figure 12.3 illustrates the relationship between states' general election votes (Figure 12.3(a)) and primary or caucus votes (Figure 12.3(b)) for the Democratic presidential candidates in 1984 and 1988, Walter Mondale and Michael Dukakis.

Except in the District of Columbia, Mondale's general election vote percentage varied in a fairly narrow range (from 25 to 50 per cent) and Dukakis's varied in a similarly narrow range (from 30 to 55 per cent). Moreover, the continuity of support for the two candidates was very considerable, as evidenced by the strong correlation between the outcomes in each state in the two elections.

The primary and caucus results in Figure 12.3(b) present a very different picture. Each candidate's support varied from less than 5 per cent in some states to more than 60 per cent in others. (Dukakis garnered more than 60 per cent of the primary vote in many more states than Mondale did, because most of his opponents dropped out of the race earlier in the primary season). But what is even more significant is that there is almost no correlation—positive or negative—between Mondale's support in 1984 and Dukakis's in 1988. Without the organizing influence of party labels, each candidate had to build his supporting coalition from scratch.

The comparison in Figure 12.3 suggests quite vividly that, whatever real decline American political parties may have seen,

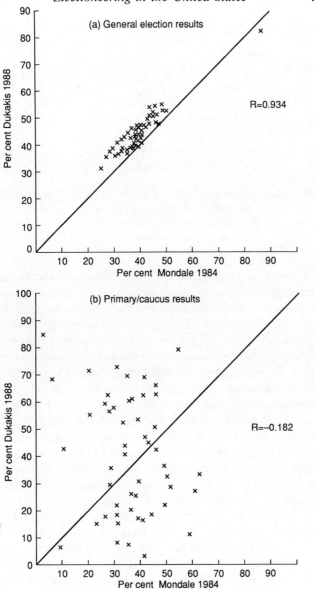

FIG. 12.3 *Continuity of democratic nomination and election coalitions, 1984–1988*

    (*a*) General election results

    (*b*) Primary/caucus results

inter-party politics remains an organized and predictable affair by comparison with the real disorganization and unpredictability of politics without party labels. The last generation has certainly seen a secular—and presumably permanent—increase in the relative salience of candidates in American politics. But what is surprising in light of this change is not that partisan loyalties have become so weak, but that they have remained so strong.

Pocketbook Voting

Of all races in an advanced stage of civilization, the American is the least accessible to long views. . . . Always and everywhere in a hurry to get rich, he does not give a thought to remote consequences; he sees only present advantages. . . . He does not remember, he does not feel, he lives in a materialist dream.[12]

Politicians have long recognized that incumbents tend to fare well when economic conditions are good and poorly when economic conditions are bad. There was more than rationalization in Richard Nixon's account of the 1960 presidential campaign: 'In October, usually a month of rising employment, the jobless rolls increased by 452,000. All the speeches, television broadcasts, and precinct work in the world could not counteract that one hard fact.'[13]

The contribution of recent scholarly work [14] has been to specify the magnitude and regularity of the impact of economic conditions on electoral politics. Indeed, the relationship between economic conditions and election outcomes is by now one of the best documented relationships in the whole field of American politics.

Figure 12.4 illustrates the most familiar version of the relationship between economic conditions and election outcomes. The figure graphs the incumbent party's margin of victory or defeat in each of the last eleven presidential elections (measured on the left-hand scale) and the percentage change in real disposable income per capita in each election year (measured on the right-hand scale). The correlation between income changes and incumbent margins is far from perfect—the standard error of the linear regression reported as Model 1 in Table 12.1 is 8.5 percentage points—but it is clear that economic conditions have had a significant electoral impact. By this estimate (the more elaborate analysis by Markus in 1988 produced a similar estimate), every 1 per cent change in real

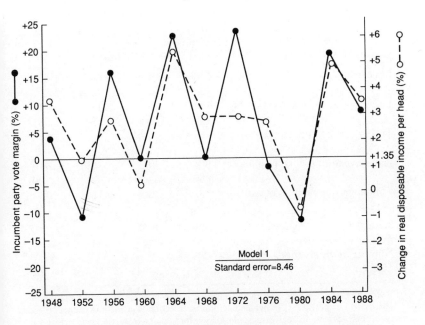

FIG. 12.4 *Income changes and incumbent party vote margins in presidential elections, 1948–1988*

income has translated into a change of 4.8 points in expected vote margin. Thus, for the incumbent party's presidential candidate, the difference between a boom year (4 per cent income growth) and a recession year (no real income growth) is the difference between a possible landslide and a likely defeat.

Should this strong connection between economic conditions and election outcomes be reassuring or disconcerting from the perspective of democratic theory? The answer to this question hinges in large part upon a matter of timing. It is customary for analysts to measure economic conditions in the election year against the conditions of the immediately preceding year. But if the voter 'sees only present advantages', as this formulation suggests, then, as Tufte warned,[15] 'There is a bias toward policies with immediate highly visible benefits and deferred hidden costs—myopic policies for myopic voters.' Conversely, if voters evaluate incumbent parties on the basis of their cumulative performance in office, then

TABLE 12.1. *Regression results for models of presidential election outcomes*

Explanatory variables	Model 1	Model 2	Model 3	Model 4
Intercept	−6.48	−15.36	−2.65	−1.67
	(4.49)	(6.08)	(1.75)	(2.93)
Election year income change (%)	4.80	0	3.18	2.71
	(1.40)	(—)	(.59)	(.98)
Three-year income change (%)	0	3.06	0	0
	(—)	(.77)	(—)	(—)
Pre-convention poll margin (%)	0	0	.369	.410
	(—)	(—)	(.060)	(.100)
Campaign spending (ln odds)	0	0	9.12	0
	(—)	(—)	(2.29)	(—)
Standard error of regression	8.46	8.08	3.00	5.08
Adjusted R-squared	.52	.65	.94	.83
Number of observations (years)	11	9	11	11
	(48–88)	(52–84)	(48–88)	(48–88)

Note: In each case, the dependent variable is the incumbent party's margin of victory (+) or defeat (−) in percentage points. 'Election year income change' is the percentage change in real disposable income per capita from the year before the election to the year of the election. 'Three-year income change' is the compounded percentage change in real disposable income per capita in the year before the election, the election year, and the year after the election. 'Pre-convention poll margin' is the incumbent party candidate's percentage point margin (+ or −) in the last pre-convention Gallup poll. 'Campaign spending' is the natural log of the ratio of incumbent spending to challenger spending. Standard errors of parameter estimates are in parentheses.

electoral incentives will tend to be in relatively close accord with voters' long-run economic interests.

What is the electorate's time horizon? The data on this point are less than definitive, but they are suggestive. In the nine presidential elections from 1952 to 1984, the incumbent party's margin of victory or defeat was positively related not only to income changes in the election year (the most common specification), but also to income changes in the years just before and—even more telling— just after the election year. As a comparison of Models 1 and 2 in Table 12.1 shows, compounded changes in income over these three years account for election outcomes even better than election year changes alone. (The analysis of Model 2 is based on the nine elections for which three-year income data are available; but the specification in Model 1 produces essentially similar results for this subset of elections as for the entire post-war era.) Since conditions in these three years taken together encompass most of what a reasonable observer could plausibly associate with the economic policy of the current incumbent, this result suggests that the American electorate is actually rather less myopic than politicians and analysts alike seem to believe.

Money

The stronghold of the general interest, the State, was invaded on all sides by money. The corporations bought legislation, 'protection,' and favours of every kind, wholesale and retail; rich men bought seats in the highest legislative assembly more or less disguisedly, obtained seats in the Cabinet, ambassadorships. It seemed as if nothing could resist the well-filled purse, that money was king in the Republic.[16]

Money has always played an uncomfortable role in democratic politics. When citizens are free to attempt to influence their rulers, it seems inevitable that, whereas some will bring to bear time and effort and others eloquence and influence, still others will prefer to pay cash. Almost alone among Western democracies the United States has treated campaign spending as a protected form of political expression; this consitutional nicety has forced American reformers to invent elaborate, indirect, and incomplete controls on the role of money in campaigns, and their record of success has been correspondingly mixed.

The sheer amount of money spent in election campaigns has troubled some observers, but that concern seems overblown. After all, as V. O. Key observed long ago,[17] 'The aggregate expended in the year of a presidential election may seem huge, yet it probably does not exceed the total of the annual advertising bills of the principal soap companies.' Moreover, although campaign costs escalated markedly with the rise of television and other expensive new campaign technologies in the 1950s and 1960s, Figure 12.5[18] suggests that presidential campaign costs were still much lower in real terms (and allowing for the increasing size of the electorate) at their peak in 1972 than in the late nineteenth and early twentieth centuries. Certainly, the dollar or so per voter spent by both

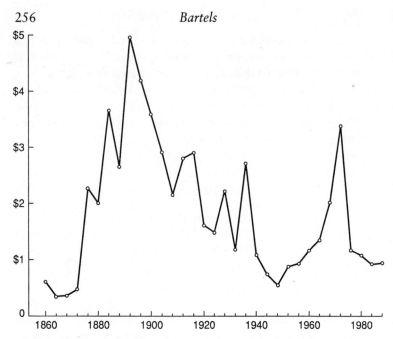

FIG. 12.5 *Campaign spending in presidential general elections,*
1860–1988 (in 1988 dollars per voter)

presidential candidates together in recent general elections does not
seem extravagant.

What does seem problematic is a system in which very wealthy
contributors dominate the campaign fund-raising process. The role
of big contributors was still relatively minor in the early 1960s, but
increased markedly in 1972, when contributions of $10,000 or
more amounted to more than $50 million (in 1972 dollars),
including more than $2 million from one wealthy insurance
executive.

The increasing cost of modern campaigns had already prompted
some congressional efforts to control campaign expenses. But the
sudden prominence of huge individual contributions, and especially
vivid Watergate era revelations about Nixon's White House operatives strong-arming corporations for bags of cash, produced new
and irresistible public support for reform. The Democratic majority
in Congress was more than happy to produce an alternative system,
in no small part because Democratic candidates had been outspent

by about two to one by their Republican opponents in each of the three most recent presidential campaigns.

There were two key innovations in the post-Watergate system of campaign finance. First, individuals are prohibited from contributing more than $1,000 to any one candidate in an election cycle or more than $20,000 to all candidates, groups, and parties per calendar year. (These limitations are held not to violate contributors' freedom of speech because they do not prohibit additional 'uncoordinated' spending in support of favoured positions or candidates). As a result, it is now impossible for a few very wealthy contributors to bankroll a candidate's campaign. Instead, candidates must attract numerous smaller contributions, both by participating in endless rounds of fund-raising dinners and cocktail parties and by organizing sophisticated direct mail solicitations.

The second key innovation in the post-Watergate system is that it offers public funds—albeit to presidential candidates only—in exchange for 'voluntary' adherence to expenditure limits. Before the nominating conventions, candidates who demonstrate 'seriousness' by raising $5,000 in relatively small contributions ($250 or less) in each of twenty states are eligible for public matching funds on a dollar-to-dollar basis, if they are willing to abide by overall and state-by-state expenditure limits. Since 1976, every major primary candidate but one (John Connally in 1980) has accepted expenditure limits in exchange for public matching of private contributions in the pre-convention campaign.

Every major party nominee since 1976 has accepted additional public funding for the general election campaign. These grants are equal for both parties and fixed in advance (but adjusted for inflation in each election cycle, so that in 1992 each nominee will get about $55 million, plus allowances for convention and accounting costs). The cost to the candidates of receiving these public funds is that they must limit their campaign expenditures to the same fixed amount. There are some loopholes—for example, presidential candidates can and do raise money for other candidates' campaigns, and they can and do benefit from uncoordinated expenditures by 'independent' individuals and groups—but the system has generally been considered effective.

With presidential elections off the agenda, recent efforts to reform campaign finance have focused on Congress. The impetus for reform has recently been refuelled by revelations of favours for a prominent Senate campaign contributor by the 'Keating Five', and more generally by a jump in already high inc imbent re-election rates and by the increasing prominence of Political Action Committee (PAC) money in congressional election campaigns.

The role of PACs is to channel contributions from organized interest groups such as corporations, unions, professional associations, and ideological groups. The total number of PACs increased from about 600 in 1974 to more than 4,000 by 1986, while total PAC contributions have grown from about $130 million in 1975–6 to $350 million in 1987–8 (in 1988 dollars). About 40 per cent of these contributions are to congressional candidates, with most of the rest going to candidates for state and local offices.

PACs are prominent targets for campaign reform in part because the 'special interest' groups that fund them are themselves objects of considerable popular mistrust. What is more, PAC contributions lack any appearance of principled political consistency because they are so overwhelmingly directed to incumbents of any and all stripes. In House races in 1988, incumbents took in eight PAC dollars for every one contributed to their challengers. And, as Figure 12.6 illustrates, the growing disparity in PAC contributions in recent years has been largely responsible for the fact that congressional incumbents now typically spend twice or three times as much on their campaigns as challengers do on theirs.

It is not entirely clear how much this growing disparity has contributed to the increasing security of incumbent Congressmen. Different studies provide somewhat different estimates of the impact of campaign spending in congressional elections.[19] They do agree that challengers' spending tends to be more productive than that of incumbents, presumably because many challengers are so unknown that they have much to gain simply by publicizing their existence. But this advantage seems far from sufficient to overcome the incumbents' advantage in PAC receipts, especially as it is the sort of advantage that tends, by its very nature, to disappear in races where the challenger manages to mount a serious campaign.

In any case, the most important function of incumbent fund-raising may be to dissuade serious challengers from entering the race in the first place. When the average incumbent Congressman running for re-election raises almost $400,000 and the average incumbent senator running for re-election raises almost $4,000,000, it is not suprising that many prospective challengers

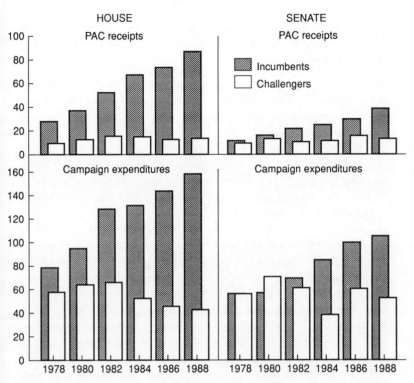

FIG. 12.6 *PAC receipts and total campaign expenditures in House and Senate elections, 1978–1988 (in 1988 $ millions)*

prefer to wait for death, resignation, or indictment to create a more level playing field.

It seems likely that any system of congressional campaign finance that provided more money to challengers would thereby make congressional elections more competitive. The most obvious remaining hurdle to reform is that any such system would have to be legislated into existence by the same incumbent Congressmen who are the main beneficiaries of the current system.

Campaign Technology

The interposition of third persons between the people and its numerous representatives, the selection of whom it did but ratify, reduced to a minimum the responsibility of the latter to their pretended constituents, and placed the real power in the hands of the election agencies and their managers, who, on pretence of helping bewildered public opinion, thus became its masters.[20]

At the local level, many American election campaigns look and work much like the campaigns of a generation ago. The slickest form of campaign technology in the average race for a seat in a county or state legislature may be the leaflet or the yard sign. But the higher the office and the larger the constituency—and, not coincidentally, the more money there is to spend—the more likely it is that campaigners will rely upon the distinctive technologies of modern electioneering: systematic polling, telephone banks, direct mail, and, above all, television.

Television emerged as a major social force in the United States during the 1950s. At the beginning of the decade, less than one American household in ten owned a television; by the end of the decade almost nine in ten did, and average television viewing exceeded five hours per day. Public responses to periodic surveys, summarized in Figures 12.7 and 12.8, suggest that in the early 1960s television surpassed newspapers both as the most important source of 'news about what's going on in the world today' and as the most 'believable' news medium. By the 1980s the percentage of the public who would 'be most inclined to believe' television reports in the case of a conflict was about twice as large as the percentage who would 'be most inclined to believe' newspaper reports.

Politicians and broadcasters alike were quick to seize upon the electoral potential of the new medium. The presidential election of 1952 saw the first television coverage of the parties' nominating convention, as well as other campaign news and candidate-sponsored television advertising. Television and radio advertising together accounted for about 30 per cent of each presidential candidate's general election campaign costs in 1952, with the fraction increasing to about 50 per cent by 1968.[21]

The pre-eminence of the mass media in modern presidential campaign strategy was highlighted in 1976, when new financial regulations drastically reduced the major candidates' general election campaign budgets. Jimmy Carter was allowed to spend about half as much as George McGovern had in 1972; Gerald Ford was

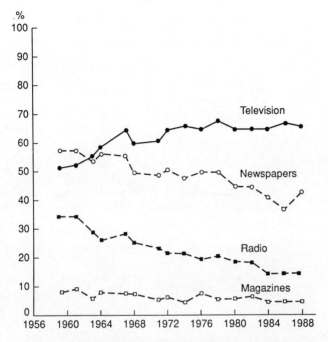

FIG. 12.7 *Primary sources of news, 1959–1988*

allowed to spend only about a third as much as Richard Nixon had in 1972. Nevertheless, both candidates managed, by drastically cutting their expenditures on everything from field staffs and local headquarters to campaign buttons and bumper stickers, to spend about as much as their predecessors had on television and radio advertising.

What have been the political effects of the rise of television, survey research, direct mail, and other new campaign technologies? One effect, recognized early on by academic analysts, is that political influence has gravitated toward the professional specialists who control these technologies.[22]

Since many of the new technologies have evolved primarily in the commercial realm, the result has been a transfer of power from the professional political operatives who managed the canvassing activities of traditional party organizations to the professional pollsters, marketing specialists, and advertisers who have applied the same new technologies to sell soap, cars, and beer. That fact in

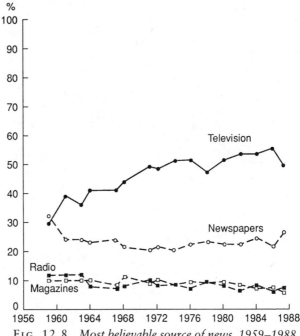

FIG. 12.8   *Most believable source of news, 1959–1988*

itself has generated considerable cynicism about 'The Selling of the President'.[23]

One index of the increasing influence of technical specialists within political campaigns is their increasing prominence as influential advisers between political campaigns. Jimmy Carter's media man, Gerald Rafshoon, continued to serve as a trusted adviser after his boss reached the White House. Pollsters Patrick Caddell and Richard Wirthlin likewise continued to consult on a regular basis between elections with Carter and Ronald Reagan, respectively. Caddell was instrumental in precipitating one of the defining episodes of Carter's presidency, the 1979 Camp David retreat and subsequent announcement of a national 'crisis of confidence'.[24]

In 1988, media consultant Roger Ailes and pollster Robert Teeter are supposed to have been the most influential boosters of Dan Quayle as a vice-presidential candidate.[25] Teeter was reportedly considered (though not selected) for a top White House staff position after Bush's election. Meanwhile, in a classic blend of electioneering, government, and entertainment in the television age, Ailes served as the co-executive producer of CBS's 1991 *All-Star Salute to Our Troops*, a blockbuster Gulf War welcome-home special featuring none other than the victorious commander-in-chief, Ailes' one-time client, George Bush. All of these examples point toward the evolution of what Blumenthal[26] has referred to as 'the true permanent campaign', with its consequent emphasis on the potential electoral costs and benefits of every policy step.

That campaign consultants and strategists are the 'masters' of 'bewildered public opinion' is much less obvious. In fact, much less is known in general about the impact of modern election campaigns on voters than one might gather from a superficial reading of the literature. Breathless accounts of brilliant campaign operatives manipulating the electorate are often based upon no better evidence than the claims of the operatives themselves. Specific assessments of effectiveness almost always take the passive voice (one consultant's campaign lyrics 'are generally conceded to be effective and entertaining' another's advertisements 'are given partial credit' for a candidate's comeback), or are attributed to 'observers', 'critics', or other consultants.[27]

When more substantial evidence is offered for the effectiveness of a particular campaign strategy, it is usually evidence of the simplest and least trustworthy sort: Campaign *A* did *X* and won. Thus, based on the evidence of the 1984 campaign, Kern[28] reasoned that 'Ronald Reagan's brand of emotional advertising' has become 'nearly indispensable in competitive races'. Of course, this reasoning overlooks many other factors that contributed to Reagan's victory in 1984—as well as the fact that Reagan won in 1980 with very simple advertisement emphasizing issues.[29]

Kern[30] similarly reasoned that 'Few can argue with the success of Roger Ailes's effort' in producing negative advertisements for George Bush in 1988. But what is the evidence of that success, other than the fact that Bush managed to win an election in a period of peace and prosperity and on the coat-tails of a remarkably popular predecessor? (Post-war patterns of presidential voting suggest that Bush should have been expected to win by nine or ten percentage points, given the state of the economy in 1988.)

In any case, negative advertisements have come and gone before in the cycle of campaign fashion. According to Kern[31] 'a recent analysis of presidential-level advertisements from 1952 through 1984 collected by the Political Commercial Archive found that fully a quarter of them were negative'. Presumably the other three-quarters were not. In 1972, one leading media specialist, Charles Guggenheim, was fired from a presidential campaign because he resisted producing negative advertisements, believing them to be 'ineffective'.[32] Guggenheim's client, George McGovern, was not obviously benefited by adopting a more negative media strategy, if in fact he did so.

Other analysts attributed the outcome of the 1988 election less to Ailes's media wizardry than to the ineptitude of his Democratic counterparts. Democratic Senator Terry Sandford's claim that Michael Dukakis ran 'the worst managed campaign in this century'[33] is an extreme example of this view. But even without the hyperbole, the explanation fails to explain how the same team that shepherded Dukakis masterfully through the 1988 Democratic primaries somehow became inexperienced, rigid, unpolitical bumblers in the autumn.

In fact, most changes in candidate support during recent presidential general-election campaigns can be accounted for nicely—without any reference to campaign wizardry or bumbling—on the basis of three simple principles:

1. Underdogs tend to gain ground. Holding a lead through four months of intensive national campaigning is no easy feat, even for a politician sufficiently skilled to have built such a lead in the first place. People will change their minds, and if most of them supported you in the first place those changes will tend to work to your disadvantage. Indeed, the regression results reported for Model 3 in Table 12.1 suggest that, other things being equal, less than 40 per cent of the pre-convention lead in the average post-war campaign has lasted until election day.

2. Economic prosperity gives the incumbent party a significant 'ace in the hole'. The effect of economic conditions on presidential election outcomes has been widely recognized; but it has not been widely recognized that much of this effect occurs during the course of the general-election campaign. In June or August, voters may have a variety of idiosyncratic concerns—or none at all. But the autumn campaign and the approach of election day tend to bring fundamental issues to the fore, and among these issues the state of

the economy is often foremost. The results reported for Model 3 in Table 12.1 show that, in the eleven post-war presidential campaigns, the incumbent party has gained or lost an average of about 1.6 per cent of the vote between June and November for every 1 per cent change in real income. In a boom year like 1964 or 1984, this effect might produce a vote shift of six or seven percentage points toward the incumbent, other things being equal; in a recession year like 1980 it might produce a vote loss of about three percentage points.

3. Candidates who outspend their opponents tend to gain ground. Although public financing of presidential campaigns has evened the playing field since 1976, previous campaigns saw significant spending differentials. The regression results for Model 3 in Table 12.1 suggest that a 25 per cent edge in campaign spending was associated with an expected vote gain of one percentage point, while a 100 per cent edge in campaign spending—the advantage enjoyed by Republican candidates from 1964 to 1972—was associated with an expected vote gain of about three percentage points. This association may be partly an artefact, reflecting the ability of good candidates to raise more money as well as the impact of spending itself. Thus, Model 4 in Table 12.1 compares the results of regression based solely upon the underdog and economic effects. Both effects are slightly weaker but still clearly significant given this specification of the model.

Figure 12.9 compares the actual change in the Democratic candidate's margin during each of the last eleven presidential campaigns with the change predicted on the basis of national economic conditions, erosion of early leads, and differential spending using the regression results for Model 3. Most of the observed change is accounted for by these three general tendencies. And much of what is left is inconsistent with the conventional assessments of journalists and other observers concerning campaign success or failure.

Harry Truman's dramatic comeback in 1948, the subject of one of the earliest and most influential academic studies of presidential campaigning[34] is more than adequately accounted for by the underdog factor, economic conditions, and Truman's spending advantage. Indeed, the three most recent Democratic campaigns—disasters all, according to the conventional wisdom—look no

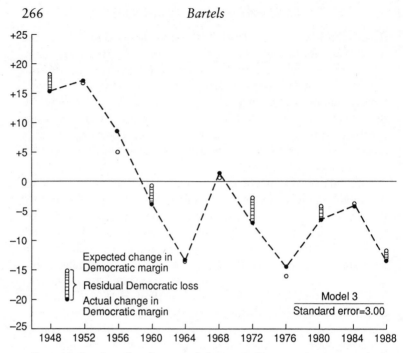

FIG. 12.9   *Actual and expected changes in Democratic vote margins*
during presidential election campaigns, 1948–1988

worse, and probably better, than Truman's campaign, once these
factors are taken into account. The wizardry of Roger Ailes and
the ineptness of Michael Dukakis together produced a residual vote
shift of less than 1 per cent in 1988. And at the outer extreme of
unexplained variation, Richard Nixon won over an additional 2.1
per cent of the electorate in a year when his opponent ran what
may really have been 'the worst managed campaign in this century',
most notably by selecting and then abandoning a vice-presidential
nominee who had been treated for depression with shock therapy.

The fact that recent presidential campaigns have not seemed to
produce many large, unaccountable changes in electoral support
should not be taken to suggest that campaigns are therefore
unimportant. Most obviously, residual vote shifts of the magnitude
suggested by Figure 12.9 are more than sufficient to change the
outcome of a close election. But in addition, it is worth bearing in
mind that even an unusually inept presidential campaign is a far

cry from no campaign at all. In a world where most campaigners make reasonably effective use of reasonably similar resources and technologies most of the time, much of their effort will necessarily be without visible impact, simply because every campaigner's efforts are balanced against more or less equally effective efforts to produce the opposite effect.

Electioneering and Governing

. . . the expression 'politics' has become a synonym for election affairs and has almost ceased to be associated with ideas of government and administration. Hence, the citizen who has been wrought into a paroxysm of excitement by the elections sinks into apathy immediately afterwards, and takes no interest in the way in which his representatives discharge their trust.[35]

American electoral politics has changed in significant ways in the last forty years. But what have been the implications of those changes for American government? Some connections seem obvious. If candidates are elected without recourse to parties, then they will tend to govern without recourse to parties. If control of the government is chronically divided, then major policy initiatives will be rare. If campaign news is filled with horse races, hoopla, and sound-bites, then politicians will not be electorally accountable for their actions.

Fortunately or unfortunately, such seemingly obvious connections between electioneering and governing often seem to dissolve upon close inspection. Divided government has been a prominent feature of American politics for most of the last forty years. But observers of contemporary electoral politics too often lose sight of the fact that it has been a fairly frequent occurrence throughout American political history. For example, different parties controlled the White House and the House of Representatives in 13 of the 19 Congresses since 1955, but also in 13 of the 27 Congresses from 1843 to 1897. In any case, the impact of divided partisan control on the outcomes of the legislative process is more often assumed than demonstrated. The only analyst to study the question in detail concluded simply and bluntly: 'It does not make all that much difference.'[36]

Have legislators become increasingly independent and unbound

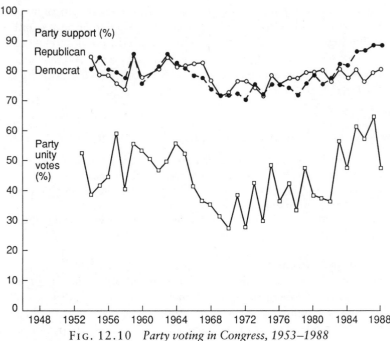

FIG. 12.10   *Party voting in Congress, 1953–1988*

by party discipline? According to a 1979 report in *Time* magazine, a Congress that 'used to operate through party discipline enforced by party leaders like Sam Rayburn' has become 'a catfight of centrifugal energies, a fractured, independent crew that in its less disciplined moments approaches the opera buffa standards of the Italian Chamber of Deputies'.[37]

The only problem with this picture is that it, too, is unsupported by the facts. As Figure 12.10 shows, party unity in Congress, which did dip significantly in the late 1960s, has returned to levels at least as high as in the good old days of Sam Rayburn—despite the fact that party identification continues to play a less important role in congressional voting. Thus, there seems to be more plausibility in the first half than in the second half of Wattenberg's suggestion [38] that 'voters reacted gradually over the last quarter of a century to the way in which politics was presented to them. Political parties themselves became less institutionally relevant and the public adjusted their views of them accordingly.'

Does the triviality of modern campaigning render democratic accountability impossible? Hoopla and tactical manœuvring certainly play a prominent role in media coverage of elections.[39] A content analysis of network television news during the heart of the 1988 presidential primary campaign (from the New Hampshire primary in early February through the New York primary in late April) found that almost 70 per cent of the stories had to do with the 'horse race'; less than 15 per cent had to do with policy issues.[40] Nevertheless, issues and ideology continue to play an important role in presidential nominating politics[41] as well as in general elections.[42]

In some respects, modern forms of electioneering have made candidates more, rather than less, directly accountable for their statements and actions. The production values of television news have increasingly made candidates the central figures in their own campaigns. Televised debates have attracted huge audiences in every presidential campaign since 1976, and in many campaigns at lower levels as well. These debates have probably focused more unmediated public atention on the candidates, their policies, and their political priorities than in any previous electoral era.

Finally, campaign consultants, however powerful they may be, provide none of the legitimizing cover of political parties. Roger Ailes and Robert Teeter may have been instrumental in picking Dan Quayle as a vice-presidential nominee, but there was never any doubt that it was George Bush whose political career rode on the consequences of that choice.

Can voters be fooled more readily by politicians wielding modern campaign technology than they were by politicians wielding the campaign technology of any earlier era? Does a simplistic televised mantra—'Read my lips: no new taxes'—communicate a candidate's commitment any less clearly or credibly than an issue paper or 'stump' speech? The case is, at least, unproven.

Perhaps, as Greenfield argued with regard to the 1980 presidential campaign,

The public had been exposed to political ads, and to their gimmicks, ever since the Eisenhower campaign of 1952 used spot advertising. They had grown in sophistication along with the medium. . . . More important, the press itself was so conscious of campaign advertising that political commercials had ceased to be isolated from the scrutiny given to speeches, position papers, and charges and countercharges.[43]

George Bush's use of the Willie Horton incident during the 1988 presidential campaign has come to symbolize the meanness, superficiality, and irrationality of modern electoral politics. One analyst, convinced that 'the electronic media give greater force and currency to scurrilities', argued that James G. Blaine's charges that Grover Cleveland 'had appointed to office 137 convicted criminals, including 2 murderers, 7 forgers, and several brothel keepers', and that the president 'beat and abused' his wife 'had nothing like the impact of a glowering Willie Horton, illustrating Republican claims that Dukakis had been "soft on crime".'[44]

It is hard to know how we might begin to evaluate this assessment of impact. In any event, it seems at least as fair to argue, as Barone and Ujifusa have, that Bush's advertisement

showed how Dukakis took a sensible and defensible policy (granting furloughs to prisoners scheduled to be released) and carried it to ridiculous extremes (granting furloughs to prisoners sentenced never to be released). It provided a valid basis for an inference that liberal Dukakis appointees would take sensible liberal policies and carry them to ridiculous extremes, with Dukakis's approval—which is exactly what many voters thought happened in the last national Democratic administration. Such an inference was neither racist nor irrational.[45]

Perhaps the most important question is whether new patterns of electioneering have weakened or severed altogether the connection between elections and government. According to one 'very prominent consultant' quoted by Sabato, 'we simply look for good candidates. Whether they become good officeholders is no longer a factor. In fact, we can compensate pretty well for their not being good.'[46] If this claim was justified by the facts, then American democracy would indeed be in sorry shape. But in fact the claim is as implausible as it is arrogant. The strong correlation between objective economic conditions and electoral outcomes documented above, and more generally the strong influence of retrospective evaluations on vote choices,[47] should be sufficient to dispel the notion that campaign consultants 'can compensate pretty well' for their clients' failures in office.

The optimistic hypothesis that electioneering and governing are not radically disjoint activities in the modern media age finds some telling support in the most famous argument offered by the most famous media candidate in contemporary American politics,

Ronald Reagan. A few days before the 1980 election, with his political future on the line, Reagan appeared in a nationally televised debate with the incumbent President. In 1979, in the midst of his period of 'malaise', Carter, had told the American people, 'Often you see paralysis and stagnation and drift. You don't like it and neither do I.'⁴⁸ Essentially, Carter based his campaign for re-election on the argument that things were bad despite his efforts rather than because of them.

In his concluding remarks in his debate with Carter, Reagan answered this claim of irresponsibility not with slickness or manipulation, but with a straightforward assertion of electoral accountability.

Next Tuesday, all of you will go to the polls, you'll stand there in the polling place and make a decision. I think, when you make that decision it might be well if you would ask yourself: Are you better off than you were four years ago? Is it easier for you to go and buy things in the stores than it was four years ago? Is there more or less unemployment in the country than four years ago? Is America as respected throughout the world as it was? Do you feel our security is as safe, that we're as strong as we were four years ago? And if you answer all of those questions yes, why then I think your choice is very obvious as to who you'll vote for. If you don't agree, if you don't think that this course that we've been on for the last four years is what you would like to see us follow for the next four, then I could suggest another choice that you have. This country doesn't have to be in the shape it is in.⁴⁹

Reagan's argument was an artful piece of partisan political rhetoric; but it was rhetoric based upon a widely shared and clearly relevant view of how America had fared during Carter's years in office. Its success represented a triumph not of campaign technology, but of substantive political accountability.

If Reagan's campaign highlighted the impact of governing upon electioneering, his performance as President, particularly in his first year in office, highlighted the reciprocal impact of electioneering upon governing. Having campaigned and won on a platform of reducing taxes, increasing defence spending, and constraining domestic programmes, Reagan proceeded to implement that platform with considerable success—in large part because the Washington community treated his election 'mandate' with a seriousness quite unfashionable among academic observers of electoral politics.

Stability and Change

American electoral politics in the early 1990s looks significantly different from American electoral politics a generation ago. Nevertheless, one argument of this essay is that these striking differences in form have tended to obscure equally striking similarities in the nature of the electoral process—and in the underlying problems facing campaigners, voters, and reformers—over long periods of time. The candidate's need to inform and mobilize potential voters may produce precinct organizations in one era and media campaigns in another, but the need itself will not go away. Differential access to money is a perennial concern, regardless of the specific technology by which that money happens to be translated into political influence. Ordinary voters in any democratic system are vulnerable to manipulation by the reigning political élites—but only up to a point.

Some evidence for the persistence of these problems can be derived from the fact that all of the observations about electioneering used to introduce them above were written at the turn of the last century by one of the very first systematic observers of mass party politics.[50]

Notes

1. See Walter Dean Burnham, 'The Reagan Heritage', in Gerald M. Pomper *et al.*, *The Election of 1988: Reports and Interpretations* (Chatham, NJ: Chatham House, 1989), 21.
2. Page 329 (see n. 50 below).
3. See Austin Ranney, *Curing the Mischiefs of Faction: Party Reform in America* (Berkeley, Calif.: University of California Press, 1975).
4. See Larry M. Bartels, *Presidential Primaries and the Dynamics of Public Choice* (Princeton, NJ: Princeton University Press, 1988).
5. Compare Paul T. David, Ralph M. Goldman, and Richard C. Bain, *The Politics of National Party Conventions* (Washington, DC: The Brookings Institution, 1960) and Byron E. Shafer, *Bifurcated Politics: Evolution and Reform in the National Party Convention* (Cambridge, Mass.: Harvard University Press, 1988).
6. Page 329 (see n. 50 below).
7. Burnham, 'The Reagan Heritage', 24.

8. See Cornelius P. Cotter, James L. Gibson, John F. Bibby, and Robert J. Huckshorn, *Party Organizations in American Politics* (New York: Praeger, 1989).

9. See Martin P. Wattenberg, *The Decline of American Political Parties, 1952-1988* (Cambridge, Mass.: Harvard University Press, 1990), 95.

10 See Angus Campbell, Philip E. Converse, Warren E. Miller, and Donald E. Stokes, *The American Voter* (New York: John Wiley & Sons, 1960).

11. See V. O. Key, Jr., *Southern Politics in State and Nation* (1949, repr. Knoxville, Tenn.: University of Tennessee Press, 1984).

12. Pages 302–3 (see n. 50 below).

13. See Edward R. Tufte, *Political Control of the Economy* (Princeton, NJ: Princeton University Press, 1978).

14. See Gerald H. Kramer, 'Short Term Fluctuations in U.S. Voting Behaviour, 1896–1964', *American Political Science Review*, 65 (1971), 131–43; Tufte, *Political Control of the Economy*; see also Steven J. Rosenstone *Forecasting Presidential Elections* (New Haven, Conn.: Yale University Press, 1983); and Gregory P. Markus, 'The Impact of Personal and National Economic Conditions on the Presidential Vote: A Pooled Cross-Sectional Analysis', *American Journal of Political Science*, 32 (1988) 137–54.

15. Tufte, *Political Control of the Economy*, 143.

16. Page 299 (see n. 50 below).

17. See V. O. Key, Jr., *Politics, Parties and Pressure Groups*, 5th edn. (New York: Thomas Y. Crowell, 1964), 487–8.

18. Based on data compiled by Herbert E. Alexander, *Financing Politics* (Washington, DC: Congressional Quarterly Press, 1980).

19. See Gary C. Jacobson, *Money in Congressional Elections* (New Haven, Conn.: Yale University Press, 1980); see also Donald Philip Green and Jonathan S. Krasno, 'Rebuttal to Jacobson's "New Evidence for Old Arguments"', *American Journal of Political Science*, 34 (1990), 363–72.

20. Page 323 (see n. 50 below).

21. Alexander, *Financing Politics*, 5, 10.

22. See Stanley Kelley, Jr., *Professional Public Relations and Political Power* (Baltimore: Johns Hopkins University Press, 1956).

23. See Joe McGinniss, *The Selling of the President, 1968* (New York: Trident Press, 1969).

24. See Nelson W. Polsby and Aaron Wildavsky, *Presidential Elections: Contemporary Strategies of American Electoral Politics*, 7th edn. (New York: Free Press, 1988), 121.

25. See Montague Kern, *30-Second Politics: Political Advertising in the Eighties* (New York: Praeger, 1989), 207.

26. See Sidney Blumenthal, *The Permanent Campaign* (New York: Simon & Schuster, 1982).
27. See Larry J. Sabato, *The Rise of Political Consultants: New Ways of Winning Elections* (New York: Basic Books, 1981), 128, 134, 140–2, 157.
28. Kern, *30-Second Politics*, 310.
29. See Jeff Greenfield, *The Real Campaign: How the Media Missed the Story of the 1980 Campaign* (New York: Summit Books, 1982).
30. Kern, *30-Second Politics*, 210.
31. Ibid. 93.
32. Sabato, *The Rise of Political Consultants,*121.
33. See Michael Barone and Grant Ujifusa, *The Almanac of American Politics 1990* (Washington, DC: National Journal, 1989).
34. See Bernard R. Berelson, Paul F. Lazarsfeld, and William N. McPhee, *Voting: A Study of Opinion Formation in a Presidential Campaign* (Chicago: University of Chicago Press, 1954).
35. Page 292 (see n. 50 below).
36. See David R. Mayhew, 'Does it Make a Difference whether Party Control of the American Government is Unified or Divided?', a paper prepared for delivery at the Annual Meeting of the American Political Science Association (Atlanta, 1989), 139.
37. Quoted by Nelson W. Polsby, *Consequences of Party Reform* (Oxford: Oxford University Press, 1983), 106.
38. Wattenberg, *The Decline of American Political Parties*, 125.
39. See Thomas E. Patterson, *The Mass Media Election: How Americans Choose Their President* (New York: Praeger, 1980).
40. See S. Robert Lichter, Daniel Amundson, and Richard Noyes, *The Video Campaign: Network Coverage of the 1988 Primaries* (Washington, DC: American Enterprise Institute for Public Policy Research, 1988), 17.
41. Bartels, *Presidential Primaries*, chs. 5, 8–10.
42. See Paul R. Abramson, John H. Aldrich, and David W. Rohde, *Change and Continuity in the 1988 Elections* (Washington, DC: Congressional Quarterly Press, 1990), 172.
43. Greenfield, *The Real Campaign*, 248-9.
44. See Wilson Carey McWilliams, 'The Meaning of the Election', in Pomper *et al.* (eds.), *The Election of 1988*, 177–206.
45. Barone and Ujifusa, *The Almanac of American Politics 1990*, p. xxxvi.
46. Sabato, *The Rise of Political Consultants*, 337.
47. See Morris P. Fiorina, *Retrospective Voting in American National Elections* (New Haven, Conn.: Yale University Press, 1981).
48. Quoted by Polsby, *Consequences of Party Reform*, 118.

49. Greenfield, *The Real Campaign*, 242.
50. M. Ostrogorski, *Democracy and the Organization of Political Parties*, ii: *The United States*, ed. Seymour Martin Lipset (Garden City, NY: Anchor Books, 1964). The original edition of Ostrogorski's book was published in 1902.

References

Every presidential election cycle brings book-length chronicles by political reporters hoping to mine the vein first worked by Theodore H. White in his best-selling book *The Making of the President, 1960* (1962). The latest volume from the most persistent and consistent of White's successors is J. Germond and J. Witcover, *Whose Broad Stripes and Bright Stars?* (1989). Two especially good journalistic accounts of recent campaigns are M. Schram, *Running for President 1976* (1977) and J. Greenfield, *The Real Campaign* (1982).

Recurring sources of academic analysis include the volumes on electoral politics by Abramson, Aldrich, and Rohde (most recently P. R. Abramson *et al.*, *Change and Continuity in the 1988 Elections*, 1990) and the collections of essays by Pomper and colleagues (most recently G. M. Pomper *et al.*, *The Election of 1988* (1989)). Standard textbook treatments include N. W. Polsby and A. Wildavsky on *Presidential Elections* (1988) and G. C. Jacobson on *The Politics of Congressional Elections* (1987). Most of the numerical data presented above were taken from H. W. Stanley and R. G. Niemi, *Vital Statistics on American Politics* (1990).

Abramson, Paul R., Aldrich, John H., and Rohde, David W., *Change and Continuity in the 1988 Elections* (Washington, DC: CQ Press, 1990).

Alexander, Herbert E., *Financing Politics* (Washington, DC: Congressional Quarterly Press, 1980).

Barone, Michael, and Ujifusa, Grant, *The Almanac of American Politics 1990* (Washington, DC: National Journal, 1989).

Bartels, Larry M., *Presidential Primaries and the Dynamics of Public Choice* (Princeton, NJ: Princeton University Press, 1988).

Berelson, Bernard R., Lazarsfeld, Paul F., and McPhee, William N., *Voting: A Study of Opinion Formation in a Presidential Campaign* (Chicago: University of Chicago Press, 1954).

Blumenthal, Sidney, *The Permanent Campaign* (New York: Simon & Schuster, 1982).

Burnham, Walter Dean, 'The Reagan Heritage', in Gerald M. Pomper *et al.*, *The Election of 1988: Reports and Interpretations* (Chatham, NJ: Chatham House, 1989), 1–32.

Campbell, Angus, Converse, Philip E., Miller, Warren E., and Stokes, Donald E., *The American Voter* (New York: John Wiley & Sons, 1960).

Cotter, Cornelius P., Gibson, James L., Bibby, John F., and Huckshorn, Robert J., *Party Organizations in American Politics* (Pittsburgh: University of Pittsburgh Press, 1989).

David, Paul T., Goldman, Ralph M., and Bain, Richard C., *The Politics of National Party Conventions* (Washington, DC: The Brookings Institution, 1960).

Fiorina, Morris P., *Retrospective Voting in American National Elections* (New Haven, Conn: Yale University Press, 1981).

Germond, Jack, and Witcover, Jules, *Whose Broad Stripes and Bright Stars? The Trivial Pursuit of the Presidency, 1988* (New York: Warner, 1989).

Green, Donald Philip, and Krasno, Jonathan S., 'Rebuttal to Jacobson's "New Evidence for Old Arguments"', *American Journal of Political Science*, 34 (1990), 363–72.

Greenfield, Jeff, *The Real Campaign: How the Media Missed the Story of the 1980 Campaign* (New York: Summit Books, 1982).

Jacobson, Gary C., *Money in Congressional Elections* (New Haven, Conn: Yale University Press, 1980).

—— *The Politics of Congressional Elections*, 2nd edn. (Boston: Little, Brown, 1987).

Kelley, Stanley, Jr., *Professional Public Relations and Political Power*, (Baltimore: Johns Hopkins University Press, 1956).

Kern, Montague, *30-Second Politics: Political Advertising in the Eighties* (New York: Praeger, 1989).

Key, V. O. Jr., *Southern Politics in State and Nation* (Knoxville, Tenn: University of Tennessee Press, 1984).

—— *Politics, Parties and Pressure Groups*, 5th edn. (New York: Thomas Y. Crowell, 1964).

Kramer, Gerald H., 'Short-Term Fluctuations in U.S. Voting Behaviour, 1896–1964', *American Political Science Review*, 65 (1971), 131–43.

Lichter, S. Robert, Amundson, Daniel, and Noyes, Richard, *The Video Campaign: Network Coverage of the 1988 Primaries* (Washington, DC: American Enterprise Institute for Public Policy Research, 1988).

McGinniss, Joe, *The Selling of the President, 1968.* (New York: Trident Press, 1969).

McWilliams, Wilson Carey, 'The Meaning of the Election', in Gerald M. Pomper *et al.*, *The Election of 1988: Reports and Interpretations* (Chatham, NJ: Chatham House, 1989), 177–206.

Markus, Gregory B., 'The Impact of Personal and National Economic Conditions on the Presidential Vote: A Poll Cross-Sectional Analysis', *American Journal of Political Science*, 32 (1988), 137–54.

Mayhew, David R., 'Does it Make a Difference whether Party Control of the American National Government is Unified or Divided?', paper presented at the Annual Meeting of the American Political Science Association (Atlanta, 1989).

Ostrogorski, M., *Democracy and the Organization of Political Parties*, ii: *The United States*, ed. Seymour Martin Lipset (1902; repr. Garden City, NY: Anchor Books, 1964).

Patterson, Thomas E., *The Mass Media Election: How Americans Choose Their President* (New York: Praeger, 1980).

Polsby, Nelson W., *Consequences of Party Reform* (Oxford: Oxford University Press, 1983).

—— and Wildavsky, Aaron, *Presidential Elections: Contemporary Strategies of American Electoral Politics*, 7th edn. (New York: Free Press, 1988).

Pomper, Gerald M., Baker, Ross K., Burnham, Walter Dean, Farah, Barbara G., Hershey, Marjorie Randon, Klein, Ethel, and McWilliams, Wilson Carey, *The Election of 1988: Reports and Interpretations* (Chatham, NY: Chatham House, 1989).

Ranney, Austin, *Curing the Mischiefs of Faction: Party Reform in America* (Berkeley, Calif: University of California Press, 1975).

Rosenstone, Steven J., *Forecasting Presidential Elections* (New Haven, Conn: Yale University Press, 1983).

Sabato, Larry J., *The Rise of Political Consultants: New Ways of Winning Elections* (New York: Basic Books, 1981).

Schram, Martin, *Running for President 1976: The Carter Campaign* (New York: Stein & Day, 1977).

Shafer, Byron E., *Bifurcated Politics: Evolution and Reform in the National Party Convention* (Cambridge, Mass: Harvard University Press, 1988).

Stanley, Harold W., and Niemi, Richard G., *Vital Statistics on American Politics*, 2nd edn. (Washington, DC: CQ Press, 1990).

Tufte, Edward R., *Political Control of the Economy* (Princeton, NJ: Princeton University Press, 1978).

Wattenberg, Martin P., *The Decline of American Political Parties 1952–1988* (Cambridge, Mass: Harvard University Press, 1990).

White, Theodore H., *The Making of the President 1960* (New York: New American Library, 1962).

13

Conclusion

DAVID BUTLER and AUSTIN RANNEY

Each chapter in this book has described the unique way in which particular democracies conduct some aspects of their elections today. But every chapter has also highlighted some common elements in electioneering; and everywhere there can be found similar changes which have overtaken electioneering since 1945. It remains for us to explore the similarities and the differences, the main themes and the principal variations.

Continuity and Change

The goals of electioneering have not changed. The contending parties and candidates, today as in 1945, seek to consolidate their own following and to activate it to vote, while trying to convert or neutralize their opponents' support.

They do this within an institutional framework that has altered little. The duration of formal campaigns has not changed; it still ranges from four to five months in the United States down to a month or so in most parliamentary democracies. Elections come about in the same way: they occur on rigid timetables, prescribed by law, in the presidential systems and in Norway; on relatively fixed timetables, established by custom, in most parliamentary democracies; and, in a few, such as Great Britain, and Denmark, on a date that the incumbent government finds convenient.

Electoral laws are tampered with less than is supposed. Only France among the seventeen countries considered here has experienced major changes in the way in which votes are converted into seats. No major alterations have been made anywhere in the laws governing electoral conduct, except in regard to money and to the use of the media.

In general the new techniques have had more impact in the United States than elsewhere because America has always had an electoral system that is uniquely personalized and candidate-based and this produces a greater experimentation in campaigning.

The public financing of party activities, and in particular of electioneering, is one of the major innovations of the last generation. Germany has gone furthest in the comprehensive funding of parties, while the United States (though only in the arena of presidential primaries and elections) has moved a long way in funding electioneering. But Sweden, Finland, and Australia have started public funding and the trend seems likely to continue.

Most countries provide some support in kind for electioneering: this usually takes the form of free postal facilities or rent-free meeting halls, and much more important, free time on television for parties to present their cases as they wish. Only the United States and Italy provide no practical direct back-up to the contestants.

Ceilings on campaign expenditure are widely prescribed but less widely observed. The total amount spent has everywhere increased, but most of all in the United States. The new technology has, of course, greatly added to the cost of campaigns and therefore to the importance of fund-raising. This has done far more to change the nature of politics in the United States than elsewhere: the unlimited amounts that a full-scale television advertising campaign can consume has turned more and more of the energy of incumbent members of Congress (but not presidents) to building up a large enough war chest to frighten off potential challengers.

In most parliamentary democracies, where the essential battle is between national parties rather than between individual candidates, some limit seems to have been put on competitive expenditures, either because of the rules of access to television (or of access to public funds) or through a tacit sense of mutual self-preservation. However, complaints about the distorting problems of fund-raising seem everywhere to be on the increase.

A tendency towards the centralized and unified direction of campaigns has continued even in countries like Great Britain and France, where it has long been the norm. In countries such as the United States, where direction of campaigns used to be relatively local and fragmented, there has been a movement towards a greater role for the national party in congressional (but not presidential) elections.

In most countries, including the parliamentary democracies, the national campaigns of most parties have more and more focused on party leaders' statements and personal qualities, diminishing the attention paid to lesser leaders and to the parties as collectivities.

Party loyalties seem to have weakened everywhere. Consequently, they matter less as cues for making voting decisions; appeals to them are not so prominent in electioneering tactics.

None of these changes has been dramatic. They are manifestations, rather than causes, of the conspicuous alteration in the nature of elections that has taken place in recent decades. The fundamental cause of the widespread 'Americanization' of electioneering, both in vocabulary and in technology, lies in the revolution in communications. Even in India, the poorest and least developed of the democracies considered here, some of the language and the gimmicks, so obvious elsewhere, are manifest.

The main devices of the new 'high-tech' electioneering include the following:

1. Direct mail to targeted citizens, individually addressed and configured by computer, has been used everywhere, principally for fund-raising but sometimes, especially in Scandinavia, to publicize party stands on issues to selected audiences.

2. Sample surveys have been employed to help in determining strategic needs and to assess the likely impact of specific campaign themes or phrases. Focus groups can explore in depth how voters feel about parties, issues, and leaders. Daily tracking polls provide quick feedback on how new tactics are working. Exit polls allow the news media to make quick predictions of the outcome soon after the polls have closed.

3. Computers are programmed to construct data banks on the electorate, constituency by constituency, as a basis for strategy and tactics, and direct mailing.

4. Fax machines and cellular telephones have in the last decade greatly enhanced the co-ordination of campaigns, with the orchestration of daily themes echoed nation-wide by all the party spokesmen; they are particularly helpful in securing quick agreement on damage limitation when an untoward event or an oratorical gaffe embarrasses a campaign.

Television, however, has done more than anything else to transform electioneering. Since the 1950s in America and most of Western Europe, television has superseded the press, radio, and the public meeting as the prime conveyor of political information. Developments in the structure, ownership, and control of television have varied widely in different countries, but in general it has been more politically neutral than the older sources of information and it has also been more centralized and more inclined to focus on visual images and personalities. It has intensified the concentration on leaders as the sole spokesmen of their parties.

In countries where political advertising has been permitted on television, repeated spot announcements have made possible extraordinarily swift build-ups of an image or theme. Television communication is still in transition. Political advertising, at first confined to the Americas and Australia, is now being allowed in some European countries; and with the advent of satellite and cable networks, it is bound to increase. Most of the countries that ban paid television advertising allow free time for party-controlled broadcasts, debates among party leaders, and journalistic interrogations. The party-controlled election broadcasts in Great Britain and Australia may be of diminishing importance, but the leaders' confrontations in France, Germany, and Scandinavia still draw enormous audiences and plainly have the power to sway the outcome of any election.

But the most far-reaching effect of television has been on campaign coverage. 'Coverage' implies the recording of autonomous events like a natural disaster or a boxing match. But in the television age, the coverage has become the campaign. The contestants' behaviour is continuously conditioned by the need to catch space in the news bulletins, the main source of communication with the voters.

Some changes are due, not to new technology, but to the exploitation of old possibilities. One example is provided by the development of press advertising in recent British campaigns, where in the final days full-page displays in the national papers accounted for over half of the total campaign expenditures by the Conservative and Labour parties.

But on the whole the new technology has been accompanied by the concomitant decline in the importance of old low-tech methods. Attendance at public meetings in Scandinavia has declined in the last forty years from over 30 per cent in 1945 to under 10 per cent in 1985. In Great Britain it fell from 30 per cent in 1950 to 3 per cent in 1987.

Canvassing, always considered improper or impolitic in some countries, has declined spectacularly even in Great Britain, its traditional home. Posters and window-bills are less and less in evidence. Journalists complain that in most countries an election is now invisible (except, of course, on television). The output of party literature—pamphlets, position papers, and fly-sheets—is still vast, but in most countries less than it used to be.

On the other hand, technical experts in electioneering have developed into a profession in the last generation, even though they have had varying impact. Paid consultants have increasingly taken over from party leaders the design of their campaigns in the United States and in Latin America. They have had a major impact on electioneering in Germany and, to a lesser extent, in Great Britain. Their role in Scandinavia has been small and in India negligible. But everywhere, including India, public and private polls have had a significant effect on campaign strategy and campaign reporting.

New techniques have transformed the role of volunteers. The addressing of envelopes, once a major function for party workers in Great Britain and Australia, can now be done by machines from computer tapes of the electoral register. If money and election laws allow, professional distribution firms can deliver literature more efficiently than party volunteers. The decline of meetings has ended the need for stewards and bill-posters. The one new role for party workers may lie in the systematic development of telephone canvassing (wherever it is legally and socially acceptable).

The role of the media has changed, and not just through the advent of television. It has moved increasingly from being merely a channel of communication to being a major actor in the campaigning process, as it selects the persons and issues to be covered and as it shapes its portrayal of leaders. One key to successful electioneering lies in campaigners' skills at providing news editors and producers with newsworthy and telegenic material. Campaigns are designed to attract good coverage in the television bulletins and the press headlines, with photo-opportunities and news events to yield compelling pictorial copy and with well-honed sound-bites to fit into quick-fire bulletins. Our Scandinavia chapter makes this point in the plainest language, and it was equally illustrated by Labour's innovations in the British campaign of 1987.

Opinion polls, ever-increasing in frequency and number, have added to the horse-race flavour of campaign coverage. The ups and downs in the party standings prove more newsworthy than the subtleties of the rival leaders' debating points.

Electioneering has become more complicated as the contestants absorb and usually obey the advice of sophisticated media experts—and even read the works of academics. If elections are, for many citizens, theatrical performances, they inspire subtle critical notices. The tactics of the campaign seem to be reported and discussed almost as much as the policy issues at stake. How the candidates are projected is sometimes as salient as what they are projecting.

From the production end, the way in which party leaders and party strategists occupy themselves during the campaign is very different from forty years ago. Consultations with advertising firms and pollsters, preparations for television interviews, briefings for radio phone-ins, and other relations with an ever more demanding media make new demands on their time. Campaigns have speeded up even more than the planes which whisk the leaders around the country.

From the consumption end, the voter now relies, to an overwhelming extent, on the television screen to learn what is at stake. In the last forty years, the behaviour of voters in most countries has changed appreciably, but it is not clear how far this is in response to the new style of electioneering and how far new styles of electioneering have developed in response to changing political cultures among voters. This book bears ample testimony to a continuing uncertainty about which is cause and which is effect.

In many countries, but not in all, there is evidence of increasing volatility. The strength of party loyalty has declined, and the willingness to change parties or split tickets has grown. In most places people now seem to vote less on ideology and tradition and more on personalities and issues of the moment.

The Impact of Electioneering

Larry Bartels' chapter raises a number of questions about the impact of the changes in electioneering technology on the outcome

of elections and the conduct of government in the United States—
questions that to some extent can be raised about electioneering in
any democracy. While Bartels does not quite say that electioneering
has changed very little and in any case continues to have no
significant impact, he rightly calls attention to the often flimsy and
sometimes absent evidence on which some commentators base
their notions, implicit or explicit, that electioneering is a highly
powerful weapon in electoral politics, made more powerful by the
new technology, and that elections are won by good electioneering
and lost by bad electioneering. For example, Bartels notes the view
of many commentators that the much-remarked Willie Horton
advertisements in the 1988 presidential campaign so cleverly, if
shamelessly, exploited the racism and fear of American voters that
it made a major contribution to Bush's victory. But Bartels points
out that such claims are warranted only if we have clear evidence
that the Horton advertisements were watched, understood, and
absorbed by millions of voters and that many of those voters were
thereby induced to switch to Bush from Dukakis; but in fact no
such evidence has been convincingly adduced.

He is right to be sceptical about this and other claims for
electioneering, for it must be confessed that political scientists as
well as political journalists have often failed to prove unequivocal
cause-and-effect relationships among the institutions, processes,
and events they study; and none of us has proved, by the demanding canons of science, that good electioneering wins elections and
bad electioneering loses them.

However, it is plain that electioneering must matter more in
candidate-dominated contests than in party-dominated ones; when
a candidate has to sell himself and cannot rely on loyalty to a party
label, campaign communications matter more.

Yet we cannot prove that the recent 'Americanization' of electioneering observable in most democracies (including the United
States!) has made voters more ignorant and alienated, weakened
party loyalties or destroyed the accountability of elected officials.
Many of these questions, we believe, are amenable to social science
research; but, so far as we know, they have been researched very
little.

Any truly satisfactory answer to the question, 'Does electioneering make a difference?' must be complicated. Looking only at the
United States, for example, it seems likely that electioneering is

more important in primary elections than in general elections. In primaries, party affiliations cannot serve as cues for helping the voters to choose, and so voters need some other reason to vote for a particular candidate over the others; accordingly, simple name recognition is a much greater asset in primaries than in general elections. Another example is the fact that, with thousands of nominations being made in primaries and hundreds of candidates being elected in general elections for national, state, and local offices each year, the news media can cover only a small fraction of the races. Hence, it is likely that the importance of electioneering varies inversely with the amount of media coverage: that is, in elections usually covered extensively by the media, such as those for president, governor, and US Senator, the media coverage probably has much more impact on voters than what the campaigners do; but in the many hundreds of contests hardly mentioned by the media, whatever the campaigners do to bring their causes to the voters' attention has a greater impact. Let us be clear that we cannot *prove* that these propositions are true, but we think that they make reasonable hypotheses worth confirming or disconfirming by research. In any case, we strongly suspect that the proposition 'electioneering has no impact' is just as oversimple and inaccurate as the proposition 'electioneering makes all the difference'.

Yet our present lack of scientific knowledge does not mean that electioneering is not important enough to be worth studying. There is no question that in all modern democracies the people in the campaign trenches—the candidates and the party leaders and workers, the people who contribute money to campaigns, and the journalists who report and interpret what the campaigners are doing—have little doubt that electioneering has a great impact on election outcomes. Why else would they bother? Many of them would ruefully agree with the old remark, 'Half the money spent in campaigns is wasted', but many would also add, 'the trouble is you don't know *which* half'. To them the stakes of the contest are high, and they see the opposition electioneering as hard and as well as it can. Who can blame them for feeling that their side simply cannot afford to stand idly by and let nature—or the basic economic forces in the models Bartels cites—take their course. You have to do all that you can even though you doubt its efficacy.

In short, there is no denying that, whether it makes sense or not, electioneering is in fact a major component of the democratic electoral process everywhere. That in itself is sufficient justification for giving it the kind of attention that it receives in this book. What we and our authors have said is certainly not the last word about electioneering, but we hope that it will help to illuminate a substantial part of what is going on in modern democratic electoral systems.

Electioneering and Democracy

High-tech electioneering has its pluses and minuses. It can be argued that the tendency of the last forty years has been to substitute images for substance and to focus on personalities at the expense of parties and policies. It can be argued that advertising hucksters have increasingly intruded into political and electoral decision-making at the expense of party leaders, and that they have sometimes trivialized politics to the level of deodorant or beer commericals.

But it is easy to fall victim to a Golden Age myth. Elections have always seemed more an emotional orgy than a feast of reason. Voters today are better informed about issues and candidates than they were in 1945, when party loyalties were more dominant. When all allowances are made, turn-out has not fallen significantly and there is little evidence of alienation. Any decline in electoral activity at the local level has been more than matched by greater participation in issue groups and protest groups.

In the final analysis, those who deplore the changes in election-eering in established democracies should take note of the eagerness of the rest of the world to emulate their practices. Established democracies no less than aspiring democracies should recognize that electioneering, warts and all, is an integral part of the democratic electoral process. No electioneering, no elections. The democratic electoral package has to be bought as a whole—or not at all.

Appendix

	AUSTRALIA	NEW ZEALAND	INDIA	JAPAN	FRANCE	GERMANY	ITALY	DENMARK	FINLAND	NORWAY	SWEDEN	UK	USA	BRAZIL	COLOMBIA	VENEZUELA
Electoral system	AV	FPTP	FPTP	Maj	2nd Ballot	PR	PR	PR	PR	PR	PR	FPTP	Prim. FPTP	PR	PR	PR
Parliament Term 1990	3	4	5	5	5	4	5	3	4	4	3	5	2	4	4	5
Campaign Duration (av.)	3w	4w	5w	2w	3w	9w	8w	3w	4w	4w	5w	3w	3w	4m	12m	6m
Members Lower House 1990	148	97	542	512	577	656	630	179	200	165	349	650	435	503	209	19
National Parties	4	2	4	5	5	4	10	8	8	6	6	3	2	8	4	3
Regional Parties			8			1	4					4			1	
Opinion polls Importance	High	High	Med	Med	High	High	Low	Med	High	High	High	High	High	High	High	High
no. of major orgs.	4	2	3	8	6	4	4	4	3	4	4	5	20	3	2	5
any restraint	no	no	no	No % for Cands	No % for 1 week ban	none now	no	no	no	no	no	no	no	no	month ban	no
Turnout %[a]	94–97	80–84	55–64	68–75	66–88	78–91	84–91	83–88	78–81	80–84	86–92	73–76	35–53	83–87	45–50	82–91
Absent vote %	11	10	none	4	11	none	none	4	15	5	37	2	5	none	none	none
TV: first major use	1963	1963	1989	1960	1962	1965	1963	1960	1966	1965	1960	1959	1948	1974	1986	1960
saturation 1960 %	64	50	none	33	15	35	20	34	52	5	42	60	88	5	5	5
saturation 1990 %	98	96	80	99	98	94	96	96	98	90	90	98	98	90	85	90
TV: paid ads	yes	yes	no	party only	yes	yes	yes	no	no	no	start 91	no	yes	no	yes	yes
free party time	yes	yes	yes	Cands only	yes	yes	yes	no	no	no	yes	yes	no	yes	yes	yes
leader confrontations[b]	1990	1984	1990	1990	Pres only	no	no	no	no	no	no	no	Pres only	1989	1986	1969 1984
right to reply	no	no	no	yes	some	no	no	no	no	no	no	no	yes	yes	no	no
Public finance parties	no	no	no	yes	no	yes	yes	yes	yes	yes	yes	no	no	yes	yes	yes
campaigns[c]	yes	no	no	some	no	yes	yes	no	no	no	no	no	Pres only	yes	no	no
Expenditure limits party	no	ignored	no	ignored	no	no	no	no	no	no	no	no	no	ignored	no	no
candidate	no	ignored	ignored	ignored	since 1988	no	no	no	no	no	no	tough	no	ignored	no	no

[a] Voting is compulsory in Australia, Brazil and Venezuela; it is semi-compulsory in Italy
[b] In Scandinavian countries airtime is made available to question the leaders collectively
[c] In several countries help in kind (e.g., free postage) is available

Index